Social
Anthropology

Social
Anthropology

Chris Hann

TEACH YOURSELF BOOKS

Every effort has been made to contact the holders of any copyright material but if any have been overlooked, the publisher will be pleased to make the necessary alterations at the first opportunity.

For UK order queries: please contact Bookpoint Ltd, 39 Milton Park, Abingdon, Oxon OX14 4TD. Telephone: (44) 01235 400414, Fax: (44) 01235 400454. Lines are open from 9.00–6.00, Monday to Saturday, with a 24 hour message answering service. Email address: orders@bookpoint.co.uk

For U.S.A. & Canada order queries: please contact NTC/Contemporary Publishing, 4255 West Touhy Avenue, Lincolnwood, Illinois 60646–1975, U.S.A. Telephone: (847) 679 5500, Fax: (847) 679 2494.

Long renowned as the authoritative source for self-guided learning – with more than 30 million copies sold worldwide – the *Teach Yourself* series includes over 200 titles in the fields of languages, crafts, hobbies, sports, and other leisure activities.

British Library Cataloguing in Publication Data
A catalogue record for this title is available from The British Library.

Library of Congress Catalog Card Number: 98-65237

First published in UK 1998 by Hodder Headline Plc, 338 Euston Road, London, NW1 3BH.

First published in US 1998 by NTC/Contemporary Publishing, 4255 West Touhy Avenue, Lincolnwood (Chicago), Illinois 60646–1975 U.S.A.

The 'Teach Yourself' name and logo are registered trade marks of Hodder & Stoughton Ltd.

Copyright © 2000 Chris Hann

Typeset by Transet Limited, Coventry, England.
Printed in Great Britain for Hodder & Stoughton Educational, a division of Hodder Headline Plc, 338 Euston Road, London NW1 3BH by Cox & Wyman Ltd, Reading, Berkshire.

Impression number   10 9 8 7 6 5 4 3 2 1
Year   2004 2003 2002 2001 2000

To: Raymond Firth
Philosophiae Doctor Honoris Causa
Jagiellonian University of Cracow

CONTENTS

PROLOGUE

Anthropology is not taught in schools and many people have only the vaguest idea of its subject matter. For some it deals with the biological unity of the human species, with the evolution of *homo sapiens* and his relationships to other primates. For others, on the contrary, it deals with the diversity of human cultures, as documented historically and observed in the present through fieldwork.

Some may believe that anthropology means the study of 'small-scale' societies in faraway places, of communities threatened with extinction, perhaps with the implication that such studies can tell us something about how the large-scale societies that predominate in today's world used to work in the past. Others imagine the field of anthropology extending to all human social contexts in space and time, including the modern industrial societies in which most anthropologists themselves live.

For some, anthropology is politically suspect if not reactionary, given its origins in an age of European imperialism. Others may argue that anthropologists no longer exploit or patronise the people they study (often nowadays their own people) and that the discipline is at the forefront of campaigns to protect minorities and to promote human rights generally.

In spite of all these conflicting views, there is widespread agreement that the discipline of anthropology, which took shape in the nineteenth century and was consolidated in the twentieth, is likely to expand and attract more students and practitioners in the twenty-first century. This introduction concentrates on the tradition of social anthropology as it evolved in the twentieth century in Britain. The larger-than-life figure who did more than anyone else to establish this tradition was not originally British at all.

Bronislaw Malinowski was born in 1884 in Cracow, nowadays a Polish city but until the First World War governed from Vienna as part of the Habsburg province of Galicia. Malinowski was educated at the famous Jagiellonian University, but he did not become an anthropologist there. Like other parts of Eastern Europe, Galicia was being explored by ethnographers and folkorists, but not by modern anthropologists. The research that earned Malinowski fame in London was carried out in Melanesia. By the end of the twentieth century, however, a social anthropologist might equally well choose to work in Cracow as in the Trobriand Islands, and the discipline was well established at the Jagiellonian University. This provides some of the context for this book. The use of various Polish illustrations is not meant to provide a comprehensive picture of one post-communist society, but merely to convey a sense of the range of social anthropology and the sort of knowledge it generates. References to post-communist Poland were much more numerous in the first draft of this book, in which the chapters were cast as lectures at an Anthropology Summer School in Malinowski's native Cracow. For reasons of space and style this plan had to be abandoned. The deleted materials included practical assignments and a narrative of a fieldtrip undertaken by Summer School participants in Galicia. Readers of this book can assess this supplementary text electronically at: **http://era.anthropology.ac.uk/ Teach-Yourself/ (Discovering Social Anthropology in Galicia)**.

Readers are encouraged to think of analogous illustrations in settings familiar to them and – the greater challenge – to begin to think anthropologically about a wider world that remains full of surprises.

Part I

INTRODUCTION

1 | WHAT'S IN A NAME?

Defining the field

This opening chapter introduces some of the basic issues in modern social anthropology and assumes no previous familiarity with the subject. Some readers may not be comfortable with the very name anthropology. In dictionaries and some of the older textbooks you will be told that it means 'the study of man', and even if we substitute 'humanity' or 'humankind' for 'man', the formula reveals very little. It is better if you try to suspend your natural inclination to have a concise definition of the subject at this point. We can try to formulate something more satisfactory by the end of the book. By then you will know much more about how this field of study has developed and what animates its contemporary practitioners.

The question of names is actually rather complicated. The emphasis in this volume is on *social* anthropology, and this tradition is particularly strong in Britain. In America, however, it is normal to speak of *cultural* anthropology. Nowadays the two are largely but not entirely identical. American cultural anthropology has been traditionally taught as one of 'four fields', the other three being archaeology, physical (or biological) anthropology, and linguistics. In most other countries these are classified as separate disciplines. In Germany the equivalent tradition to social or cultural anthropology is known as *Völkerkunde* or *Ethnologie*. However, the Germans have a separate tradition of *Volkskunde* to describe research into the customs of their own people (*Volk*). Poland and most other European countries maintain a similar distinction. In other countries similar research projects might be organised by departments of sociology, or of cultural studies. In other words, the academic packaging of our field is muddled. Actually it always has been. This is a field that has always been open to influences from other subjects on almost all sides, and you cannot expect to find much international consistency. Sometimes the same name is used when there are big differences in substantive research agendas. Equally, different names may conceal a basic similarity of interests and approaches.

This volume, then, is concerned with social and cultural anthropology, which for most purposes can be treated as one and the same subject. In this chapter we shall outline how this branch of anthropology is related to other branches and to the three standard groupings of academic disciplines: the natural sciences, the social sciences and the humanities. A more detailed account of anthropology's history will be found in Chapter 2. You will learn that anthropologists place great emphasis on field studies or *ethnography*. The same word is used for the descriptive account they publish when their fieldwork is completed. At the end of the book, we shall summarise some of the most exciting contemporary developments in anthropology and assess the subject's prospects now that humanity has entered the third millennium.

Ethnocentrism and relativism

Let us pursue this reference to the millennium to take us very quickly into the central concerns of anthropology. It probably seems natural to most readers that we measure time according to the Gregorian calendar and count our years from the year in which (we think) Jesus Christ was born. But why should billions of people around the globe who do not share Christian, European intellectual traditions accept a method of time reckoning based on this event? It may well be the case that, thanks to the current power of these western traditions, some sense of entering a 'new millennium' has penetrated the consciousness of most people around the world. But there is nothing uniquely rational about our system and not many westerners can explain the details of it. For example, assuming you come from a country in which western traditions are dominant, do you know why we should have a calendar based on 12 solar months, when the lunar year contains 13? How many people can explain why February should have three fewer days than the months which precede and follow it? Other systems of timekeeping are also historically specific and they may be just as interesting as our own; but these others have mostly fallen out of use because they had less power to back them up.

Bronislaw Malinowski studied the Trobriand Islanders, nowadays citizens of Papua New Guinea. Like many people without writing and therefore without the possibility of developing a formal calendar to measure time, they measured time by counting lunar months. However, they had specific names for *ten* lunar months, no more. This may seem odd, but the system seems to have worked well enough for the Trobrianders. Although very different from our own system of time reckoning, this sort of difference does not entitle us to assume that a Trobriander's subjective experience of time was radically different from that of Malinowski, or of us today.

It would be ethnocentric to assume that Trobrianders were somehow behaving illogically or irrationally in having developed only ten named lunar months. Modern anthropologists try hard not to approach and evaluate other people's customs in terms of their own. Ethnocentrism is just about the worst sin they can accuse each other of.

Instead, anthropologists try to understand how other people make sense of their world. The underlying assumption is that people behave consistently, some scholars would say 'rationally', given basic orientations which they learn in the course of their socialisation. These orientations include norms and values, guides to what is considered appropriate behaviour, which vary greatly across human communities. For example, Trobriand Islanders have certain norms of exchange as a result of which large quantities of yams are given to relatives on the mother's side after the harvest, and this detail may have some bearing on Trobriand time reckoning. The point is to see how the details of the Trobriand world view make sense when they are taken together. This does not mean that everything must fit harmoniously together: that was a common mistake made by anthropologists in the past, and we are nowadays much more sensitive to elements of tension, and even contradiction. We are sensitive, too, to the amount of individual variation that may exist: but it is not necessary that every individual should hold the same views about time and yam exchanges for us to be able to identify a configuration of Trobriand norms, customs and beliefs, and to describe these as systematically as we can. We shall then be in a position to talk about a 'Trobriand model' or a 'Trobriand tradition', and to compare this with models developed for other people in other places, including perhaps our own.

At this point some anthropologists like to take a step further, and you may wish to follow them. You may wish to say that the Trobriand model is not simply different from our own, but that it is equally valid in all ways. You may feel that it is impossible to make comparisons with other models, because there can be no basis for such an assessment. This position is usually known as 'cultural relativism' and it has a long history. For the extreme relativist, there are *only* particular models, and the scientific knowledge that has developed and spread from modern Europe is itself another local model, a somewhat bloated one, with greater technical capacities in most fields, but perhaps significant deficiencies in other fields. The extreme relativist may also embrace ethical relativism and argue that, given the values of the group in question, female circumcision, not to mention headhunting and cannibalism, must all be considered acceptable forms of behaviour. Examples such as these bring the relativist into conflict with those trying to formulate universal human rights. In practise, few anthropologists have taken up such extreme positions. Many are active in global human rights movements, but seek ways to reconcile what they consider to be of universal value with respect for cultural diversity.

Cultural diversity

The Trobriand Islanders are a 'small-scale' society, the sort of society that most people associate anthropology with (if they have heard of the subject at all). Yet for a long time now, starting in the age of Malinowski, anthropologists have been trying to change this image. They do not want their discipline to be restricted to the study of remote, exotic, primitive societies. You might see this as a survival instinct on our part. The present world offers few possibilities for discovering and documenting previously unknown ways of living. The political and social circumstances in which anthropological research is conducted have changed enormously, particularly following the dissolution of the major European colonial empires by the early 1960s. In an age of accelerating globalisation the boundaries which distinguish anthropologists from other social scientists and from historians have inevitably become fuzzy.

Anthropologists in countries such as Britain have often argued that their studies of the exotic were aimed not only at obtaining a better understanding of some 'other' society, but also a better understanding of their own. Nowadays even British anthropologists work increasingly within their own country. A good deal of the work that has been undertaken in Britain, and indeed in Poland, has concentrated on relatively unusual communities, such as groups of migrants or remote villagers, while large urban and suburban populations have been overlooked. You may wonder what is going on here. Are the anthropologists deliberately seeking some exotic 'other' within their own societies? Can an anthropological perspective be applied to absolutely any form of human group? If our subject is the study of cultural differences, is it really possible to do anthropology at all in contemporary Europe, now that even the historic city of Cracow has its own McDonald's?

Our argument is that anthropology can be carried out anywhere, including apparently 'ordinary' social contexts in the most economically advanced countries. Despite all the evident pressures promoting homogenisation, human diversity need not diminish in the course of these globalisation processes. It may even increase, as new forms of diversity develop. Many readers of this volume may have an interest in older forms of diversity which have disappeared or are seriously threatened nowadays, such as the lifestyles of people who hunt in tropical rainforests. But you may also be interested in new forms of diversity, such as those of urban youth groups in your own countries, and in how all forms of diversity, old and new, interact in our contemporary world.

> Culture or Civilization, taken in its wide, ethnographic sense, is that complex whole which includes knowledge, belief, art, morals, law, custom, and any other capabilities and habits acquired by man as a member of society.[1]

One key concept in anthropology for understanding all forms of human diversity is culture. This concept has a long and tangled history. It was used in the singular by Edward Tylor in the nineteenth century as the equivalent of civilisation. Most twentieth-century anthropologists, including Malinowski, have used the term in the plural. In the USA, particular attention is paid to the values and meanings that people share, which enable us to identify them as forming a single group. Sometimes we refer to the group itself as 'a culture'. For example, following Malinowski we can identify 'Trobriand culture' and compare and contrast it with 'Polish culture' or even 'American culture'.

Historically, the concept of culture has not been as dominant in Britain as in the USA. Some people who call themselves social anthropologists do not find the concept of culture very helpful at all. We shall debate these issues throughout the book, but without losing sight of the ground that social and cultural anthropologists have in common. The areas of agreement will emerge if we try to see how both social and cultural anthropology fit into the wider academic map, beginning with the so-called 'hard' or 'natural' sciences, and concluding in the humanities.

Anthropology on the academic map

Biology

Like all other creatures, humans have biological characteristics and these have been the object of expert sudy, both inside and outside anthropology. The extent to which humans form a unique case on the basis of their more elaborate cultural capacities is much debated. From time to time strong claims have been made from the biological side. A movement known as 'sociobiology' was briefly influential in the 1970s. Its proponents tried to explain human diversity solely in terms of biological adaptation. Social and cultural anthropologists do not deny the constraints which biological universals impose on all humans, e.g. as the organism matures and ages, or in the field of sexuality. However, they argue that these constraints do not determine cultures. We shall illustrate this point later when we come to explain the difference between sex and gender.

Some biological approaches emphasise the selection of genes rather than the adaptations of groups. However, it has yet to be demonstrated that a Darwinian 'selectionist' perspective can provide a convincing explanation for the rise and fall of social and cultural traits (sometimes called 'memes'). Humans can choose to modify or delete their social and cultural traits. This can happen over short time spans. By no means all changes of this kind are conducive to the reproductive success of the individual or the group. Applying evolutionist models may generate new insights in certain cases, but as a general explanation for human diversity they are far from convincing. Moreover the implication that some cultures are 'maladaptive' compared to others raises disturbing ethical issues.

Ecology

Similar points apply in other subdisciplines. It is important to study the interplay between human populations and the material environments in which they reside, but it is too simple to assume that culture and society are simply determined by the environment. Tropical rainforests are not conducive to dry grain farming, but they are compatible with a variety of other gardening techniques, very different styles of hunting and gathering, and different forms of human community. Like human biology, the biology of the environment imposes *limits*, but it does not *determine*.

Psychology

Some mental capacities, such as the capacity for language and logical thought, are common to all human beings, but just how much is held in common, and which mental processes are susceptible to local cultural influence, is a continuing area of debate. Some scholars in cognitive or evolutionary psychology put forward strong causal claims along the lines of the sociobiologists mentioned earlier; most social and cultural anthropologists reject such strong claims, without, however, denying that our neural 'hardware' plays a large role in shaping the behaviour that we study.

Archaeology

Archaeologists study the material remains of past societies. In cooperation with biological (physical) anthropologists, archaeologists can illuminate the emergence and development of *homo sapiens*. Particularly in the case of non-literate societies, the research of archaeologists may also yield important clues about the recent past. Work on the tools used by humans in the past may give us clues to other aspects of their culture, but it cannot give us the sort of rich knowledge of values and beliefs that can be obtained by a fieldworking anthropologist.

Economics

Mainstream economic theory is founded on concepts of rational, decision-taking actors. Critics have emphasised that beliefs and values are also important, that economic action is 'embedded' in society and culture. Anthropologists can accept the basic premises of rationality, linked to the biological and psychological capacities already noted, and yet find these inadequate to explain the diversity of economic behaviour that we observe in the world.

Sociology and other social sciences

Some psychologists and economists are willing to accept the designation 'social scientist', but many prefer to be associated with the 'natural sciences' rather than with social sciences such as sociology and political science. The majority of social and cultural anthropologists are content to classify themselves with the latter. The intellectual links to sociology are particularly close. Radcliffe-Brown, for instance, liked to define social anthropology as 'comparative sociology'. He argued that it should be a 'natural science of society', but this aspiration is not considered appropriate by many contemporary anthropologists. The main differences between anthropology and sociology lie in the methods we use, and in anthropological studies tending to range more widely, both geographically and temporally.

Humanities subjects

There are also many links at the non-science end of the academic spectrum. Close ties to history will be emphasised throughout this book. Ties to philosophy may seem less obvious, yet we investigate in the context of real human communities many of the problems that our philosopher colleagues contemplate in the privacy of their office or in the library. Finally, some anthropologists have pursued a rapprochement with various branches of literary studies. In particular, the expanding field of 'cultural studies' has an agenda that partly overlaps with that of anthropologists; but as with sociology, most specialists in this field limit themselves to contemporary western societies.

These recent trends, sometimes labelled 'postmodern', have brought new insights and opportunities. Anthropologists have become more aware of the literary devices and biases concealed in their own writings. As you begin to read books by anthropologists, ask yourselves in what way they deserve to be considered as science, how they differ, if at all, from the accounts that a journalist or a novelist would produce. Certainly, for some purposes social and cultural anthropologists must adhere to the same standards of science that one expects in other subjects. They must gather their data conscientiously, analyse them in clear, value-free terms, and dig out the causal relationships which will help us explain the patterns in their data. All this is much the same as basic scientific procedure in the so-called hard sciences. But anthropologists and sociologists are also interested in understanding the groups that they study in their own terms, so far as this is possible. This further goal of *understanding* the behaviour of other human beings shifts the anthropologist closer to the position of the historian and the literary critic than to that of the physicist.

We can sum up by saying that social and cultural anthropologists have close links to all three of the academic federations we have identified here. They must pay attention to what the natural sciences have to teach us about characteristics we share as members of a common species. But human cultural diversity seems much richer than that developed by any other species and it is not reducible to ecological or environmental adaptation. It must be explored using a combination of social science techniques, without which accurate documentation and explanations of differences will be impossible, and humanities techniques, without which it will not be possible to understand and communicate the uniqueness of a culture, whether strange or familiar, as it is lived by its members.

A word on words

One problem which affects anthropologists at all levels, from the pioneers of advanced theory to the authors of introductory texts is the problem of language. In essence the problem is this. This book will discuss issues in the English language. Inevitably, we shall make use of many English terms that have no exact equivalents in other languages. We shall also use terms that have been a source of controversy in the discipline, some of which have come to acquire a rather different meaning in anthropology from that which they have for the majority of English speakers.

It is important not to assume that, when we apply a word such as 'law' or 'marriage' to societies remote from our own European experience, we shall be able to locate and describe phenomena that correspond neatly to the usual sense of the English speaker. As we shall see, 'marriage' in parts of South India and 'law' in Albania were, certainly until the recent past and perhaps even now in some respects, quite different. There is a danger that the use of an English term may lead to a serious distortion of our comparative investigations, because we end up analysing and evaluating the 'remote' data by reference to the English model. There is no simple way to deal with this problem. The most important thing is to be aware of the dangers, to be continuously aware of the risk that ethnocentric bias is introduced through using the everyday terms of one language.

Apart from the problem of translation there is the problem that a great many terms commonly used by anthropologists have been mulled over, contested, sometimes rejected altogether, by different scholars over generations. It is impossible in an introductory volume to convey this adequately, to pause every time we come to words such as 'religion', or 'society', or 'magic', and explain the past controversies. Sometimes foreign words have been adopted to fill a perceived gap in the English vocabulary, but here too you must be very careful. Certainly it is not safe to assume that the present English meaning of the word *taboo* is identical to either past or present usages in Polynesia, where the term originated. Since definitional exercises tend to be tedious, having given you this warning we shall proceed largely on the assumption that words have the meanings that ordinary speakers of English attribute to them. In only a few cases do we need to outline more specialised usages.

Abstractions that refer not to social institutions, as marriage and law do, but to intangible ideals such as 'rationality' or 'justice' should be treated with special caution – perhaps you should put a *taboo* on them! Such terms are often the subject of an extensive philosophical literature in English and other languages. Anthropologists may learn much from such debates. A few anthropologists have made original contributions to them, usually on the basis of their fieldwork results. For the anthropologist, concrete engagement with other people and other places has priority over theoretical reflection. It is entirely possible, indeed a very respectable activity, to spend an academic lifetime defining and refining a concept such as rationality in the context of academic debates alone. But this cannot be the path of an anthropologist.

Attention is drawn at the outset to one word in particular. In the case of 'culture', after wondering if we should try to avoid the term altogether, we decided eventually to discuss it in one form or another in almost every chapter. We do this quite deliberately, because it seems to us to be absolutely central to the study of anthropology. It is, however, an increasingly problematic concept. At the end of the book you should make up your own mind as to its continued usefulness.

2 HISTORY OF ANTHROPOLOGY

Beginnings

You cannot hope to understand what anthropologists are doing today unless you have some idea of where they are coming from, of the intellectual traditions and practical and political circumstances which have shaped the discipline. The precise starting point is almost bound to be arbitrary. Humans have no doubt been trying to understand the customs of groups other than their own for as long as there have been humans on earth. They have only been able to record their views for posterity in the last few thousand years. Herodotus was a Greek who described Scythian nomad 'barbarians' in the fifth century BC with a degree of understanding and respect for their 'otherness'. He therefore has some claim to be viewed as a pioneer of anthropology (he is also sometimes hailed as the first historian). The Chinese and other ancient civilisations have also left fascinating accounts of the barbarian neighbours with whom they interacted.

Another possible starting point would be the writings of Jesuit priests and others on the native peoples with whom Europeans began to interact in many parts of the world from the sixteenth century onwards. The European Enlightenment, reaching its peak in France in the second half of the eighteenth century, had a decisive impact on almost all branches of art and science. Its implications for anthropology were complex. On the one hand, the Enlightenment emphasised the power of reason and ideals of 'liberty, equality and fraternity' that were to apply in principle to all humans. Our contemporary discussions of human rights stem directly from these ideals. On the other hand, these universal ideals were not translated into practice. Jean-Jacques Rousseau, with a bare minimum of anthropological knowledge at his disposal, invoked the image of the 'noble savage' to criticise intellectual universalists. A little later, the works of Johan Gottfried Herder in Germany proved to have lasting significance for anthropology. His innovation was to use the term culture in the plural. You could almost describe him as the first modern cultural relativist. Like his French contemporaries he was a well travelled, cosmopolitan man, with a commitment to progress. Unlike them, he thought not in terms of universal rights, but of the vital qualities of diverse cultural communities, each with its own equally valid ways of living and ways of thinking. His approach can be viewed as part of a 'romantic' reaction to the modern ideals of the Enlightenment: in place of rational universalism, Herder emphasised traditional cultures.

> Anthropology is not the bastard of colonialism but the legitimate offspring of the Enlightenment.[2]

At this point it is still too early to speak of a coherent anthropological tradition in anything like the modern sense. Those who began to identify themselves as such later in the nineteenth century did not develop Herder's relativism. Instead, in Germany and elsewhere they still thought in terms of a fundamental divide between the savage and the civilised, between *Naturvölker* and *Kulturvölker*. Culture was restricted to the peoples that had attained a higher level of civilisation, notably literacy. Nevertheless, the subject made considerable progress in the nineteenth century. The Royal Anthropological Institute was founded in 1843 as the Ethnological Society of London. Similar societies of enthusiasts, very few of them engaged in a full-time, professional way, followed in other European countries and in the USA. The study of what we nowadays term social or cultural organisation was not clearly separated from the study of physical anthropology and archaeology. The dominant theoretical orientation of this period was evolutionism and it took many different forms. In the USA, Lewis Henry Morgan based his theories on the evolution of property relationships, an approach that was congenial to Karl Marx and Friedrich Engels, who quickly incorporated Morgan's ideas into their communist texts. In Britain James Frazer argued in terms of a long-term evolution from beliefs in magic to religious faith and finally to rational science.

Specifically Darwinian ideas had little direct influence upon these anthropological theories, though some researchers with biological training argued that social customs spread around the world in adaptive processes of *diffusion*.

Bronislaw Malinowski and the fieldwork revolution

This brings us more or less into the twentieth century and the contribution of Bronislaw Malinowski, who was born in Cracow in 1884 and educated at that university, obtaining a doctorate with distinction in 1908. He then went on to study in Germany and in England, before carrying out field studies in Melanesia. He is the man who made the Trobriand Islanders famous in the anthropological literature, following the intensive studies that he carried out there during the First World War. In the course of this study he set new standards for fieldwork. Pitching his tent among the natives and mastering their language enabled him to move closer than any predecessors to the 'savages' he was studying. He argued that this full immersion into the community was necessary if one wanted 'to grasp the native's point of view, his relation to life, to realise his vision of his world.'[3]

Malinowski dismissed all forms of diffusionism and what he regarded as 'speculative history'. The important thing was to understand how a particular culture functioned in the present. He called this approach *functionalism* and we could also call it *presentism*. For example, if a group of Trobrianders told a story about how one of their ancestors emerged from the ground at a certain place, this could not be understood as revealing useful information about the history of the group, but as a mythical 'charter' supporting, or one might say legitimating, the location of those people in the present.

Malinowski became known internationally in the inter-war decades as Professor of Social Anthropology at the London School of Economics. It seems no exaggeration to see him as a revolutionary. Victorian anthropologists had used the data sent to them by missionaries and explorers to support their general theories about the evolution of humanity. Malinowski rejected this and argued for a shift of focus to the present. The task of the fieldworking anthropologist was to provide meticulous descriptions of how customs made sense to the natives in the contemporary context, and not to speculate on origins and evolution. Malinowski defined this modern anthropology as 'the scientific study of cultures', and ethnographic fieldwork was the basis of this science.

Great man though he certainly was, it is not entirely correct to see him as a single-handed revolutionary. For one thing, others in British anthropology were already developing the techniques of fieldwork before Malinowski appeared on the scene. For another, we must look more carefully at developments in North America. Nowadays this part of the world has more professional anthropologists and more people studying the subject than the rest of the world put together. The key figure in the emergence of the American tradition of cultural anthropology was Franz Boas, who received his education in Germany before moving to New York in 1889. In fact, some of the people who taught him also taught Malinowski a few years later: Boas and Malinowski had common intellectual roots in Central Europe. Boas, too, was a pioneer of fieldwork. He worked over several decades on the customs of the Indians he called the Kwakiutl, who lived on the North West coast of North America. Most of this work was undertaken in partnership with a literate native of this region, George Hunter, who deserves some of the credit for the rich documentation that Boas amassed for these people. Boas did not himself undertake extended periods of fieldwork in the manner later undertaken by Malinowski, but he, too, was a superb linguist, who sought to grasp the Indian's view of the world in which he lived. Unlike Malinowski's view of Trobriand culture as an integrated whole, (the Herderian view of the world). Boas did not assume that cultural traits would necessarily coalesce to form an integrated totality.

The concept of culture was developed in the first half of the twentieth century by Boas's pupils, anthropologists such as Alfred Kroeber, Ruth Benedict and Margaret Mead. They established the foundations of American cultural anthropology, which have been much modified but not fundamentally altered since. This was the age in which anthropology became institutionalised as a university discipline.

Social structure and structural-functionalism

If Malinowski's concept of culture was so similar to that of his American contemporaries, why then did the subject develop in Britain as *social* anthropology, and not as *cultural* anthropology? In the early days Oxford did recognise 'cultural anthropology', and 'ethnology' as a subfield of it. It was mainly due to intellectual influences originating in France, in the sociology of Émile Durkheim, that priority was eventually given to the term social. While Malinowski had the charisma of a prophet and was undoubtedly the driving force in consolidating anthropology's presence in the universities, the intellectual direction of this British school was at least as strongly influenced by an English disciple of Durkheim, Alfred Reginald Radcliffe-Brown. For Radcliffe-Brown, culture was never the central concept that it was for Malinowski. He stressed the study of social structure, the goal being to formulate typologies and laws analogous to those of the natural sciences.

Malinowski, for his part, was also interested in formulating laws and in comparison. But it was perhaps the inevitable consequence of the energy with which he prosyletised on behalf of his functionalism and the fieldwork method that most of his major works are detailed studies of particular elements of the world of Trobrianders. He did not produce any large-scale comparative studies; indeed, he did not even produce a single synthesising study of the Trobrianders. Radcliffe-Brown, by the same token, did not produce any satisfying ethnographies (he seems to have lacked the personal skills to be a successful fieldworker) and his attempts to derive scientific generalisations from disparate case studies, his own and others, have not proved very influential. What did prove influential over several decades, roughly speaking over the last generation of Britain's colonial Empire, was the notion that the anthropologist should focus on the study of structural form and *social relations*, and that these were somehow more concrete than the *cultures* studied by the Americans. Eventually the term *structural-functionalism* came into use to describe a synthesis of Malinowski and Radcliffe-Brown, and this was the core of the British school in its heyday in the later years of the colonial Empire.

You can see the distinction most readily if you compare a British monograph with Ruth Benedict's generalisations about the values of the Japanese in *The Chrysanthemum and the Sword* (1947), or with Margaret Mead's writings on the Samoans. In many cases, however, the distinction between cultural and social anthropology remained fuzzy. A curious situation arose in which Americans tended to see an emphasis on social relations as one element within a broader programme of research into 'culture', while the British school tended to view culture as one element in their broader programme of research into 'society'. In any case, definitions of culture shifted away from the very broad type offered by Tylor in the nineteenth century, and retained by Malinowski in the twentieth. The new, narrower definition of culture neglected such elements as technology to emphasise the ideas, values and symbols that people held in common: the mental, rather than the material. Clifford Geertz, Marshall Sahlins and David Schneider have been among the leading figures of this 'idealistic'current in the last decades of the twentieth century. During this period the distinction between the American cultural and the British social traditions weakened. The British school accepted that those concrete social relations, like everything else they investigated, were in some sense culturally constructed. There was a retreat from the scientific goals of Radcliffe-Brown. For example, in Oxford, Edward Evans-Pritchard's early writings on the Nuer of the southern Sudan (1940) showed a Durkheimian concern with social structure. Later works placed a stronger emphasis on the Nuer as a unique cultural configuration.

Structuralism

It is difficult to reduce the theoretical orientations of anthropologists in recent decades to tidy schools, but four -isms stand out and deserve brief summary. Structuralism as advocated by Claude Lévi-Strauss (b.1908) was an orientation with goals quite different from those of Radcliffe-Brown, with his emphasis on social structure. Drawing inspiration from modern linguistic theory, Lévi-Strauss was less interested in mapping and comparing social relationships than in understanding how they reflected universal mechanisms of the human mind. He believed that these followed logical patterns and he sought them at first in kinship systems and later in myths. This orientation was dependent for its raw material on ethnographic data, and Lévi-Strauss himself was an active fieldworker among Brazilian Indians. However, the structuralist attached less weight to a full rendition of the 'local model', i.e. the native's own view of his social world, than he did to a further level of analysis, in which the fundamental oppositions of this model were decoded by the external analyst, the anthropologist. In contrast to the historian, the anthropologist was not concerned with the details of actual change through time, but with specifying the principles of *structural transformation* at a deeper level.

Marxism

Structuralist approaches can and have been combined with other orientations, including that of Marxism, which was particularly influential in the western social sciences in the 1960s and 1970s. Western Marxists were free to modif or ignore the continuing Soviet preoccupation with evolutionary schemata, a nineteenth-century legacy, and able to concentrate instead on the inequalities generated by capitalism in contemporary societies. Marxist terms such as 'mode of production' were also applied to precapitalist societies in an effort to demonstrate that, for example, the tribal chief was exploiting the 'labour power' of those who performed more manual work than he did. Some of the more influential work, much of it undertaken in France, explored the interactions between traditional modes of production and the dominant capitalist mode. Marxist anthropologists argued that the basic relationship between the so-called first world, i.e. that of the developed capitalist countries, and the underdeveloped, so-called third world countries, was a relation of exploitation. They differed as to whether those in the so-called second world offered a genuinely alternative path, or whether they too were part of a single 'world system', dominated by the capitalist countries of the North Atlantic. The collapse of the Soviet bloc seems to have made it quite clear that no alternative is available, but the Marxist orientation had lost much of its earlier popularity even before the dramatic political changes of 1989–91.

Feminism

The radicalism of the Marxists was to some extent recaptured in the impact of feminism on anthropology from the 1970s onwards. Ever since the work of Morgan and Engels in the nineteenth century, theories about the subordination of women have been commonplace. However, for a long time it was rare to come across detailed studies of the values associated with women in different societies or of the actual political options open to them. Even studies carried out by women, and there was no shortage of excellent female ethnographers in the twentieth century, often focused more on the activities of men, because they seemed to play the more important role in regulating the public affairs of the group. Feminists rejected the idea that inequalities between men and women had a simple explanation in biology (*sexual* differences) and instead explored the many subtle ways in which shared ideas (ideologies) created *gender* differences that reinforced subordination. They have shown, for example, how folk ideas about the respective contributions of men and women to the reproduction of human life often reflect male domination, and how metaphors derived from gender relations can be extended to many other fields of social life.

Postmodernism

The orientations we have mentioned so far, from evolutionism and functionalism to Marxism and feminism, form a very mixed bag, but the last -ism to which we wish to draw attention in this chapter belongs in a very special category all of its own. Postmodernism is not so much a coherent orientation intended to advance knowledge in the field as the claim that such an aspiration is hopelessly misjudged, at least in a subject like social anthropology, where so much depends upon the particular perspective, values and literary techniques used by the anthropologist. Many classical contributions have been reappraised, including Malinowski's work on the Trobrianders. When the private diary he kept during his fieldwork was published in the 1960s, long before postmodernists appeared on the scene, some thought that passages in which he noted his boredom and appeared to disparage the natives would forever tarnish his reputation. Such passages may indeed change our picture of Malinowski the man, but they have not affected the lasting value of his Trobriand ethnographies. More generally, postmodernists make a valid point when they remind us that a subject in which human beings are studying the behaviour and customs of other human beings is unlikely ever to achieve the precision of a laboratory science, a subject in which experiments can be repeated and all the constitutive elements described with clinical precision.

Political contexts

It should already be clear that, like all academic subjects, but probably rather more than most, anthropology has always been sensitive to the social and political contexts in which it has been researched and taught. The connections can be explored at many levels. In the nineteenth century, for example, over and above the influence of particular texts, such as the writings of Darwin, there was a more diffuse climate of intellectual opinion emphasising progress and the emancipation of humanity from previous bonds, which helped to establish evolutionism as a basic framework in anthropology. The reluctance of most social anthropologists to engage with such theories in the twentieth century must have had something to do with wider changes in the intellectual climate. At the same time, improved global communications and geographical mobility have also influenced theoretical developments, including increased questioning of the concept of culture.

Sometimes the links between anthropology and politics or ideology have been extremely close. The anthropologists of the Soviet Union were always obliged to work within an evolutionist framework adapted by Engels from the work of Morgan, no matter how difficult it proved to squeeze fresh ethnographic data into this straitjacket. In western countries, too, it is possible to detect ideological influences at work, perhaps more subtle, but in some ways all the more effective because partly disguised. British social anthropology in its heyday depended on the favourable conditions for research provided by the last decades of colonialism. It is not difficult to detect the paternalist values of the colonial power in the writings of Malinowski and his students. Perhaps it is not accidental that

American cultural anthropology is currently the most influential style. America has many more anthropologists than any other country and it is the dominant world power. The democratic, pluralist values of American society have had a great impact not only on the formal ethical code of the American Anthropological Association, but on the causes for which many anthropologists have become engaged and the style in which they have worked. For example, the growth of feminist anthropology is clearly related to the rise of the women's movement and its influence on American society.

Context can influence the course of anthropological history in very practical ways. In the inter-war years it was relatively easy for Malinowski to obtain grants from the Rockefeller Foundation to finance his students' projects on the impact of colonialism upon African societies. By the end of the century it was perhaps easier to obtain grants for anthropological projects in Europe, for example projects investigating the impact of the expansion of the European Union. Of course, not all research is driven directly by such pragmatic issues as the availability of sponsors. We are simply saying that you cannot understand the history of anthropology without paying attention to the changing social and political circumstances in which anthropology is practised.

This means also looking carefully at the way it is packaged in different education systems. Anthropology remains conspicuously absent from the school curriculum in most countries. Many anthropologists regret this absence, and believe strongly that instruction in cultural diversity should become a prominent part of national education systems. Others feel that the subject does not lend itself to popularisation for immature audiences, and that its proper place is therefore in the university, where it became successfully established over the twentieth century. But what sort of training should universities give in this subject? Should social anthropology be studied on its own, or always in combination with some other branch of anthropology, or with another discipline? Should the course include a practical, fieldwork assignment, or should such projects be reserved for postgraduate studies?

Anthropologists do not agree on the answers to these questions and courses in the subject vary accordingly.

3 | TIME AND SPACE COORDINATES

Three time frames

Our basic point in the last chapter was the need to understand how the academic discipline has developed if you want to understand what anthropologists are doing today. But the same point applies to everything that anthropologists study. No people exist outside real historical processes. The Malinowskian model of a *synchronic* study that ignores the historical context in favour of the ethnographic present must be rejected. Using the present tense in later published accounts compounds this error. Soon it will be a century since Malinowski did his fieldwork, yet on the basis of his books the anthropological literature is full of statements such as, 'Trobrianders give...' and 'Trobrianders believe...' as if the observations made by Malinowski were eternal truths.

In fact it is unfair to attribute the extreme 'presentist' position to Malinowski. He argued against 'speculative history', in order to emphasise the task of showing how the elements of the culture that an anthropologist observed in fieldwork fitted together. They made sense when studied in context, not if removed from context and treated as the 'survivals' of some earlier form of society. But Malinowski was not so foolish as to deny the usefulness of historical and archaeological research. In his later work he conceded that he should, himself, in his work on the Trobrianders, have made more effort to place them in real historical time, i.e. to make plain the influence that traders and missionaries had already had on local people, before the anthropologist appeared on the scene.[4] He remained fundamentally an evolutionist, in that he never challenged the basic nineteenth-century view that human societies had evolved from 'primitive' into increasingly complex forms. We can see this in his late writings, where he makes it very clear that, in his view, liberal capitalism is the highest form of civilisation that humanity has yet achieved.[5]

No ethnographic study is actually undertaken like a photographer's flash. Time is built into the fieldwork and some anthropologists have taken much trouble to document processes of short-run change that they observe during their fieldwork, in other words to produce a *diachronic* analysis. They may try to distinguish causes of change that are internal to the society (*endogenous* change) from factors that are external (*exogenous*). For example, the emergence of a new ruling élite might have an endogenous explanation, or it might be related to the impact of new regulations brought in by an outside power, or it might be some combination of the two. The first temporal frame, then, concerns dynamic processes that can be studied within the period of one or two years of fieldwork.

The second time frame is concerned with diachronic processes over a longer period, for which collaboration with historians is usually essential. Many anthropologists themselves collect oral histories and/or varieties of archival data, in order to build up a picture of long-run change.

> By and by anthropology will have the choice between being history and being nothing.[6]

Some argue that there is no essential difference between the work of the historian and that of the anthropologist. Many anthropologists have contributed to better understanding of the impact of colonialism. Thanks to the work of scholars such as Eric Wolf we also have a much clearer picture of the deeper political and economic causes of the expansion of European populations to other parts of the globe in recent centuries, and the terrible consequences that this brought for most of the native peoples they encountered. Anthropologists cannot ignore this history, in which they themselves sometimes played a role, however minor.

In addition to short-run processual change and long-run historical change, a few social anthropologists are also interested in much longer time spans. Most social and cultural anthropologists have preferred to turn their backs on evolution altogether. You could say that this has been a defining feature of the subject in the twentieth century. We have been swept along by the fieldwork revolution and left the really long-term issues to be discussed by biologists and others. We have criticised them when they come up with oversimplified accounts, such as the notion that human social evolution is simply a matter of our genes seeking reproductive advantage. But we, that is social and cultural anthropologists, have not come up with powerful alternative explanations.

When we suggest that it is time to take evolution seriously again we do not mean to suggest a revival of the Frazerian spirit, of the assumption common in Victorian times, that evolution means qualitative changes in the human mind, in terms of logical, rational thinking. But we do want to suggest that the shallow time frame of modern anthropology leads to problems with the concept of culture. The fieldwork revolution led anthropologists to stress the particularities of the people among whom they worked. More than half a century after Malinowski, fieldworkers in the highlands of New Guinea and in Amazonia were able to document small societies that were, at this time, still substantially different from their neighbours (although hardly uninfluenced by the outside world). The tendency to emphasise, in cases like this, the uniqueness of a culture, was not seriously weakened by the call to add historical depth. The sources to write histories for societies of this type were often scant but even elsewhere, where the possibilities for understanding the past using historical methods were greater, research did not affect the tendency to think in terms of separation and *difference*. Even when the historical work showed the influence of external forces, this did not alter the tendency to think in terms of *separate cultures*.

This tendency can be countered if we pay more attention to the study of long-term change, i.e. longer than the usual time scale of a historian, although perhaps still shorter than that of the evolutionary biologist. Anthropologists may look to archaeologists for help in this time frame.

The world we have lost

The world which Malinowski explored in the Western Pacific in the early twentieth century was not so very different from that which

Captain James Cook had explored on his famous voyages a century and a half before. Many people, even whole societies, had not seen whites and not been significantly affected by their technology. The expeditions of Europeans were perilous adventures in a way that very few anthropological fieldtrips can be nowadays. Islands were especially popular locations for anthropological work but even those who did not work on islands wrote about 'the X' as if they were a unified and bounded entity, to be compared to 'the Y' and 'the Z'. The world was a mosaic of these bounded 'peoples', 'cultures' or 'societies'. This fitted with the idea of the nation as it was then gaining strength in Europe. While anthropologists studied societies that were geographically remote, the 'national ethnographers' in Eastern Europe sought out the most primitive communities of peasants in order to uncover what they claimed were the essence of their national traditions.

What has changed over the twentieth century? First, the numbers have multiplied dramatically. At the beginning of the twentieth century the world contained just over one billion people. By the end of it, it contained more than 6 billion and the rate of increase continues to accelerate. We say this without any apocalyptic overtones, but simply to make the point that the world has become a more crowded place.

It has also become a much more mobile place, in which persons and groups with quite different backgrounds are more mixed up together than ever before. Of course, humans have always been mobile and intermingled. There was a considerable amount of long-distance mobility before the twentieth century, such as the involuntary movements of large numbers of West Africans to the American colonies and the Caribbean during the years of the Slave Trade, or the almost equally coercive methods used later on to transfer hundreds of thousands of people from South Asia to the same sugar plantations. This was movement from one 'peripheral' part of the world to another. Within European societies movement from the countryside to the town accelerated as capitalist industrialisation intensified. The resulting transformation of earlier forms of society was no less dramatic than changes on the periphery

One of the most dramatic changes brought by the twentieth century was the movement of large numbers of people from colonies or ex-colonies into European societies. The precise conditions of their reception, the measure of their integration, and the extent to which close links were maintained with the homeland varied greatly. In some respects these migrations brought to European societies conditions similar to those which had developed over earlier centuries in the USA. Just as earlier theories of a 'melting pot' failed to recognise the extent to which immigrant groups from Europe and elsewhere would strive to hold on to their distinctive identities in their new setting, so European societies have developed notions such as 'multiculturalism' in order better to understand the new forms of diversity. Most non-migrants seem to view the presence of these newcomers as an enrichment of their society, although there are difficult debates about how better to integrate them, and to what extent they should be allowed to deviate, on cultural grounds, from the norms of the majority. Is it acceptable, for example, for young people from South Asia to be required to make marriages arranged for them by their parents, when the norms of the European societies in which they have grown up emphasise individual choice?

These processes have been unevenly distributed. Fifty years ago the population of the cities of southern Sweden was overwhelmingly Swedish. Today roughly one-quarter of this population has some foreign affiliation. This is a big change, even if we bear in mind that the host Swedish population is itself the product of complex past migrations of people and of customs. The twentieth-century history of Poland followed a very different course. When it began there was no Polish state: Poles were divided between the states of Russia, Prussia and the Habsburg Empire. Nonetheless, the intelligentsia kept the idea of the Polish nation alive and Poland regained its statehood after the First World War. This was the occasion for a more general wave of pride in Polish culture. At this point, however, Poland was in reality rather multicultural, in that rather more than one-third of the population was made up of people who did not consider themselves to be Polish in an ethnic sense. The largest minority groups were Ukrainians and Jews, but many others were also present. This changed during the Second World War and its aftermath. After the extermination of the Jews, and the elimination of most Ukrainians through the imposition of new borders and population transfers, socialist Poland considered itself, with some justification, to be one of the most ethnically homogenous states in Europe. Remaining minorities were not recognised; it was assumed that problems of cultural differences in Malinowski's homeland would simply dissolve.

The situation has changed again following the collapse of socialism: multicultural elements are beginning to re-emerge, for example Turks and Chinese. These are not yet as numerous in Poland as the Jews used to be before the 1940s. They seem, however, to form similar kinds of grouping: they are people who will retain their own language, marry each other rather than Poles, and assert that they have a right to be different, to maintain their different culture. Once again, culture seems to be the key term.

Globalisation

Many social scientists, however, have rejected the older anthropological notion of a world made up of different cultures. Alongside the economic and political forces that seem to be making the world a smaller place and undermining the power of individual countries to regulate their own affairs, it is alleged that cultures are becoming cosmopolitan. The media can transmit the same films or soap operas to virtually all parts of the world. It is increasingly clear that 'globalisation speaks English'. It is not possible to organise a summer school in Central Europe in any other language, at least not if one genuinely wants to recruit internationally. Is it not time to speak of a 'world culture'?

The answer is both yes and no. Yes, in the sense that so many things are now organised in basically the same way all over the world. It isn't just that people almost everywhere drink Coca-Cola and listen to similar pop music. The very fact that people everywhere now consider it normal that they should be citizens of a state, and that all these states have broadly similar structures and interact with each other to form a world order, creates a situation quite different from that of the diversity of the past.

Yet the claims of uniformity and fluidity in flows of culture are sometimes exaggerated. Can we be so confident that the same soap opera is received in the same way in Bali as it is in Belfast? Is it not possible that new cultural configurations may emerge in place of the old? For example, in regions such as the Caribbean, which were among the first to experience the major convulsions of the modern world, the old Indian cultures have been largely replaced by elements originating in Africa and South Asia. The dominant language is English, the dominant sports also originate in Europe. Large migrations in the twentieth century have given many inhabitants close links to Europe and North America, yet the region as a whole, and particular islands within it, have developed their own identities, which they show no sign of giving up.

Just as much early anthropological writing exaggerated the remote and exotic character of the people under discussion, so a lot of recent writing under the banner of globalisation has exaggerated the opposite. The great majority of people still feel a strong attachment to particular groups, which are in turn attached to places, even if, as with many migrants, these are not the places in which people live for most of their lives. It is often precisely the experience of migration and displacement which increases consciousness of belonging to a group and to a place.

Claims to cultural distinctiveness often place the anthropologist in something of a quandary. She may see, for example, that the distinctively Vietnamese culture which small groups of immigrants developed in the German Democratic Republic, and more recently in Poland, has little in common with the mainstream of Vietnamese culture in Southeast Asia. In Europe these migrants are participants in a quite different social system. We can hardly expect the cultural characteristics to be the same as those of Vietnamese speakers elsewhere in the world. Yet we notice that they show no sign of assimilating into their 'host' societies in Europe and members of the group constantly emphasise their otherness. Examples can be found in the Polish diaspora. In the nineteenth century, when part of Poland was governed by Russia, in a manner experienced by many Polish intellectuals as deeply offensive, many Poles were deported for political reasons to remote parts of the Russian Empire, notably Kazakstan. These people kept their language and religion alive, through all the difficulties of the socialist years. Since the collapse of the Soviet Union, a few of these Poles have been able to return to their 'fatherland', as they call it. However, the society in which they arrive is likely to seem as alien to them as it does to Vietnamese or other arrivals. Knowledge of a few classics of Polish literature hardly qualifies them for everyday life in contemporary Poland. On the contrary, members of the German minority may be much better qualified in this sense, despite all the friction that has existed in the past between the Polish and German nations.

These examples suggest that the large-scale migrations of recent centuries have made it much more difficult to identify the members of a particular nation, or linguistic community, with participation in a shared culture. The assertion of a common culture, however, is increasingly made, despite realities that contradict the usual anthropological understanding of the term.

One solution is to move away from the concept of culture as the main focus of anthropological research. Some anthropologists prefer to talk about the organisation of social life. Virtually all countries contain groups that differ in their customs and practices. We can study these differences, but if we do so from the starting point that they are different cultures we are likely to miss some of the ground they have common and the ways in which they work together. The term 'society' is open to the same objections as 'culture' if we think of it as referring to a bounded unit, so it is preferable to speak of social organisation or simply social relations. Having said that, there is little doubt that, for a country such as Poland at the present time, the national society is the primary reference point, the anchor, for most of the people who live here. The same seems true for most western European countries, even after their integration into the European Union. Even anthropological investigations with a quite different focus, e.g. one village in a distinctive region, or a transnational enterprise, must usually acknowledge the continuing force of 'nation states' in one way or another.

Anthropology at home

Most anthropological studies continue to follow the patterns established in earlier years, whereby researchers go out from relatively wealthy countries to study some aspect of the social organisation of a rather poorer country. Despite the increased amount of anthropological research carried out 'at home', much of this has concerned the local equivalent of the 'exotic', e.g. migrant groups such as those we have just mentioned and remote rural populations. Studies of middle-class majorities or of élite groups remain exceptional, while fieldwork projects in Europe by anthropologists from former European colonies are virtually unknown. Yet, until we have more such studies, the discipline will continue to bear its colonial legacy.

> Anthropology is interested in what is most exotic in mankind, but equally in ourselves, here, now at home.[7]

In the meantime, is anthropology still anthropology if it is undertaken among groups whose language and interpretations of the world are close if not identical to those of the investigator? Does it not make more sense for anthropologists to concentrate on people quite unlike themselves? The challenge of mastering a language very different from your native tongue in order to approach a very different view of the world is very demanding, but it is also very rewarding. Anthropological fieldwork can certainly generate new insights into one's own society. It may be a big challenge for a Pole, say, to learn how to communicate effectively with novices in a Catholic monastery, or with the directors of a Warsaw bank, or with members of the Wisla soccer team in Cracow, although all of these groups communicate with each other in Polish. All of these projects are potentially interesting, and fieldwork at home is not necessarily easier, a soft option in comparison with work elsewhere. On the contrary, leaving aside the physical conditions of the research, the effort of immersing oneself in the group studied and justifying the project to them may be greater than that normally required in a 'foreign' project. That said, a genuinely foreign experience may initially help in making students better equipped to look with an anthropological eye on their own societies later on.

What do we mean by genuinely foreign? Of course, many varieties of culture and identity exist within large countries such as Britain and the USA. Perhaps in these countries you can find the 'foreign' experience without leaving your country. This is much less true in Poland, after the convulsions of recent history. Of course there are significant differences to be explored. You may, for example, compare the rivalry between Cracow and Warsaw to the rivalry in England between Oxford and Cambridge – but no one would say that the cultural differences there are very profound. What is certain is that even if you study a group that is quite distinct from your own, if you stay in your own country to do so the experience is likely to be very different from what it would be if you undertook a similar project elsewhere.

If our world were already so globalised that the familiar and strange existed in more or less the same mixture everywhere, then it really would not matter any longer where we carried out our fieldwork. In many parts of the world fieldwork can be carried out entirely in English, because locals either speak it as their first language or have learned it as their second. If the latter, however, the anthropologist is likely to miss a lot if she does not also master the mother tongue.

Cultures and traditions

Ultimately, our task is to establish new, post-Malinowskian temporal and spatial coordinates for social anthropology. We can summarise the Malinowskian coordinates as 'presentism' and 'islandism', in other words the study of cultures as snapshots in the present, and as islands, each forming a separate world from the others. This perspective has elevated the plural concept of 'culture' to be the master concept of the discipline. Most of the many currents in later twentieth-century anthropology that were critical of details of Malinowski's programme, notably his functionalist doctrines, were faithful to the master concept of culture. But we cannot feel comfortable with a notion of culture that has come to be used as a bounded entity, analogous to a nation, that can be reified to justify the exclusion of others and/or the application of different moral standards. Culture is, nowadays, in most languages, not a scientific term in the domain of anthropologists but a highly controversial term in public discourse.

At the end of the twentieth century accelerating globalisation was undermining the idea of cultures in the plural. Attempts to tie culture to place were seen by many as increasingly untenable, and we shall address the challenges of globalisation throughout this book. Yet differences in behaviour and values between different groups obviously still do exist in our world. Anthropology will continue to define itself as the discipline that investigates and explains these differences, and it seems reasonable to call them cultural differences. It would be nonsense to turn away from cultural differences precisely when their assertion seems to be becoming more important for so many people all over the world. But the tendency of nationalists and religious fundamentalists to use a concept of culture to support their boundary-drawing stratagems should be a warning to anthropologists. Their response must be to extend the time frames and to insist on the *contingency* of all these cultural boundaries. Culture in this sense is nothing more than an aspect of the social relations, not something that hovers above the real world of social interaction, exercising some mysterious power over the human beings in its thrall.

So, the anthropological approach to terms such as 'culture' and 'tradition' must always have a critical edge. Of course anthropologists study culture and tradition. But it is a mistake to assume that all people at all times have such a notion themselves, of customs that have gathered strength over time and therefore built up a case to be preserved. This sort of consciousness of tradition goes together with the perception of possessing *a culture*: both tend to emerge as the specific products of modern social conditions, in the age of the nation state. Anthropologists have been involved in these processes; they have helped to construct, and sometimes even to invent, the tradition(s) and culture(s) they have documented.

4 DOING SOCIAL ANTHROPOLOGY

Theory

The development of anthropology, like that of any academic discipline, is fuelled by theoretical and intellectual debates. The modern discipline has emerged primarily from within a European tradition. Contemporary anthropologists proceed on the basis of the knowledge accumulated and the questions asked by their predecessors. They are also influenced by developments in neighbouring disciplines. While some are sceptical concerning the claims sometimes made for 'progress' in the social sciences, others believe that both the questions we ask and the way in which we formulate them have improved. There has always been a healthy variety in the precise research orientations that anthropologists have pursued. Theoretical debates are sometimes linked to the development of distinctive regional traditions, such as controversies over the concept of caste in India. But even in cases like this, when non-western researchers do anthropology in their own societies they usually operate within a framework that owes as much to the development of the discipline in a western context as to 'indigenous' intellectual traditions. The research may aim to document and engage with those local traditions, but it does so on terms that are established elsewhere.

It is hard for us to imagine that a time might come when anthropology will sever the links to its own past and enter into a new phase where it is not so tied to what we are loosely describing a western intellectual tradition. Certainly that point has not been reached yet. The theoretical framework used in this volume is a very conventional one that reflects some of the most common distinctions used in teaching and research in anthropology. The remainder of the book will look in turn at economic anthropology, political anthropology, religion and kinship. This does not mean that the subject matter of anthropologists can in reality be so neatly carved up. Social life itself does not allow such subdivisions and many anthropologists, including Malinowski, insist that their discipline must be 'holistic'. Western intellectuals only began to separate out economic from political aspects of social organisation relatively recently. In many other traditions, this division may make no cultural sense at all. Nonetheless, this fourfold division is a convenient way of presenting the field. It is what we term an external model.

External models

The most vital distinction to bear in mind as you begin to study social anthropology is that between external and local models. The latter are those elicited during fieldwork. It is often immensely difficult to represent them in language that western readers can comprehend. The external models are in this respect rather less of a problem. They consist of concepts and explanations that are found helpful for some purpose or other by the investigator, irrespective of whether such ideas are found among the people concerned, or whether they would even make sense at all to those people.

The Marxist tradition is rich in external models, most of them devised with modern capitalist societies in mind. Anthropologists disagree concerning their usefulness for other types of society, for example applying terms such as 'ruling class' to societies where the economy remains rudimentary and everyone is consuming more or less the same sort of goods. It would not have occurred to Malinowski to use Marxist terminology in his analyses of Trobriand society. The Trobrianders do have a social hierarchy, with a 'paramount chief' at the top. But this chief has rather little power to issue commands to others. A Marxist might also view ritual specialists in this society, such as the garden magician, as belonging to a class that exploits the labour of others. But that is certainly not how things seemed to Trobrianders themselves: for them the spells of this hardworking figure were a vital ingredient of their productive system. Similarly, one might from a certain external standpoint consider that Trobriand women are in some ways subordinated, since the most prestigious positions in this society are barred to them. Yet the Trobrianders trace their descent through the female line and a high evaluation of women and women's activities is demonstrated in many of their customs. In short, the local model of the society, the way that natives understand their own social world, is very different from the external model offered by the theories of Marx and Engels. But this sort of evidence need not undermine the usefulness of the external model in providing an overall analysis of how increasingly complex divisions of labour are linked to social and gender inequalities.

Since Marx never undertook any anthropological fieldwork, there is little danger in his case of confusing external and local models. His research was concerned with the formulation of a materialist theory that would explain people's subjective experience of capitalism, but apart from some perceptive remarks about 'commodity fetishism' in the opening chapter of *Das Kapital*, he paid little attention to local models. Engels once applied the term 'false consciousness' to local models that did not fit with the analyst's external model. They were so confident that their own model was accurate and true that they dismissed all other models as 'ideology'. Not all external models aspire to this sort of truth, but the makers of such models do generally claim to have a knowledge of at least some aspects of the workings of a society that is not readily available to the members of the society. In some, perhaps very limited ways, the analyst *knows more*.

Cases where an anthropologist claims some sort of relationship between external and local models are even more complex. For example, it may be claimed that an analytic model based on the structure of kinship groups offers an explanation of how some societies manage to dispense with centralised rulers. The local model is unlikely to be phrased in such terms, but the anthropologist may, with some creative interpretation, insist that the external model is in effect *implicit* in local ideas. We shall consider exactly this case in a later chapter. The main point is that, however we derive them, we do need to have external models if we are to achieve two fundamental goals of anthropology: namely, to address effectively the big questions of human social evolution and to make systematic comparisons.

Local models

> Evidently, Australian savages cannot have any idea of the
> objective aim of these ceremonies from a sociological point
> of view. Nevertheless each institution is somehow reflected
> in the collective ideas of the community, especially if
> expressed in external palpable forms, as ceremonies or rites.
> The initiation ceremonies are likely to be the object of
> collective ideas. We cannot, however, assume the latter at
> will, but must infer them methodically from facts. Some rites
> express certain ideas very plainly; it is allowable to suppose
> that the meaning of these rites is clear for the savages
> themselves. The supposition becomes certitude when it has
> been ascertained by the observer that the natives themselves
> formulate this meaning.[8]

Of course, when an anthropologist comes along with an elegant
external model, there is a strong likelihood that many rich subtleties
of the society will be neglected or ignored. It can, therefore, be
rewarding to give priority to the local models, i.e. to the way in
which people conceive the social worlds in which they live and
their subjective experiences. How can any external analyst claim a
better understanding of any particular life-world than the people
who live within it? It may seem to many that such claims are built
on arrogance. They are themselves local models, the models that
have emerged in the course of the development of western social
science traditions. Anthropology itself springs from these traditions
and we cannot simply wish them away. Many, however, feel that the
external models should take second place to the effort to grasp the
life worlds of the people we study. To document cultural diversity in
this way is even more important than addressing issues of social
evolution and worldwide comparison.

Let us give some examples in relation to themes we have discussed
so far. The three time frames that we identified in Chapter 3, namely
the present/short term, an intermediate 'historical' term, and a long
'evolutionary' term, may be useful devices for organising our work.
But it might be more useful to come to grips with culturally distinct
experiences of time, such as that of the Trobrianders, and to see if

subjective experiences of time passing vary significantly across human groups. Some structuralists, notably, Lévi-Strauss, tended to contrast the 'linear' and 'irreversible' time of modern western societies with the 'cyclical' and 'reversible' time of 'savage' societies. But is such a dichotomous external model actually borne out in subjective experiences? People who live and work in preindustrial settings are likely to be more tied to the rhythms of the seasons but this experience of agricultural cycles may not significantly qualify their sense of living in a time that is forever moving them forward, linear and irreversible. Communist regimes proclaimed a strong ideology of progressive development over time, but only careful enquiries though fieldwork can reveal how far this lineal model impacted on 'ordinary' people. In short, external models may be flawed and ethnocentric when we examine people's actual time experiences.

Understandings of the past are in all societies inextricably bound up with constructions of the present. Even the details of individuals' memories are necessarily affected by the way knowledge of the past is structured in the community. History books play a major role in most countries nowadays, but anthropologists also investigate 'social' or 'collective' memory in non-literate societies. Most groups select particular events as having special salience for them. Some events acquire significance for many different groups – think, for example, of the continuing affects of the Holocaust on both Jewish and non-Jewish identities.

Understanding the subjective dimension of space is just as important, for this is why so many people do maintain a loyalty to particular places. These attachments are well attested, for example in the wish of many migrants to return in their old age to their village of origin. Let me develop the point with an illustration from recent research undertaken by Zdzislaw Mach in the region of Lower Silesia, a region which, until the end of the Second World War, had a large German population. After these Germans had fled or been deported, their houses and farms were allocated to Poles. The research focused on how these Polish immigrants came to terms with a natural and built environment radically different from that to which to they had been accustomed. It was extremely difficult for the first and second generations of Polish settlers to make the necessary adjustment, particularly since there was still some cause to worry about their long-term prospects for political and economic security in this location. They simply did not feel at home in settlements where the cemeteries were foreign (the significance of the bones of the ancestors is similarly attested in many other societies). The third generation, however, raised within this environment, shows a stronger identification with its landscape. Unlike their parents and grandparents they are investing in their futures there.

According to the old cliché, anthropologists are concerned only with remote and exotic societies. Some economists and political scientists are happy to work with anthropologists in third world countries. They recognise that, in a culture very different from our own, the anthropologist's study of the local model may generate some useful information concerning, for example how best to spread some new knowledge about agriculture or birth control. However, investigations into local models can also have beneficial effects at home. Certain Polish economists and political scientists, for example, held strong external models concerning the kind of society that would and should emerge in Poland after the collapse of communism, based on western democracy and market economy. The realities of post-communist development turned out to be much more complicated. Many of the 'deviations' from the external models could be explained if you took account of the local models that determined everyday social behaviour.

Generalisations about local models in post-communist Eastern Europe are very difficult to make. Even within Poland there are considerable variations between social groups and also between regions. Even within different institutions and enterprises it is sometimes possible to identify distinct local cultures or world views. Anthropologists need to engage with all this local diversity and point out the inadequacies of the dominant external models.

Synthesis

The emphasis upon understanding human communities in their own terms is important. It is the most distinctive and in some ways the most important part of anthropology, but two points must also be borne in mind. First, neither external nor local models are sufficient in themselves. Good anthropological work will always deal with both. The important point is to keep the distinction between them clear: the anthropologist must make it clear when he or she is no longer outlining the local model and, instead, introducing external terms.

Second, let us be clear that local models are not the same sort of thing as the external ones. The latter are intellectual constructions, specifically designed to serve a particular theoretical purpose. It is doubtful, however, whether people are guided in their everyday lives by anything like a model, with the implication of internal coherence. In some cases, perhaps, but many people lead social lives that are not entirely coherent; they are muddled, chaotic even. But if this is so, then the search to identify local models could be basically mistaken.

Participant observation

Thanks above all to Malinowski, fieldwork is the hallmark of modern social anthropology. Our theories are tested and new ideas emerge in the course of intimate contact with other people, usually quite 'ordinary' people in small-scale settings. This is what makes anthropology so different from its closest neighbours in the social sciences. Sociologists, if they do fieldwork at all, seldom do so over a long period in the context of one restricted social group, the usual practice for anthropology. Some anthropologists feel uncomfortable about defining their discipline primarily in terms of its methods. What do fieldwork and the term 'participant observation' really involve?

At one level the meaning is simple and obvious. The anthropological fieldworker tries hard to participate in the everyday lives of the people that he or she is studying, while at the same time being an attentive observer of all the interaction that goes on. Good knowledge of the local language is indispensable. On the basis of this participant observation the anthropologist amasses data, often in the form of diaries and fieldnotes, which serve as the basis for the articles and books that he or she goes on to publish. Why are these sources better than others, for example the distribution of a questionnaire? Because people may not always understand the standardised formulations of a questionnaire. Or they may understand them well enough, but not give truthful answers. Most anthropologists find that people trust them more as they spend longer in their community, and so the quality of the information obtained is much higher in the later phases of research. Another problem with questionnaires is that people may give answers that truthfully express their views at some level, but which do not correspond to what they say in other contexts, or to what they actually do. Moreover, in questions about topics such as religion and belief, it may be very hard to express everything in words. The anthropologist who is able to observe and participate stands a better chance of understanding what is going on.

It may sound simple but, in reality, fieldwork is beset with difficulties at every stage. Just how does the anthropologist gain acceptance? Leaving aside problems of obtaining political or administrative authorisation, there is a more basic human problem of adaptation. It can take very different forms in different types of community, but the task of building up relationships of trust with 'informants' is always delicate. No doubt some anthropologists, by virtue of their personalities, are better at this than others. Adaptation may involve, for example, particularly in the early stages of a project, sitting patiently through long rituals of hospitality, in which no useful new information is gathered, in the hope that more fruitful phases of research will follow later. Even if it gradually becomes easier for the anthropologist to move about and conduct conversations more freely, he or she always remains an outsider. Much of the interaction that takes place in the presence of the anthropologist is bound to be influenced by the outsider's presence; so he or she cannot pretend to be the 'fly on the wall', observing events invisibly. The anthropologist is likely to get to know some people much better than others and to use some as 'key informants'. But this is often a highly serendipitous if not arbitrary process. Sometimes data collected may not even be representative of one small community, but only of particular individuals within it. Then there is a host of problems concerning the translation of different cultural experiences, a vital part of the anthropologist's work if the main aim is to achieve insight into local models.

All in all it is not surprising that fieldwork, the nuts and bolts of our trade, has come in for much critical scrutiny in recent decades. Later researchers have returned to classical works, such as those of Malinowski, or of Mead among the Samoans, and found them deficient in important ways. Malinowski's diary was written in Polish and, indeed, was not intended for publication, and it shows that fieldwork was not always a pleasant and rewarding experience, and that he did not always have feelings of empathy towards the people he was living among. He made mistakes; Mead may have made rather more. Fieldwork is an imperfect craft. To take another classic, Edward Evans-Pritchard lived for about a year in the early 1930s among the Nuer of the southern Sudan. He revealed little in his books about the conditions of the fieldwork, beyond hinting at major difficulties, and he has been much criticised for his almost complete neglect of the social and political context. Like others in that period, he presents his case study outside of historical time. To judge from his later reminiscences and from photographs, the fieldwork of this colonial Englishman was not founded on close personal rapport with native people. Fifty years later Sharon Hutchinson worked among the Nuer in quite different conditions. She paid close attention to the recent history of the people and she says much more than Evans-Pritchard about how she actually undertook her work. Establishing warm personal relationships seems to have been relatively easy for her. Indeed, to some extent the course of her work was directly influenced by her interactions with the informants. This must also have been true for Evans-Pritchard but it is largely suppressed in his narrative. In preparing her major book, Hutchinson unlike her predecessor benefited not only from the advice of many external authorities on the people and the region but also from the comments of educated Nuer, people who knew the culture well from the inside. On the whole her evidence shows the lasting value of Evans-Pritchard's contribution, but it is clear that half a century has made an enormous difference in the way these anthropologists have practised their discipline.

Co-operation with local scholars is one way in which the nature of anthropological fieldwork has changed for the better, particularly if it can be sustained over a long period with follow-up studies.

Sometimes it may be enough to have preliminary discussions and then later to share the results with these scholars, without the latter actually joining the foreign researcher in the fieldwork location. In other cases, teamwork in the location may be a better solution. Such cooperation is sometimes problematic, for example in cases where a foreign researcher is not free to choose partners but must work with those chosen by the local political authorities. In some cases the foreigner might take the view that all local researchers have a quite false perception of some important matters, such as the myths of their own group, but even in difficult cases it should be possible to establish some form of dialogue. If the anthropologists of different countries cannot engage in dialogue, then what are the prospects of effective communication among politicians and others?

For some projects, regardless of whether or not they involve a combination of local scholars, an interdisciplinary team may be optimal. However, larger teams of investigators cause more disruption than the 'lone ranger' fieldworker and this drawback should be kept in mind. There is also a trade off in the use of modern technology. To have a video film of a particular ritual may facilitate meticulous analysis later, but it may only be worth doing if the performance is not significantly distorted by the presence of a camera team. An unobtrusive tape recording may generate more authentic, albeit less colourful data.

Ethics

This brings us to the problem of research ethics. In the example just given, a ritual is being recorded by a tape recorder. If the tape recorder is hidden, there is a stronger likelihood that people will speak and behave as if it were not there, which is what the anthropologist ideally wants. Should he or she then not ask for the hosts' permission to make the recording? Such a procedure would be ethically indefensible. We obtain all our data from the people we study and we have obligations to inform them and consult with them at every stage. We also have obligations to protect the people who give us information from possible adverse effects when we publish. In some cases not using real names would smack of condescension and deny recognition to persons who deserve and expect to have their true identities stated. Sometimes, however, it is appropriate to change the names of people and places. In extreme cases, the possibility of negative consequences may be so great as to lead a conscientious anthropologist to decide not to publish the data at all. Many anthropologists nowadays feel an obligation to make the results of their work available to the community they have studied, so they present them with copies of the texts they write or the films they make. In all of these ways anthropologists attempt to cultivate a climate of partnership in their research and they reject the often exploitative patterns of the colonial period.

Some contemporary anthropologists go further. Aware of how little they give in return, they feel an obligation to become 'advocates' for the people with whom they work. This, too, can be problematic. It may be, for example, that an anthropological study uncovers cases of injustice and corruption that lead the investigator to campaign for remedies. But, especially if the community itself is not united on the issues and in cases where the anthropologist is not a citizen of the country concerned, this can easily lead to trouble, including greater difficulties of access for future researchers. Advocacy is usually better pursued in one's own country and in one's professional associations.

Maintaining a certain political detachment may also help the anthropologist in those situations in which the people being studied have privileges or hold values with which the investigator disagrees. It may be much more difficult to build up relationships of trust with people you really do not care for, but such groups may be no less deserving of study. The anthropologist should be able to describe, explain and understand the social organisation of any human group, or, if you prefer, the local culture, including the values that people hold; it really is not necessary to take the additional step of *evaluating*. In this sense, a large element of relativism is indeed built into the subject.

SUMMARY OF PART I

Anthropologists study the full range of human societies in time and space. They are interested both in the fundamentals that unite all members of the species *homo sapiens*, and in the extraordinary diversity of human behaviour. They aim to understand these by transcending the bias of their own particular background and avoiding ethnocentric judgements. They resist the seductive claims of extreme relativists. Perfect translation between different cultural worlds is not a realistic goal, but neither is it necessary for understanding and explanation. It is ethnocentric to imagine that our values are superior, or that we go about our everyday lives in a more rational manner. It is not ethnocentric to point out that in many ways contemporary industrial societies have superior knowledge of the world to that of their predecessors.

The discipline grew out of European intellectual traditions and took shape gradually in the course of the nineteenth and twentieth centuries, stimulated partly by the contacts made by Europeans with other peoples and partly by nation-building forces within Europe. The most decisive point in the institutionalisation of the discipline came in the early decades of the twentieth century when, above all in the case of Bronislaw Malinowski, the emphasis shifted away from speculative reconstructions of the past toward comprehensive analyses of societies in the present, as observed in fieldwork. From this point the main concerns of social anthropology (known in North America as cultural anthropology, the difference being mostly, but not entirely, a question of name) diverged from those of physical (biological) anthropology and archaeology.

The 'presentism' that is fostered by an emphasis on 'participant observation' needs to be supplemented by expanded time horizons. Social anthropologists also pay attention to dynamic processes and some still take seriously the issues of long-run change (evolution) that engaged their nineteenth century predecessors. The history of European colonisation of the world over the last half millennium has been in large part a story of destruction and exploitation. The Europeans who conquered most of the rest of the world rendered its peoples as 'peripheral', 'exotic' and 'other'. Anthropologists have begun to transcend this definition of their discipline. They are as likely nowadays to study modern elites as they are to study 'primitive tribesmen', though there may still be good reasons for doing one's first fieldwork in a setting that is unfamiliar. The anthropologist should make a distinction between external and local models, but all models should be treated with a degree of scepticism, for social life is usually far more muddled than any models allow.

From its inception, social anthropology has found itself in the awkward position of being concerned with group differences that were in some process of erosion or disintegration. In this respect the recent discussions of globalisation have not brought anything new, although accelerating homogenisation has no doubt contributed to a certain idealism in the discipline: both a romantic concern with preserving past distinctions, and a focus on ideals and values as the hallmarks of continuing cultural distinctiveness, when other, more tangible signs of difference were rapidly fading. A contemporary perspective from Cracow, Malinowski's home city, located in the heart of Europe and yet 'peripheral' to the main centres of power and European overseas expansion, suggests that some of the claims made for globalisation are exaggerated. Most people nowadays, as in past centuries, have strong roots or 'anchors' in particular places, among particular named groups of people. Rapid communications and greater mobility may encourage people to reflect more explicitly on the nature of their collective loyalties than they did in the past. This often leads to the formulation of local models of a unitary 'culture' and an exclusive 'tradition'. These basic concepts may need rethinking in the anthropology of the twenty-first century.

Part II
PRODUCING AND CONSUMING

5 ECONOMIES AND ECONOMISING

Malinowski and the challenge to economics

Crucial to the organisation of any society are the means of production, of destruction, and of communication. Production is one of the main concerns of the subdiscipline of economic anthropology, and especially of Marxist approaches. In the era when Eastern Europe was officially governed by Marxist régimes, ideologists claimed (some of them may, indeed have believed) that all social phenomena could be explained by their material causes. Such economic determinism has been rare in anthropology, but whatever one's orientation, economic factors are too important to be ignored completely. This was certainly the view of Bronislaw Malinowski, who devoted the first and the last of his monographs on the Trobriand Islanders to economic matters (exchange and production respectively).

Unlike anthropology, the discipline of economics has an annual ritual in the form of the award of a Nobel prize: a sign of prestige and influence. Yet, little more than a century ago no separate discipline of economics existed. For scholars such as Adam Smith and Karl Marx the study of economic phenomena was inextricably bound up with questions of politics and the distribution of resources in society. Similarly, for early anthropologists, material culture and subsistence strategies were aspects of the general study of human societies, to be investigated as part and parcel of general social organisation. This insistence on placing economic matters in a wider social context has not been abandoned with the emergence of the sub-discipline known as economic anthropology.

What do anthropologists study when they study economies? The word economy derives from the Greek *oikos*, meaning a household. A term that once referred to the management of a household is now habitually applied to peoples and states; we even speak of 'the global economy'. Anthropologists can and do study economic activities at all of these levels, and at varying stages of 'development', from the most primitive technologies to the most sophisticated. Although there is often disagreement about the exact importance of material factors in explaining particular aspects of social life, the physical environment and the technologies available for making a living within it clearly set constraints for other institutions. Economies in which people subsist from hunting and gathering cannot support large populations and complex institutions such as the state, or belief systems disseminated through written texts. Conversely, our economies cannot exist without sophisticated forms of political organisation. The pre-eminence of the state may be weakening, but increasing globalisation does not mean that complex infrastructural supports and political restraints on economic activities become any less important.

For some purposes it makes sense for economic anthropologists to classify economies into general types. For example, all economies based on hunting and gathering could be considered as basically of the same type. For other purposes, however, it is important to make finer distinctions. Hunting techniques in tropical rainforests are bound to be very different from those found in polar regions. Moreover, if hunting and food collecting are practiced alongside other activities, the case for lumping these societies together as if they all demonstrated a common early stage of evolution becomes very weak. Sometimes anthropologists make comparisons that extend across the boundaries of these types. For example, they may compare how labour is divided between the sexes in hunting economies with the equivalent division in pastoral societies.

Some economic anthropologists have investigated how economies change from one type to another but, on the whole, nineteenth-century evolutionist work has had little direct impact on later developments. As in so many other fields, Malinowski was a pioneer. Many before him had contributed valuable descriptions of the material culture of exotic societies, but he was the first to pose the economic organisation of a 'savage' society as a theoretical challenge to the discipline of economics. In an article published in 1918 in the *Economic Journal*, he argued that the behaviour of

Trobrianders could not be explained within the framework of modern economics. Whereas the central actor of a modern capitalist economy was the entrepreneur whose goal was to maximise his profits, the central actors of the Trobriand Islands were concerned with elaborate ceremonies in which they gave goods away to others. It seemed that 'economic man' did not exist among the Trobrianders, or rather, that economic considerations were outweighed by political and cultural factors.

A few years later in *Argonauts of the Western Pacific* (1922) Malinowski presented detailed classifications of the types of exchanges practised by Trobrianders. Some of these, notably *gimwali*, glossed by Malinowski as haggling, seemed roughly comparable to market exchange in a modern industrial economy in that participants negotiated to obtain the best deal they could – even though the Trobrianders had no formal marketplaces and nothing resembling a modern currency. Another important form of exchange in this matrilineal society was the *urigubu* seasonal giving of yams by a man to his sister's husband. Such transfers served to maintain marital alliances and enabled chiefs, who often had several wives, to accumlate yams for ostentatious storage and eventual distribution. The most famous of all Trobriand exchanges was the ceremonial exchange of valuables known as *kula*. In the *kula* 'ring', through which Trobrianders were linked to a number of other islands, including mainland Papua, individuals exchanged shell necklaces (known as *soulava*), which could only be passed on in a clockwise direction and armbands (known as *mwali*, which circulated counterclockwise). The *kula* rules left individuals with plenty of room to manoeuvre, determining the size and timing of their gift in order to gain as much prestige as possible. This system of exchange has fascinated many later commentators, and *kula* has continued to flourish since Papua New Guinea became an independent state in 1975. Its origins probably owe much to its political functions in the age when there were no effective states in this region. Without the 'umbrella' of security created by ceremonial *kula*, the simultaneous (but separate) organisation of utilitarian barter might have been too risky.

The economic ethnography of Malinowski, later extended to the fields of production and land tenure in the monograph entitled

Coral Gardens and Their Magic (1935), raised more questions than he himself was able to resolve. In some respects, his challenge to modern 'neoclassical' economics was less radical than he thought. In Robbins' famous definition:

> Economics is the study of the allocation of scarce resources between alternative ends.[9]

The theory only assumes that individuals make choices that maximise their utilities. An emphasis on scarcity may seem misplaced in a context where piles of yams are left to rot, but Malinowski's analysis is consistent with a focus upon maximising individuals. In place of the stereotypical capitalist entrepreneur, allegedly motivated by the desire to maximise *profits*, Malinowski substitutes a political entrepreneur, whose decisions are driven by his desire to maximise *status*, *prestige* or *power*. He emphasises reciprocity in Trobriand interaction, but this in no way contradicts the utility maximising theories of the neoclassical economists.

Not until the second half of the twentieth century, some time after Malinowski's death, can we really speak of a distinct subdiscipline of economic anthropology. It has been a lively field of debate in which four main approaches or paradigms have struggled for supremacy. Although many economic anthropologists adhere more or less closely to just one of these approaches, they are not alternative products in a market, from which just one can be purchased. On the contrary, these approaches are not substitutable rivals at all. They can and should be combined. The optimal combination will always depend on the specific problem that the investigator wishes to address.

Four paradigms

Formalism

The first paradigm is the 'formalist' or 'decision-taking' approach. It amounts essentially to the generalisation of the modern economist's toolkit to the entire range of human societies. The fundamental axioms of neoclassical economics are scarcity and utility maximising. The constraints within which economic actors make their decisions obviously differ from case to case. However, at a certain level of abstraction it is assumed that African pastoralists, Australian hunter gatherers and European capitalist firms all make choices in fundamentally the same way, in order to maximise utilities given the information available to them. This universalist assumption has some appeal to anthropologists who, always sensitive to accusations of possible ethnocentricity, do not wish to argue that the economic decisions of pre-industrial peoples are in any way less 'rational' than our own.

But what do we learn from postulating that the ultimate foundation of decisions is utility maximising? Some actions that are not rational within one culture may be entirely rational in another. Within one and the same culture, behaviour that for one individual would be irrational might maximise the 'utility function' of a neighbour. These utility functions are subjectively determined and they change. At the end of the day this approach is tautologous. It simply states that what people do is the best they can do at that moment, given their preferences and the knowledge available to them.

> In my view an analysis of a primitive economic system or of an African or Oriental peasant system can be made without sacrifice of the basic approach of modern economics. Most assumptions about resources, wants and choices made by an economist in his formal analysis, are so general that they can apply to any human society.[10]

At lower levels of generality, anthropologists have made constructive use of many concepts from neoclassical economics, sometimes in unlikely contexts. For example, in his study of *Primitive Polynesian Economy* Raymond Firth used the concept of capital in his discussion of coconut trees on the island of Tikopia. When a chief imposed a taboo on the harvesting of coconuts, this had the effect of increasing the savings rate and augmenting the stock of capital. The fact that the people of Tikopia had no acquaintance with money or markets did not prevent them from making this rational adaptation. Firth, who had some training in economics, provided a fuller and more explicit statement of the position implicitly developed by his teacher Malinowski and numerous other commentators on 'primitive economics'.

Substantivism

The second paradigm emerged as a direct challenge to the first. Karl Polanyi (1886–1964) was primarily an economic historian, born and brought up under the Habsburgs, in the same Central European empire as Bronislaw Malinowski. He was never a fieldworker, but he did experience social life in England in the Depression years, before moving on to America during the Second World War. As the leader of an interdisciplinary group at Columbia University in New York, Polanyi provided the inspiration for a powerful counterblast to the formalists. His manifesto is outlined in the essays he contributed to the volume he coedited, *Trade and Market in the Early Empires* (1957). Polanyi argued that there were two distinct senses of the word 'economic'. The formalist meaning was that which had become central to neoclassical economies – maximising utility in conditions of scarcity. However, in its 'substantive' sense, economics was simply the study of how humans obtained a living from their environment. Polanyi argued that this was the more important sense of the word for the anthropologist. He did not deny the importance of the formalist meaning. On the contrary, he accepted that this had primary significance in the study of economic life in modern industrial societies. Such societies, he thought, were dominated by the impersonal mechanisms of self-regulating markets. Following the onset of industrialism, economies had escaped from the social and political controls in which they had previously been 'embedded'. The scientific toolkit of the economist was appropriate to this kind of economy, but for preindustrial economies different tools would be required. Polanyi suggested that reciprocity and redistribution were the basic 'modes of economic integration' in preindustrial societies.

> The format of the substantive concept is the empirical economy. It can be briefly... defined as an instituted process of interaction between man and his environment, which results in a continuous supply of want satisfying material means.[11]

Polanyi's 'substantivism' was pitched at a lower level of abstraction than the formalism he attacked. Whereas formalists asserted universal human proclivities to maximise, applicable to any society at any point in history, Polanyi pointed to a unique 'great transformation' and maintained that different concepts were needed for different types of economy. Some of the polemics generated by Polanyi's critique failed to acknowledge this difference in level of abstraction. Those who criticised him for propagating a somewhat romantic, anti-market philosophy were probably close to the mark. The substantivist approach in economic anthropology was an echo of an earlier 'institutionalist' strand in American economics, as well as of other radical traditions in Central and Western Europe well known to Polanyi from his earlier career. It is a pity that Polanyi showed little interest in applying substantivist insights to contemporary industrial economic life. He conceded this ground to the economists, since he regarded modern economies as 'disembedded' and apparently devoid of social and cultural interest. This is a blind spot in his approach, as we shall see. However Polanyi argued vigorously that modern economics was *not* capable of understanding economic life in all other social systems, where anthropologists and historians should co-operate to develop new tools. This position has proved extremely fruitful.

Political economy

The third influential approach in economic anthropology can be summarised as the political economy paradigm. Marxist theory has been particularly influential in this approach, but the aim is to return to the tradition not just of Marx but also of Adam Smith and the other 'classical' economists, who did not bracket economic issues apart from questions of social and political organisation, as their neoclassical successors did. Neo-Marxism came into western anthropology via Parisian intellectuals in the 1960s, who adapted the concepts developed by Marx for the analysis of nineteenth century industrial society to the study of preindustrial societies. All social formations, it was held, were determined 'in the last instance' by their modes of production. Each mode of production had a material base consisting of the 'forces of production' (environment and technology), and the 'social relations of production' (which in all social formations other than egalitarian hunter gatherers were taken to be class relations). Social formations changed as a result of tension (the 'dialectic') between the forces of production and the social relations of production. The neo-Marxists were critical of both formalists and substantivists for restricting their attention to the realm of exchange and failing to grasp 'deeper' issues pertaining to production. The earlier researchers were also alleged to be blind to conflict and contradiction in the societies they studied and to have paid insufficient attention to the temporal and spatial contexts of the small communities they studied. In contrast, the adherents of a political economy approach emphasised how even the most isolated communities had been affected by the global expansion of capitalism since the sixteenth century, and how most parts of the 'periphery' had come to be locked into relationships of exploitation and dependency with the capitalist, imperialist countries.

> The economic structure of society is the real basis on which the juridical and political superstructure is raised, and to which definitive forms of social thought correspond: in short the mode of production determines the character of the social, political and intellectual life generally.[12]

This broadening of the context was a valuable corrective to the common tendency of anthropologists to restrict their attention to particular localities. This is perhaps the most valuable element in the political economy approach. On the negative side, many anthropologists objected to what they considered its economic determinism. Substantivists, for example, although conceding such determinism when it came to explaining capitalist industrial society, which they saw as dominated by self-regulating markets, rejected the prioritising of economics in the study of preindustrial societies. Some neo-Marxists themselves recognised that features such as kinship or religion played such significant roles in precapitalist societies that it hardly made sense to dismiss these as items of 'superstructure', whose appearance was determined by an economic 'base'. Maurice Godelier sought to resolve the problem by allowing that, in societies such as that of the Baruya, who he studied in New Guinea, kinship might 'function as' the social relations of production; but it is not clear how far this represents an advance on the earlier substantivist idea of embeddedness. More generally, the fieldworkers who had their materials reworked by neo-Marxists were unimpressed to be told that they had overlooked the significance of class, exploitation, alienation, dominant ideologies and so on. The external models of the neo-Marxists might be applied to the whole range of human society. But, as with the tools of the formalists, such application was not very illuminating. Concepts such as 'class struggle' did not make much sense when applied to tensions between fathers and sons in an African tribal society.

Culturalism

The fourth paradigm is a response to the deficiencies of all attempts to impose external models on economic phenomena. The adherents of 'culturalist' approaches argue that the anthropologist's priority is to understand the *local* models of the people they study. People's relationships with their material environments are understood by them in terms of ideas, values and metaphors which it is the job of the fieldworker to uncover. From this perspective the complex theoretical frameworks of formalism and Marxism are themselves examples of a local model, with roots that may extend far back into European history and Judeo-Christian traditions. However, the generalisation of these models to other societies with other traditions is considered to be unwarranted and fundamentally ethnocentric by the culturalists. They are also dismissive of substantivism, principally because its practitioners do not move far enough in the direction of cultural relativism. To the extent that substantivists rely on very general terms such as reciprocity and redistribution, they too must fail in the main task, which according to this paradigm is to explore each particular culture in its own unique terms:

> The folk have economic models too.[13]

Culturalists do not deny that local models undergo changes and they may pay special attention to the disruptive colonisation processes of recent centuries. However, the export of similar capitalist ideas from the North Atlantic region to the rest of the world has led not to cultural homogeneity, but to unique combinations of old and new in each locality.

A famous early example of a culturalist approach to economic life is the German sociologist Max Weber's argument for the significance of a 'Protestant ethic' in explaining the origins of capitalism. The thesis remains controversial. Yet it is obvious to any observer of capitalism in the contemporary world that it catches on much more quickly and successfully in some places than in others, and local conditions must be at least part of the explanation for this. The fullest exposition of a culturalist approach in modern economic anthropology is that of the American Stephen Gudeman, who has carried out fieldwork in peasant communities in Central and South America. Gudeman has applied the culturalist perspective to other parts of the world using other fieldworkers' data, and also to earlier phases in the history of European economic thought. His *Economics as Culture* (1986) includes a chapter on the physiocrats, a group of eighteenth-century French scholars whose models and forms of economic reasoning were rooted in the European culture of their age. Perhaps his most successful work to date is the collaborative book with Alberto Rivera, *Conversations in Colombia*. The models which inform the economic activities of these peasants, beginning with a model of the house itself as the key unit of production and consumption, are the product of continuing 'conversations' between native peoples and centuries of European immigrants. This analysis of the cultural embeddedness of economic activities is richer than that offered in substantive approaches. However, some prefer to see the culturalist paradigm as an extension or logical continuation of substantivism, and indeed of Malinowski's original point that the economic was always influenced by a range of non-economic factors.

> No human beings, at whatever stage of culture, completely eliminate spiritual preoccupations from their economic concerns.[14]

What are the weaknesses or drawbacks in culturalist approaches? Even when its practitioners pay close attention to historical changes (which is not always the case), those who favour other perspectives often complain of an idealist bias. Much of the activity that we think of as economic involves material objects and physical labour. Culturalist accounts of how people think and talk about their economic activities often fail to engage with these practicalities, such as the pain of a difficult labour process. Formalists may criticise a lack of attention to statistical patterns in production and marketing, that modify or contradict the cultural model. Neo-Marxists may argue that the exploration of models and metaphors is no substitute for tracing the links of dependency and exploitation that exist both within small communities and between those communities, and the wider world. Some culturalists seem to replicate the old illusions of harmonious and functionally integrated communities and it is often difficult to use their analyses of local models for more general comparative purposes. Finally, there are also potential political dangers with prioritising cultural explanations. For example, if we attribute the relatively poor performance of some social groups in the marketplace and in the school system to enduring elements in their culture, this may provide policymakers with a ready excuse for ignoring other social factors contributing to the poor performance.

Four economic fields

Each of the four approaches sketched above draws on powerful intellectual traditions outside anthropology and it would make no sense to treat economic anthropology as a self-contained scientific tradition. It is doubtful whether we can speak of cumulative progress in this subdiscipline. Formalist tools have been used by a minority of practitioners all along, and each of the other approaches has enjoyed a period of dominance, influenced at least in part by the wider intellectual and political climate. Thus, the demise of the European colonial empires and the rise of student radicalism both played a part in the popularity of the neo-Marxist approaches in the 1960s and 1970s. This turned out to be short lived as the end of the Cold War and the rise of 'postmodern' approaches in other areas of academic study increased the popularity of the culturalist paradigm.

Within the subdiscipline we can identify four economic fields of work, exchange, property and consumption. Of course these familiar terms may have different meanings in different societies. To introduce a sharp distinction between work and consumption is already to introduce a western bias. It is usually assumed in the discipline of economics that people undertake a certain amount of work in order then, separately, to be in a position to undertake the consumption activities that will maximise their utilities. Yet many people do not draw such a distinction between work and consumption and it may indeed be increasingly questioned in our own societies. Bearing this in mind, these terms are nevertheless a useful external model to help us to navigate a path through the field of economic anthropology in the remaining chapters of Part II.

WORK

A problematic concept

What is work? The question may seem simple, trivial even, but the answer is by no means straightforward. The student may consider hours spent in the classroom as work. The lecturer who teaches and does research in anthropology works in various places: university office, lecture rooms, the library, and at fieldwork sites around the globe. He may also read anthropological texts in peace and quiet at home, where the activity is more of a leisure pursuit. He may also relax through gardening, and produce all his household's vegetables as he enjoys his hobby. In other words, everyone's experience of work is very different and anthropological approaches to work must take account of many complexities.

We may reasonably begin with an external model that defines work in terms of activities that have to be undertaken in order to ensure subsistence and the reproduction of a group over time. This definition must include a range of domestic tasks, often undertaken by women. Housework and work with children is still work, even though it is not for the most part in our sort of society undertaken on the same sort of basis as the work for which people receive wages or salary outside the house.

But many human groups do not distinguish work from a range of other social activities, which in their local model are equally important to their social life. They might take the view that the 'work' involved in making ritual sacrifices to their gods is actually more important that the mundane activities of putting food into hungry mouths. In short, this is a field in which the local models often challenge external definitions. The Marxist tradition provides us with good examples. Marx argued that work was central to human life. His 'labour theory of value' argued that the products of labour were worth the 'socially necessary labour time' that had gone into making them. They should therefore be exchanged with each other on that basis. But if, as in many societies, working time is not clearly distinguished from leisure activities, it becomes difficult to test this theory. It may be commonly asserted as part of a local model – 'that item is worth the labour that I put into making it' – but, as the basis of a calculus to explain exchanges, the labour theory has not turned out to be particularly useful.

Food collectors

The Marxists' external model for technologically simple societies based on food collecting was 'primitive communism'. They believed this to be the past condition of all humankind, to which in the post-capitalist future it might one day be possible to return. Again, it is hard to test the full theory. The hunter gatherer bands studied by ethnographers in recent generations typically inhabit unfavourable, 'marginal' environments. Their contemporary lifestyles have been greatly influenced by recent social contacts in these environments. They cannot therefore be taken as representative of the lifestyles of our common palaeolithic ancestors.

Despite their possible importance for questions of human evolution, detailed ethnographic accounts of food collectors were rare until the second half of the twentieth century. It was usually assumed that these people led harsh and precarious lives and had to work hard to survive. This picture was demolished by Marshall Sahlins in a famous essay called *The Original Affluent Society*. Sahlins showed that most hunters and gatherers did not in fact work long hours at all, for example in comparison with agricultural peoples. They were able to ensure the food supply needed for the band by working on average no more than a few hours daily, leaving themselves abundant time for leisure activities. Sahlins did not claim that such people were wealthy in the terms of a modern economist, who measures income in dollars per capita. The typical hunter gatherer band placed a premium on mobility and had no wish to accumulate items of property. If calorific needs could be met with ease in relatively secure environments, then from a 'Zen' point of view, argued Sahlins, such people were affluent; they were wealthy in relation to their low material wants.

Sahlins aligned himself with the substantivists. His account of hunter gatherer economics emphasised a distinctive non-western context and rejected the western economist's definitions of affluence. However, there was little in Sahlin's account to disturb a formalist. It was perfectly possible to argue that hunter gatherers make rational individual choices, given the opportunities open to them. In view of their environment and their technology, it was only sensible for them to turn their backs on the acquisition of goods and choose leisure as soon as they had satisfied their subsistence requirements.

From a culturalist point of view, Sahlins did not take his analysis of the cultural context far enough. What did hunter gatherers think about their economic activities, how did they *conceptualise* their environment? Nurit Bird-David conducted fieldwork among the Nayaka people of South India in the 1970s and found them to have a strong sense of confidence and trust in their forest environment. The forest was imagined as a parent, with a duty to provide for all its children. According to Bird-David, the Nayaka treated their natural environment like a 'bank'. Whenever they needed to withdraw deposits, they had only to enter their forest. Bird-David finds similar ideas and even similar images among hunter gather peoples on other continents. Rather than see such economies as founded on work and production, Bird-David prefered the term 'procurement' to describe how hunter gatherers set about the task of making a living.

James Woodburn developed a distinction between 'immediate return economies', those food collectors who obtained their food directly from nature, and those with 'delayed return economies', hunter gatherers who make more use of technology, e.g. in making animal traps and building storage facilities. He argued that immediate return groups tended to be highly egalitarian. However, even groups of this type, such as the Hadza of Tanzania, studied by Woodburn himself, usually feature some division of labour between males and females. The male-associated hunting tasks may not produce as many calories as the nuts and berries gathered by females, but they carry higher value or prestige. In his detailed studies of the !Kung San of Botswana, Richard Lee found some support for the Marxist notion of 'primitive communism'. Although men and women for the most part did different jobs, the total workload was very equally divided. Lee did not have much to say about the local models of the !Kung and made his complex calculations on the basis of his own, external definitions. For example, he excluded the consultation of oracles because this took place within a 'socially pleasurable context'. Yet for the !Kung themselves this was an integral part of the activity of hunting.

Very few people in the world today subsist solely from traditional forms of food collecting. Contacts with more powerful neighbours have often led to relations of dependency, as when Kalahari bushmen become employed to tend the cattle of their pastoral and rancher neighbours. But such relations may not mean the complete end of hunting and gathering as a way of life. By the time that Bird-David studied the Nayaka most of them worked in a nearby plantation as wage labourers. A Marxist might have classified them as a rural proletariat, making their living from selling their labour power to an exploitative capitalist. But this was not how the Nayaka saw themselves. They refused to conform to the discipline of a factory-type labour process, preferring to turn up for work as and when it suited them just as they had traditionally procured their living in the forest. Bird-David, therefore, spoke of 'wage collecting'. The existence of a new income opportunity did not change the economic ethos of the Nayaka. They remained obliged to share any resources they acquired with the members of their community and attached little importance to planning for the future.

Peasants

There is no concise and generally accepted definition of the term peasant. Some anthropologists reject it altogether, for the same reason that they reject terms such as 'tribal' and 'savage'. This last term certainly has objectionable connotations today, though it was standard in Malinowski's time. But the terms tribal and peasant can still serve as loose descriptive terms for social organisation based on agriculture and horticulture. The distinction between them is often fuzzy but tribal is normally applied to peoples such as Melanesian gardeners (e.g. Trobrianders) and sub-Saharan African peoples who use digging sticks rather than ploughs. The term peasant is applied principally to rural cultivators in Europe and Asia who developed agriculture based on the plough following the neolithic revolution some 5000 years ago. Both tribal and peasant economies are based on cultivation of the soil using simple, labour-intensive technology. The main unit of production and consumption is usually the household, though some produce may be sold, and a part of the 'surplus' is normally transferred as tribute to a political superior or paid as tax to the state. The household may or may not own the land that it farms but is usually strongly attached to that land and consumes a substantial portion of its own harvest.

The rural household is also the key unit in some modern farming systems, but where machines have displaced human labour the peasant character of the economy usually changes rapidly. Of course, as with hunter gatherers the pure forms may be increasingly rare in the modern world. Peasants may be found marketing the greater part of their output and buying the foodstuffs they need. They may combine their small-scale farming with forms of wage employment, perhaps through commuting to a nearby factory, or through long-distance migration on the part of one or more household members. Yet so long as attachment to the 'family estate' persists and people continue to behave according to the values of the community and the traditional rural culture, it is premature to speak of the peasantry's demise.

One powerful explanatory model of the peasant economy that has influenced many anthropologists was that developed for pre-revolutionary Russian society by A.V. Chayanov, an agrarian economist. Chayanov was much influenced by the assumptions of neoclassical economics and sought to account for peasant economic decisions in terms of the maximising of utilities. However, he recognised that a peasant household that relied upon the labour of family members rather than hired workers would define that optimum differently from a capitalist farm. Whereas the latter might rationally hire labour up to the point where the cost of more labour exceeded the marginal additional revenue the labour was expected to generate, the 'family labour farm' which did not treat the labour of family members as a cost would extend its production to the point where a subjective assessment of the 'drudgery' of additional labour exceeded the expected benefits to the family. Chayanov also recognised that the two types of farm might respond in quite different ways to a change in the commercial environment. If the price of the main crop were to fall, a capitalist farmer might be expected to produce less and cut back on his labour inputs. However, a family labour farm faced with a similar deterioration might well attempt to *increase* its output if it needed to attain a specific target, for example to meet tax burdens.

In developing such analyses Chayanov used typical formalist tools, but adapted these to the contextual features that made peasant maximising different from the profit maximising of a capitalist entrepreneur. He also offered an explanation for inequalities in the amount of land cultivated by households by describing what anthropologists were later to call the 'developmental cycle of the domestic group'. When the household was large and had many dependants to support, the old and infirm and young children, it would need to cultivate a relatively large surface and its able-bodied members would have to work relatively intensively. However, as time passed and children married and left the parental home, the intensity of labour would diminish. The commune might then reallocate land for the benefit of another household in which the ratio of dependants to workers was greater. Thus Chayanov provided a theory for explaining social inequalities in the countryside that turned on demographic factors at household level. In contrast, Lenin interpreted the same statistical data as confirmation of his arguments about the spread of capitalist class polarisation. He assumed that the households with a large acreage were an entrenched élite dependent upon the labour of poor and landless peasants. Neither Chayanov nor Lenin provided detailed anthropological analysis to support their arguments, but the general view among later commentators is that Chayanov's insights provide a better guide to the internal differentiation of the Russian peasantry in the pre-revolutionary period.

Many years after Chayanov's death in the Stalinist purges, Sahlins adapted his principle and made it the basis for an anthropological argument about a 'domestic mode of production' (see Figure 6.1).

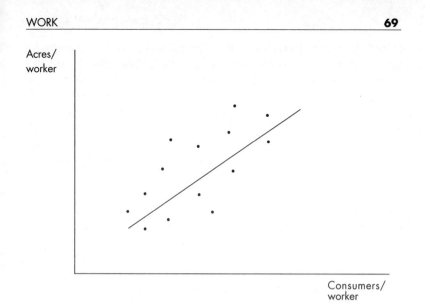

Figure 6.1   Sahlins' adaption of Chayanov's Rule[15]

Statistical evidence from a number of societies suggested that the patterns diagnosed by Chayanov in Russia could also be found among agriculturalists in other parts of the world. As the consumers/worker ratio increases, workers must labour more intensively. In Figure 6.1 the dots represent households: those above the line are producing a surplus, while those below it cannot produce sufficient to meet their current needs.

Sahlins' focus on the household deflected attention away from the constraints imposed by the environment of the village community and wider contexts. In reality, the decisions made by peasants are more complicated than his model suggests. In some cases needs can be met by hiring the labour of others. In others it may be possible to farm the land of others on a temporary basis through a 'sharecropping' contract. In all cases, the decisions of households (which are often taken autocratically by its head) are influenced by the values of their community. Some local models may inhibit community members from experimentation with new crops or technologies, on the grounds that any successful innovation will disturb an egalitarian ethic, and perhaps make some villagers worse off in absolute terms as well as relatively. Households are not 'atomised' units, as Sahlins presents them.

Factory wage labour

If the archetypal economic unit of agrarian society is the peasant household with its fusion of production and consumption roles and absence of wage labour, the archetypal unit of industrial society is the factory. The site of production is now distinct from the sites of consumption, in the household and in networks and communities. Instead of controlling their own labour, the workers are alienated from it. It is controlled by others, and the value that is extracted from their labour takes the form of profits which accrue to the capitalist owners. The products of human labour circulate as commodities. In Marxist jargon they are 'exchange values' rather than 'use values'. Labour itself is a commodity, bought and sold on the marketplace like other commodities.

The external model that Marx gave us of the capitalist mode of production contains valuable insights but as a guide to the realities of capitalist economic organisation it is even less adequate than Chayanov's theories are to the realities of a peasant economy. Contrary to Marx's expectations, workers' wages have not been driven down to subsistence levels. They have risen to allow the great majority of workers in advanced capitalist countries a high degree of prosperity. The model of a class of workers which stands opposed to a class of capitalist owners also seems seriously misleading. In particular, it does not take account of complex hierarchies within the workforce and of the role played by managers in the organisation of any complex enterprise. Another complication is that many sectors of the economy do not seem to be regulated by the model of the factory at all. For example, even in the most developed countries agriculture seems to work more efficiently on a familial basis, so the models of Chayanov may still be more relevant than those of Marx.

These problems have been pointed out by generations of social scientists. What particular contribution can economic anthropologists make? First of all, they can document the different forms that capitalism takes as it spreads around the world. You may think that a car plant in Brazil will operate in exactly the same way as its equivalent in Germany but a closer inspection is likely to reveal many differences. The differences are much greater in cases such as the Bolivian tin mine studied by June Nash, where Indian miners carried with them a world view that was entirely different from that of a European proletariat. In spite of the dangerous and exploitative conditions in the mines, Nash found that the miners were not entirely alienated. They owned their own tools and exercised a high degree of direct control over their labour process.

Economic anthropologists have found similar results in mines and factories closer to home, and even when new, highly mechanised techniques have removed the last vestiges of workers' control, the anthropologist who practises participant observation on the shop floor may be able to uncover complex local models of how the enterprise actually works, quite different from the model that is outlined in the management blueprints. The anthropologist will show how the values held by employees influence their behaviour at work and their relationships with each other. Informal aspects of these relationships are likely to attract as much attention from the anthropologist as more formal aspects of bureaucratic structure. Participant observation in the boardroom may also reveal more complex models.

For example, research in postcommunist factories in Poland shows that the discipline is tougher than it used to be in communist days. Working patterns were often harsh then, especially towards the end of the planning period when targets had to be fulfilled and everyone worked unpaid overtime. But what people also remember, and contrast with the situation today, is that under communism they also had enjoyable social experiences in the factory. The brigade often arranged parties and cultural activities for its members and whole factories might come to a standstill on namedays of popular saints such as Saint Andrew. Capitalist factories also have their 'informal' aspects, but these seem generally less significant than the elaborate alternative culture that generations of communist workers built up to help them cope with the dogmas of central planning.

The informal economy

This formal versus informal distinction has been taken up in various ways in recent decades. In particular, 'informal sector' has been widely used to refer to the persistence in industrial society of small-scale enterprises, units which fuse production and consumption in much the same way as the family labour farm, and which are similarly suspicious of outside regulation by the state. In a country such as Britain, the large informal sector of the nineteenth century gave way in the early part of the twentieth century to more structured labour markets and the large pools of the urban poor were eventually drawn into permanent jobs. Those who believed in progress and modernisation assumed that similar paths would be followed elsewhere in Europe and in 'third world' cities experiencing a massive influx of poor rural migrants.

The concept of the informal economy was pioneered by the Cambridge anthropologist Keith Hart, following his research among FraFra migrants in Accra, capital of Ghana, in the late 1960s. He was able to show how these migrants made a living when, in the eyes of economists and state administrators, they had no jobs or any other sources of income. Strategies ranged across a spectrum of legality, from brewing beer in one's neighbourhood to smuggling and theft. Hart argued that some at least of the 'informal income opportunities' had the potential to develop into viable enterprises. Far from being economic parasites, or a 'reserve army of the unemployed', as they were described by Marxists, these poor migrants could make a positive contribution to the overall development of the national economy.

This message was eventually warmly accepted by many development agencies including the World Bank. These institutions were becoming wary of aid schemes to former colonies which prioritised large-scale, capital intensive projects. Promotion of the 'informal sector' was seen as a way to unleash popular energies and promote development 'from below'. In practice, this often meant a reliance on market competition, with a minimum of political interference. This was hardly what Hart had intended but anthropologists have little control over the uses made of their work by politicians and international agencies. He was well aware of the sordid and corrupt nature of many of the activities that flourished in unregulated slum settlements. He went on to write a very different kind of monograph, *The Political Economy of West African Agriculture*, in which he explained the economic failures of the states of this region in terms of their failure to support agriculture and create an adequate revenue base for the state.

In the period after the end of the Cold War a new kind of informal sector has developed in Russia and other ex-socialist countries. Some of those active formerly in the 'underground economy' have assumed the roles of new capitalist entrepreneurs in the formal sector, but others have become more like mafia bosses. These states, like the post-colonial states of the third world, have few means of controlling the activities of their informal sectors. It requires a long-term perspective and a lot of faith to claim that, on the model of Dickens's London, more stable conditions for work and trade will emerge eventually.

Hart's work stimulated other urban anthropologists in a variety of settings. In India, Mark Holmstrom found the labour markets of Bangalore to be sharply polarised. Those with factory jobs enjoyed security and a range of fringe benefits for family members, including good housing, education and health services. They were clearly an élite, almost a separate class, in comparison with the mass of unemployed or irregularly employed outside this 'citadel' of the formal sector. A few years later after further fieldwork in Bombay, Holmstrom modified his account. In *Industry and Inequality* he recognised the many complex linkages that existed between formal and informal sectors. For example, many of the inputs required by the large factories were produced by small-scale units. There were intimate, personal links: the people who held jobs in the larger companies had kin who worked elsewhere in the city, or who had remained behind in the countryside. Holmstrom replaced the metaphor of the citadel with that of a slippery slope. The factory workers might occupy the most desirable positions at the top of this slope, but some of those running small family businesses were doing almost as well. Lower down the slope were the unskilled who formed a proletariat in Marx's sense (although they were unlikely to recognise themselves as such). Even further down were those who could find only casual employment. At the bottom of the pile were the destitute beggars. In short, there was no clearly demarcated informal sector, but only complex 'segmented' labour markets, with varying degrees of privilege and security.

Similar points can be made about changing conditions of work in the most developed capitalist economies. The changes were nowhere more dramatic than in Britain, where, as much of the old manufacturing base disappeared, the informal opportunities open to the household acquired an enhanced significance. Economic sociologists had long been aware of the role of the 'black economy', but more detailed ethnographic explorations of work in Britain began to reveal a spectrum of activities comparable to those reported from the third world or from communist Eastern Europe. Formalists could explain these activities as rational responses to changing circumstances, such as changes in the tax system. Marxists could interpret the decline of 'Fordist' production methods as part of the deepening crisis of capitalism, and the increased numbers of unemployed as a 'reserve army', serving to limit the wages and conditions of those in employment. Substantivists could point to forms of sharing and inter-household reciprocity as ways of adapting to crises and examples of embeddedness. Finally, it is clear that cultural perceptions of what is legitimate, moral behaviour shape the various ways in which employees cheat on their employers, and different responses to unemployment. In *Being Unemployed in Northern Ireland*, Leo Howe explains that 'doing the double' means breaking the social security regulations by undertaking undeclared paid employment while drawing state benefit. The incidence of doing the double was significantly higher on the estate where Catholics predominated, since Protestants were more likely to assign moral opprobrium to an activity understood as cheating the state. Catholics, because they felt less loyalty to the British state, did not see the activity in the same terms.

Howe was also concerned, as were many feminist anthropologists, to investigate economic decision-taking made *within* domestic units, a level of analysis ignored by Chayanov and most economists. Sociologists may also address these issues, but it is hard to get to the bottom of intra-familial power struggles and the influence of cultural values on the 'hidden work' of the household, if you rely, as they usually do, on questionnaire techniques. Sensitive ethnographic investigation can yield more insight.

Finally, anthropologists have also taken an interest in those people who can be found in one form or another in most modern industrial societies and who seem deliberately to reject all conventional forms of work. Marginal groups such as Gypsies in Eastern Europe define themselves as free and egalitarian communities, in contrast to the hierarchies that work creates all around them. Gypsies had great difficulties in the communist period, when those states tried to turn them all into wage labourers. They have a little more freedom nowadays, but their resistance to conventional forms of employment remains strong. They can often be seen begging and their attitude seems to be rather like the procurement philosophy that Bird-David found among food collectors: everything that comes into the group should be shared, and there is little or no planning for the future. Members of the dominant groups often condemn the Gypsies for their laziness and irresponsibility. More sympathetic observers have sometimes explained their behaviour in terms of a 'culture of poverty'. Yet their behaviour can also be interpreted as the protest of a minority experiencing discrimination. Why should they enter wage labour jobs when this would only increase their dependency and destroy their cultural identity?

7 | EXCHANGE

Reciprocity, giving and sharing

To imagine an economy without exchange is perhaps even harder than to imagine one without work. Even the most self-sufficient of peasant farms is obliged to engage in some forms of trade with the outside world. Exchange refers not only to flows of goods but also to services and intangible transfers. These may be egalitarian and taken for granted, as when neighbours exchange greetings, or in the exchange of services between husband and wife. But not all marriages are egalitarian and exchange can also be asymmetrical, as when a wealthy patron extends protection to a client in return for his loyal allegiance. Understood in this way exchange is much more than a subfield of economic activity. It is a pervasive principle of social life that underpins all human relationships.

Malinowski often made this point, but he was not entirely consistent. After initially identifying a Trobriand form of exchange as a 'pure gift', he later retracted this view and argued instead that all gifts were made with some expectation of return. This principle of reciprocity, understood as a principle of give and take, underlay all Trobriand social interaction. This view was consistent with the formalist paradigm of neoclassical economics, based on the rational maximisation of utility.

But can all gift exchanges really be explained in relation to such a calculus? Should there not also be room for pure gifts, for altruistic exchanges? Alternative interpretations of giving were developed by the French sociologist Marcel Mauss who, stimulated in part by Malinowski, drew on a range of secondary accounts to produce his *Essay on the Gift* (1924). Mauss argued in conventional evolutionist terms that human societies have moved from conditions of organic integration to a modern age in which contract and the impersonal exchange of commodities are dominant features. The pristine conditions were exemplified, according to Mauss, by societies in the Pacific which had preserved the practice of the 'total prestation'. This 'total social fact' was characterised not by maximising individuals but by ritualised exchanges between social groups. In forms such as the Maori *hau*, Mauss argued, following, so he thought, the local model, that to give something was to give a part of oneself. The 'spirit of the gift' was a link between the object given and the donor, which ensured that the object would eventually be returned to the donor. Mauss emphasised the sense of obligation involved in all gift transactions. There was an obligation to give, but there was also an obligation to receive and to repay, and from these various obligations a kind of social order emerged.

Mauss's theses have been the object of extensive later re-analyses. He was not a fieldworker and can be charged with lifting data out of context, with imposing the theoretical concerns of a Parisian intellectual onto the narratives of Polynesian islanders. Despite such criticism, *The Gift* has continued to exercise great influence as a suggestive analysis of the fundamental importance of exchange in social life. To the extent that it displaced the choice-making individual actor, Mauss's work implied a confrontation with the assumptions of modern economic theory. The total prestation is quite distinct from an act of voluntary generosity, which is how we typically think of gifts in our market-dominated societies, although on special occasions such as Christmas we too continue to demonstrate vestiges of the prestations we made in the past.

Psychologists and others have challenged the notion of 'disinterested giving' in our own societies. They have come up with concepts such as 'reciprocal altruism' in order to explain that what may appear to be disinterested can in fact be understood as a rational adaptation in evolutionary terms. And indeed, if we think about it, even the presents that we give at Christmas are the object of calculations on our part, given the value that we attach to the relationship in the long term. Are we then merely maximising our own utilities when we give? What about, say, anonymous donations that we make to charities? Surely these are altruistic? Some economists and psychologists would answer that, in these cases too, one's decision to give is motivated by the higher subjective gratification that one receives from making this gift, instead of spending it on more consumer goods for oneself.

This is another of those examples where the formalist logic of utility maximisation is hard to refute, but not particularly illuminating. If the category of altruism exists in our local models nowadays, this in itself is reason to pay some attention to it. Mauss's evolutionism, in this case, can seem unconvincing for it may be that examples of individual generosity to others can be documented in the more 'archaic' forms of society too.

There are several reasons for *not* using exchange as a general model for studying all forms of social interaction. For one thing, it is hardly appropriate to do so when force is involved, as when obedience is exacted by a warrior who carries a gun. Second, most human groups engage in some sharing and pooling of resources. Sharing plays a particularly important role in the maintenance of social equality among food collectors. This form of sharing has been termed (by Sahlins) 'generalised reciprocity' but Woodburn has argued persuasively that it is better seen as a political principle than as a form of exchange; at any rate it is quite different from the usual sense of reciprocity.

Redistribution

Karl Polanyi and the substantivist school associated reciprocity primarily with flows of goods and services between partners of roughly equal standing in the absence of centralised political direction. They considered the principal alternative mode of integration in preindustrial societies to be redistribution, which they associated with the flow of goods and services into a political centre and then outwards from this centre.

The basic idea can be applied to any form of hierarchical society, from simple chiefdoms in which some form of tribute is paid to a ruler to the complex taxation systems of a modern state or even the planned economies of the former communist states. Polanyi noted yam transfers in the Trobriand Islands as one example, but the most famous illustration of redistribution in the ethnographic record comes from the northwest coast of North America where chiefs, in competition with each other for status, both distributed and destroyed significant quantities of goods in the course of ceremonies known as *potlatch*. A careful look at the historical record, however, suggests that the ceremonies underwent rapid changes after the impact of colonialism. The evidence recorded by early anthropologists was already seriously distorted by the expanded availability of the blankets and other items required for a *potlatch*.

Redistribution need not be confined to exchanges of final products. Like the principle of reciprocity it can play an essential role in the process of production itself, and it is often difficult in practice to see where the one principle ends and the other begins. This is very well illustrated in Donald Donham's studies of the Maale of south-west Ethiopia, based on fieldwork carried out before and after Ethiopia's 1975 Revolution. Donham set out to test Sahlins' arguments concerning Chayanov's law. Remember, the law states that households with more people to feed will have to work longer or harder than other households. To test this apparently straightforward argument Donham had first of all to resolve some formidable technical problems. To measure the intensity of work is intrinsically difficult in societies where no clear demarcation is made between working time and leisure. It was necessary to make some rough approximations, for example in distinguishing the labour undertaken by children from the labour of adults, and in dealing with different types of productive activity. After addressing issues of this kind, Donham found that his data for 1975 suggested precisely the opposite of Chayanov's law. In the Maale case the households with high consumer to worker ratios, which might have been expected to work longer, were actually working less. Donham considered several possible explanations for this surprising result, but none of them worked. For example, it was not the case that households producing a surplus presented some of this to those in need. Rather than passing on part of the harvest as a gift, Donham found that the Maale transferred labour from surplus households to those where it was most needed. In other words, although the household was the prime unit of production, it was systematically augmented through labour cooperation. The outcomes of these labour transfers are schematised in Figure 7.1, which shows that

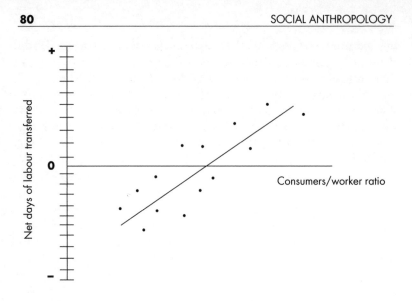

Figure 7.1   Labour transfers between households among the Maale[16]

households with high consumer/worker ratios are net recipients of labour from other community members.

The transfers were effectively transfers of the labour of junior males, controlled by their elders. Women were said to be unsuited to co-operation. Their job was to prepare the food and brew the beer with which the host household entertained its helpers whilst 'working together', making the occasion a festive one for all participants and not merely a matter of utilitarian drudgery. In one version of these work groups the same people remained together in a highly ritualised association over a lifetime, while in other types the composition of the cooperating group changed regularly. Donham made it plain that 'working together' was an important value in Maale culture. The Maale upheld an ethic of intra-community egalitarianism, inasmuch as the labour which flowed out of a household in any one period should ideally flow back in some future period, if the composition and therefore the needs of the household warranted it. However, Donham argued that some labour flows actually contributed to a Leninist path of class polarisation. In other words, in addition to a 'Chayanovian' redistribution of labour between households that helped to preserve their long-term equality, there was also a redistribution that allowed the dominant landlord faction to make use of the labour of poorer families to increase its own profits from growing new cash crops. The élite would never reciprocate this labour. Poorer people were aware of this trend, but in practise, without any direct use of force, they had no choice but to continue to participate in the work groups as if they were genuinely egalitarian.

It can be seen even from this brief summary that Donham's account synthesises several different approaches in economic anthropology. He makes least use of the formalist approach. Poorer farmers' insistence on rational utility maximising does not help us to understand why they should offer their labour when it does not seem to be in their interests to do so. Only an appreciation of their limited political options can rescue any notion of rationality here. Substantivists would approve of the way in which Donham shows the Maale to have an *embedded* economy, in which *reciprocity* was the dominant mode of integration, supplemented by systematic *redistribution* of labour between households, while a few landlords were gearing their activities to a new *market principle*. The detailed descriptions provided by Donham of the cultural bases for 'working together' meet the criteria of the culturalist school. Yet Donham does not oversimplify and homogenise 'traditional Maale culture', which he explores with a neo-Marxist's sensitivity to competition, emerging class conflict, and the role played by ideology in the disguising of such conflict. Finally, he has also been sensitive to historical change. When he returned to the Maale in the 1980s, he found that the previous pattern of labour transfers had completely changed, one of several consequences of the Ethiopian revolution on this region.

Markets

Market exchange is seen by the substantivists as the dominant mode of integration in modern industrial economies. The other modes do not disappear altogether. Reciprocity may continue in familial and some inter-household relations, while redistribution may be undertaken by the state. Nevertheless, it is the market that dominates. Polanyi and his followers accepted that modern economists, the neo-classical school, had the right tools for understanding the workings of the market. In the simplest model, with money available as a medium of exchange, the market for any particular commodity should clear at a point of equilibrium E where the demand slope of consumers and the supply slope of producers intersect (see Figure 7.2).

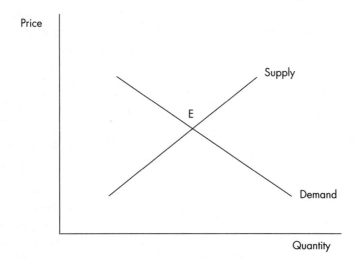

Figure 7.2   A simple commodity market

Numerous questionable assumptions underpin Figure 7.2 as a model, let alone a realistic description, of the market for, say, shirts, in an economy such as that of modern Britain. Economists of a formalist persuasion face even greater difficulties in economies that lack markets and currencies altogether. As we have seen in the case of the Trobrianders, a formalist may claim that in exchanges of the *gimwali* type ('haggling') individuals seek to maximise their returns in a way that directly resembles the way that modern Europeans behave in impersonal market settings; but this is very hard to demonstrate. The more important point is that many economic transactions in modern Europe are not of this type at all. Sellers have long-term motivations in retaining customers and this inhibits them from maximising of profit in any particular sale. Buyers do not have the free time to shop around and bargain for every item they purchase, but turn to retailers and brand names that they have learned to trust. Consumers leave tips for waiters, even in restaurants to which they know they will never return, so it would not seem to be in their individual rational interest. These are pointers towards the many other sorts of exchange identified by Malinowski which are based not on haggling but on customary obligations and fall outside the sphere of the market. Implicit in Malinowski's work, and later made explicit in the work of Raymond Firth, is the notion that every economy is made up of separate 'spheres of exchange'. The market sphere is a wide one in our sort of society, but even for us it does not include everything. The spheres of reciprocity and redistribution have their place. In most preindustrial societies these spheres or principles will play the more significant role.

Whether or not one one sees a market principle at work in the haggling that takes place in a moneyless society such as that of the Trobrianders, genuine markets clearly did exist and were important for economic integration in many preindustrial societies. Paul Bohannan and George Dalton addressed this problem from a substantivist viewpoint in their volume *Markets in Africa*. They distinguished between societies with 'peripheral markets' and societies where the 'market principle' was the dominant mode of economic integration. In many colonial African societies, the political, social and even religious significance of the marketplace was as great as its specifically economic significance. Bohannan and Dalton pointed to the apparent paradox that the rise of a capitalist *market principle* often spelled the decline of traditional forms of peasant *marketplace*. The reason was that the market principle was associated with more specialised production for more distant markets, often for export. The replacement of traditional street markets by new forms of chainstore retailing is a product of the same tendency in the most developed and urbanised capitalist economies.

The changes to which the substantivists draw attention, notably the impact of the market principle on societies previously characterised by distinct spheres of exchange and only peripheral markets, are also central for the adherents of a political economy approach. Neo-Marxists emphasised the sharp contrast between the logic of the gift economy, or that of the production of use values, as in a relatively self-sufficient community of cultivators, and that of the commodity economy, driven by the production of exchange values. They explained the transformation not in terms of the impact of markets *per se*, but in terms of the spread of a capitalist mode of production.

Culturalists question the assumption that markets can ever be completely impersonal phenomena for the competitive determination of prices. All markets depend upon political authorities, just as the Trobrianders who practised *gimwali* depended upon the security created by the *kula* system. Even in an age of sophisticated information technology, economic decisions are taken by individual agents. These agents may be members of bureaucratic organisations, but they are also members of families, networks and social classes, whose shared values and culture necessarily affect their strategies. Those who interact in markets normally seek to establish relationships of trust with each other. It is often easier to establish such relationships if people come from the same social class or ethnic group. The use of common ethnic background to establish the trust required for successful market activity is well documented all over the world, for example in the case of the Chinese diasporas throughout Southeast Asia. This dimension of market activity is as important nowadays as when long-distance trading relationships first developed in early millennia.

Money

Most economists simply take it for granted that the most important function of money is to serve as a medium of exchange, in order to overcome the practical difficulties of clearing many different markets at the same time. Historical and anthropological evidence, however, suggests other possibilities. Money may in some cases have emerged as a means of payment, for example to resolve political disputes between neighbouring groups, or it may function as a standard of value without playing an important role in facilitating everyday exchanges. On this basis *kula* valuables can be seen as a type of money. They are not a medium of exchange, but they do represent a store of value and a means for paying off one's long-term debts. Another fact that casts doubt on the usual economist's assumption of the origins of money is that, far from being everywhere superseded by money, barter remains a phenomenon of considerable importance at all levels of the world economy, as the post-communist countries illustrate very well.

Formalists usually emphasise the medium of exchange function of money. For example, Harold Schneider argued in his *Economic Man* that cattle functioned as money among many East African peoples, who used them to make purchases in the market for women. Schneider was able to demonstrate that a reduced supply of the 'commodity' in question led, exactly as neoclassical logic would predict, to an increase in the price. A rapid expansion of the stock of money, as occurred following the influx of shells into the New Guinea Highlands, had similarly predictable effects on nominal prices. Through such examples, formalists claim that their insights into the operation of money and markets have a universal validity.

George Dalton drew a clear distinction between 'general purpose money' and 'limited purpose money', the latter being more common in most forms of preindustrial economy. Limited purpose money lacked the full range of functions undertaken by the modern dollar. It was also likely to be technically deficient, compared with the advantages of coins and paper in terms of divisibility, portability and 'fungibility'. For example, the Rossel Islanders had a sophisticated shell currency system, in which shells had numbers, with the higher number having the greater value. But the fact that it was not possible to convert a large quantity of low value shells for one of higher value meant that this money was lacking one of the fundamental features of a general purpose money. In another famous example, Mary Douglas showed that raffia cloth might serve the Lele, a Central African people, as a store of value and a necessary means of payment for young men to obtain wives; but it did not serve as a more general medium of exchange. Paul and Laura Bohannan reported a more complex case among the Central Nigerian Tiv in the late colonial years. The Tiv used iron bars to facilitate the exchange of a range of luxury goods, including tobacco, cattle and slaves. However, it was not considered appropriate to use this currency either for the purchase of subsistence goods or for the acquisition of wives. Traditional Tiv society had three morally ranked spheres of exchange comprising subsistence goods, luxuries and, in the highest sphere, women. Although it was always possible to make 'conversions' between spheres, it was the impact of modern forms of money in the late colonial period which, according to the Bohannans, broke down the traditional moral barriers and made a general purpose money an effective common denominator for all types of goods (although land and labour continued to resist commoditisation).

Culturalists insist, as in the case of markets, on the importance of local differences in the way that even general purpose money is handled and deployed. For example, in Polish families, as in many countries, there are significant gender divisions. Money that is earned in unpleasant factory conditions by a factory commuter undergoes a sort of cultural transformation when it is handed over to his wife for general household use. Expenditure on the maintenance of the household is commonly a female responsibility. The male 'breadwinner' may retain some money for his individual use, for which the woman is allowed no equivalent. Such patterns depend not simply on a domestic balance of power and changing patterns of work and income, but also on deeply held cultural notions.

New technologies of money, notably the use of plastic credit cards, are explicitly repersonalising everyday exchanges: you can only make your purchase if the photo matches and the computer gives the authorisation after checking your balance. The controversy in many European countries that has accompanied the introduction of a common currency shows that modern forms of money also have symbolic features, capable of generating strong loyalties.

'The great divide'

In these ways, contrary to the substantivists, who were prepared to leave the study of modern economies to the economists, culturalists can show that markets and money are always embedded in particular contexts, in which local models and power relations will influence economic behaviour. Does this mean that Polanyi exaggerated the extent of the 'great transformation' which he saw as dividing modern, market-dominated societies from all their predecessors? Did Mauss exaggerate the differences between traditional forms of gift exchange and the modern variants? John Davis rejected the Maussian view that exchanges of the 'total prestation' type can be considered symbolically 'thicker' than the exchanges people make in modern Britain. Davis himself studied the operation of the 'gift sector' in Britain and generated some suggestive data which indicated that expenditure on certain kinds of gifts and cards might rise in times of economic recession. A possible cause was that people were more conscious at such times of their need to 'invest' in their social relationships. Davis also explored some of the cultural criteria determining people's choices of gifts, and the social consequences when taste and judgement were found wanting. The gift sector is only a relatively small sector of the modern British economy, far outstripped not only by other parts of the market sphere but also by the state's taxation of its citizens in order to finance a range of public services. But changing cultural attitudes influence all of these sectors, as they do the extent of state redistribution and reciprocity between households that never enters the national income statistics. In short, all of these subsectors of the economy, or spheres of exchange, can be illuminated by enquiring into the local models that shape the activities and the motivations of the agents.

8 | PROPERTY

Ownership as a social relationship

After discussing the fields of production and exchange, we now come to consider the importance of property. Relationships of property depend on legal and political frameworks and show even more clearly than the fields we have considered so far why the study of economic organisation is extricably linked to the study of social organisation as a whole.

The concept of property provides a good example of that difficulty to which we have already alluded. It is a word with a range of meanings in modern English, familiar to ordinary citizens but also carrying more technical senses, particular for lawyers. If it is to be used for comparative purposes by anthropologists we need to be careful to avoid ethnocentricity. We need to distil some core reference from the term property, discarding cultural meanings that are specific to one particular society or type of society, while recognising that what constitutes property in any actual case is necessarily variable and contingent.

The most common, everyday usage of property in modern Britain is that which postulates a relationship of exclusive ownership between a person or persons and some kind of 'thing'. A property relation is therefore cast as a relation between persons and things. Anthropologists, however, have preferred to define property relations as 'social relations *between people* with *respect to things*'. This nuance actually makes a big difference. It is the recognition that the modern western idea of private property is the product of a particular tradition – a tradition which itself contains numerous strands that modify and conflict with the concept of pure private ownership. The very words 'property' and 'own' are among the most difficult to translate into many languages. There is tremendous cultural variety in ideas about proper ways of 'holding' or 'possessing' or 'disposing of' things, and of the kinds of goods, intangible as well as tangible, that can qualify as 'things' in different societies. The only common feature is that all these ideas depend on a context of social relations.

This diversity has led some culturalists to raise objections to the idea of property altogether, on the grounds that it presupposes certain western assumptions which are bound to distort the analysis of non-western cases. Marilyn Strathern has argued that the very identity of persons as isolable subjects does not hold among the people she studied in the highlands of New Guinea. She therefore dismisses neo-Marxist arguments that allege exploitation in the case of a woman whose labour goes into raising pigs that are later handed over for exchange by her husband. The charge of exploitation could only stick if the woman could be said to 'own' her own labour power, which Marx assumes to be the case for western proletarians. But this Melanesian culture does not recognise individuals in this sense. According to Strathern the woman in this case does not own her own labour power any more than she owns the pig she has raised as her private property. On the contrary, her husband is understood to have played a part in the raising of the animal, and she is understood to share in the prestige he gains by making a successful exchange.

This challenge to the use of an English language term for comparative analysis is important. If Melanesian notions of how people relate to each other and to material objects are so very different from our own, in what sense if any can we speak of property relations among them? But Melanesians, like us, do produce, exchange and consume objects and it seems reasonable to wish to investigate the ways in which they do so in some kind of comparative framework. An external model which asserts that property is a matter of social relations does not prejudge the question of cultural forms.

It would be unrealistic, however, to pretend that European ideas about private property are just one of a long list of cultural variants. This is a variant which has been very extensively disseminated all over the world in the last few hundred years, and with the recent demise of socialist systems it no longer has any serious rivals. We are therefore justified in paying particular attention to the modern western idea of exclusive private property. What we must not do, however, is impose this unwittingly in cases where it is not appropriate. Unfortunately the earlier literature on property is replete with anthropological examples of just this.

Primitive communism

We have already noted work on food collectors by Richard Lee, who has described !Kung Bushmen of the Kalahari as practising a form of 'primitive communism', while James Woodburn has referred to egalitarian hunter gatherer societies as 'disengaged from property'. Individuals may have exclusive rights to use a few items essential to survival, but these are not assigned a high cultural value. These societies make it impossible for individuals or groups to use their control over things as a basis for exercising power over other people: those who try to do so are ostracised or ridiculed. The Hadza spend a lot of time gambling, to ensure that highly valued goods circulate between members of the band. Woodburn does detect some elements of individual ownership among them, for example in the claim of a successful hunter to the animal he has killed. However, as soon as the meat is taken back to camp the individual has no choice but to share. Similarly among the !Kung, the basic principle is one of 'demand sharing'. The anthropologist may be included in this system. Many, including Lee, have described the pressures they experienced during fieldwork to share out their own material possessions among groups such as the Bushmen. Individuals were clearly interested in acquiring new and valued goods, but they were seldom allowed to retain possession for long.

This degree of communism is not, however, characteristic of all hunters and gatherers. Those with 'delayed return' economies allow investment in tools and storage facilities, which are then controlled by particular subgroups or even individuals. Such people usually develop stronger forms of *exclusive* rights over territory, for example the more fertile stretches of forest or watering holes. Similar tendencies are found among pastoral and fishing peoples.

Nomadic pastoralists may, for example, allow individuals or their households to exercise ownership rights over animals, while rights over standardised migration routes are vested in larger kinship groups. The domestication of animals frequently proceeds hand in hand with the domestication of plants, but even when pastoralists settle and begin to farm on 'private' fields, they typically continue to use large areas of 'common' land as summer pasture ('transhumance').

Expanding populations of people and herds have led in many parts of the world to environmental degradation. Western advisers have sometimes argued for stronger private property rights as the only solution to problems such as overgrazing and overfishing. Anthropologists have shown, however, that systems of communal management can also work well. They do not necessarily open the door to unlimited access. On the contrary, political agreement to regulate the use of common resources can be effective without leading to the marked social inequalities which normally follow the shift to a more private system.

Bundles and hierarchies

This distinction between communal forms of land management and forms based on private ownership is valid and important. However, anthropological understanding of property evolution has often been hindered by misplaced and exaggerated use of the western dichotomy between *communism* and *individualism*. The Marxist tradition has contributed to this, of course. All the communist countries of Eastern Europe were built up on the assumption that communal forms of ownership were superior to private forms. So most private industry was nationalised, with unfortunate consequences. Recently the opposite policies have been implemented but the consequences of ideologically driven privatisation have been almost equally bad.

In an earlier age, western ways of thinking about property permeated the work of colonial administrators. The British in Africa and India took it for granted that the 'things' of the people they governed, including their most important resource, the land itself, were either owned collectively (by the tribe), or privately, by its king or paramount chief. This was a misjudgement of a more complex situation. Officials who treated a chief as the private owner of all the territory that he claimed as his chiefdom later came to appreciate that this was a mistake. The subjects of the chief did not consider him as a private landlord, with the power to intervene and dispose of land that they regarded as belonging to their group. It took a long time before Europeans realised that it was their own dichotomy and insistence upon an exclusive notion of ownership in the western sense that was creating the problem.

More constructive approaches were found by following legal historians and approaching property in terms not of exclusive ownership but of a 'bundle of rights'. Different persons and groups could exercise rights over the same 'thing'. Land in tribal societies was typically farmed by domestic groups. Sometimes plots might be assigned to specific individuals. Families exercised 'use rights', which might be inherited. Those who farmed the land did not have the freedom to sell it or to dispose of it by any other means, so they did not enjoy anything approaching modern capitalist ownership rights. Land was commonly redistributed between households, in Africa as in prerevolutionary Russia, by some community-level authority. In the event of tracts of land falling out of cultivation, for example due to depopulation, then rights over this land would typically 'revert upwards' to a political authority such as a king or a chief. This individual was in some sense an 'ultimate owner', but in practice he was more a trustee or custodian on behalf of his people. He was not in a position to sell land as a commodity to strangers, and his obligations to provide his people with as much land as they needed severely constrained his ability to allocate the land that they used. He might, however, receive some payment of tribute, perhaps a portion of the harvest, as a sign that he too had some rights over the land and over the people who farmed it, in return for providing them with security and perhaps magical services.

It is inadequate to label such a system of land tenure as either collectivist or individualist, because it contains elements of both. This point was grasped by Malinowski during his work on the Trobriand Islands, and it was developed in detail in *Coral Gardens and their Magic*. Similar points were made by Raymond Firth in *Primitive Polynesian Economies*. A fuller theoretical elaboration was provided later by Max Gluckman, an Africanist who had the advantage of having had some training in law. Gluckman distinguished an 'estate of production', referring to how a piece of land was actually cultivated, from 'estates of administration', referring to rights to manage and control. The former was vested in the household or the individual. The latter were distributed between the individual and his household, headmen and local chiefs, and ultimately a king or state power. In general there would be as many estates of administration as there were significant levels of political hierarchy in the society. For example, Gluckman did much of his own fieldwork in Barotseland (now part of western Zambia), where the estate of production and the lowest of the estates of administration were vested in the household. If a household no longer needed the land allocated to it, this would revert back to the level of the community for reallocation by its headman (most Barotse lived in clearly demarcated mounds in the Zambezi valley where fertile land was scarce). If an entire community reported that it no longer needed land, the area in question would revert back to the king, the 'ultimate owner'. The system clearly had individualistic aspects, particularly in the assignment of responsibilities for production. This might help to explain some later failures of 'African socialism', when post-colonial élites tried to organise production in communal ways. But the system also had its collectivist aspects and land was not available to anyone as alienable private property. The king received tribute annually from all of his subjects, in return for fulfilling his obligation to provide them with land.

Where a neo-Marxist might interpret such payment of tribute as *prima facie* evidence of economic exploitation, most anthropologists would interpret such patterns as examples of how economic relationships are embedded in political and social dependencies. The people themselves might plausibly explain the payment of tribute in the language of reciprocity: 'The king is working for us, his magical actions make our land fertile; so it is right that we pay tribute to him.' If the tribute accumulated by a ruler is then reallocated by him, a substantivist might wish to speak of 'redistribution'. A culturalist might, in this case, be more interested in pursuing the particular cultural ideas of fertility and magic of the people in question. Once again each approach has its own validity, and the anthropologist is perfectly at liberty to combine them all.

Property and citizenship

Gluckman's framework has been adapted to fit the circumstances of a wide range of tribal and peasant societies in which property relations are overlapping and thoroughly embedded in custom and tradition. It has also been ingeniously applied by Caroline Humphrey to the somewhat different forms of hierarchy that prevailed on a Soviet collective farm. But can the main insights of this model be extended even to the advanced capitalist societies, with their strong ideas of exclusive ownership?

This brings us again to the vexed controversies concerning a 'great divide'. Some anthropologists tend to the view that there is really no difference between tribal societies such as those of Barotseland and the way that we organise our economies today. All human communities have their local models and rich symbolism, in economic fields as in other aspects of their community life. On the other hand, something significant occurs when land that was formerly 'held' at various levels of a tribal hierarchy is precisely mapped and recorded in a cadastral survey document as being the exclusive property of X, regardless of whether X is an individual, a family or an entire tribe. Even when this happens, the land is unlikely to become just another market, on a par with, say, the market for shirts. But the very possibility of its sale, like the commoditisation of labour, may reflect more pervasive changes in human social relationships and, usually, greater inequalities.

Property relations are much influenced by distinctive local cultures, even in the most economically advanced European societies. This is particularly the case with land, where owners often feel themselves to be 'stewards' of a resource that has been held and passed down in one family over generations. Strong sentiments inhibiting sale (commoditisation) are also attached to other forms of inherited property ('heirlooms'). If property ownership is modified in these ways in our own societies, where markets and legal sytems to support private property have evolved over centuries, it is hardly surprising that modifications elsewhere are still more striking. Sometimes the efforts of an individual to accumulate private property are rejected by the community: he is ostracised and his crops are burned. Elsewhere conditions may seem more favourable. In Papua New Guinea, for example, it was sometimes suggested that the apparent individualism and competitive aggression of traditional political leaders would equip them well for careers as capitalist entrepreneurs. Many of them did indeed take entrepreneurial initiatives. However, many businesses became rapidly bankrupt because their owners simply could not enforce modern criteria: they could not, for example, deny credit to anyone claiming a relationship of kinship.

Western ideas of exclusive private ownership, though now widely disseminated, do not provide a full picture of *actual* property relations, not even in the advanced western countries. This external model is also an ideology, with a number of powerful associations and metaphors (individual autonomy, the 'home as castle' etc.) that culturalists can unpack. It is not simply that private ownership is not as absolute as we imagine it to be. Your house and garden can be appropriated by the authorities to build a new road, and provided due legal process is followed this will be sanctioned by the wider community. Your freedoms to use your property are curtailed in countless ways, from the colour you use to paint your doors and windows to noise pollution. In other words, the holding of the archetypal property items in modern Britain depends on wider contexts of political and social relations. These items cannot be enjoyed except to the degree that owners are protected against theft, by the legal system and by the state. In a formal, legal sense the monarch can still claim 'ultimate ownership' rights over all the real estate in Britain, and indeed rights *in* her subjects.

We need to stretch the term property and take it beyond its primary associations with large, 'lumpy' things such as houses, cars, land. In modern European states, as in any preindustrial society, there is a social context of educational, medical and other welfare entitlements, which needs to be drawn in to the discussion of property relations. The legal context may reflect changes taking place in society, or it may obstruct them, or be used to promote them. For example, changes in the law may strengthen the rights of a tenant vis-à-vis the person who is the formal legal owner of a house, to the point where it might seem realistic to say that the tenant, too, has property rights over this accommodation, from which it is almost impossible to evict him. The right of contemporary British citizens to a minimal provision of social security benefits is analogous to the right formerly enjoyed by communist citizens to employment, and to the rights of the tribesman of Barotseland to be allocated enough land to feed himself and his family. These are all 'public law' forms of property right.

You might think that this is to stretch the term property too far, by equating property relations with all the various rights of citizenship. However, the connections between welfare entitlements and the things people own as property are sometimes brought home forcefully to the wider public: according to the current regulations in Britain, if you own property worth more than £12,000 you may be obliged to sell this to pay for your terminal care. Examples of this sort are being carefully studied by those responsible for organising post-communist health care systems in Eastern Europe.

Peasants in Eastern Europe

Let us explore one example of changing property relations in this region in a little more detail. Eastern Europe since the collapse of communism in 1989–91 has provided anthropologists interested in property relations with a wonderful laboratory for research. Substantivists can interpret this latest example of the impact of capitalism, in which an ideology of private ownership seems to go hand in hand with that of free markets, as yet another case of the destruction of previously well-integrated, 'embedded' economies. Much of the recent anthropological work shows that people are suspicious and fearful of new property systems and 'the market'.

The overlapping rights and responsibilities of a collective farm certainly had economic drawbacks. Hungarian villagers often complained that, under collective arrangements, people did not treat resources with the same care and attention they would show if they were in private ownership. The sheep which starved in a harsh winter due to neglect, people said, would have survived if the 'estate of production' had been left in their hands. Similar attitudes to collective property have been widely documented in urban factories, and this is supposed to provide the justification for the insistence of all the western 'experts' who now operate in the region, that everything should be privatised. However, as these policies are implemented it becomes apparent that people also recognised a positive side to the old arrangements, which provided them with great flexibility, space to practise reciprocity, and above all with basic existential security. When land and labour became capitalist commodities there is a strong sense of moral loss, reported particularly from the Russian countryside where communal traditions were most deeply embedded. The values of the peasant community emphasised equality and the virtues of hard work on the soil. It is understandable that Russian villagers are suspicious of the new private owners, some of whom have obtained land only thanks to political connections, who obtain equipment and credit from the new authorities, and who are seen to be making money through exploiting the labour of others and through 'speculation', rather than through their own honest labour.

Hungarian rural society is rather different. This is partly because private property in land was well established before the socialist period, when the distribution of land was very unequal and some large estates had thousands of landless workers and servants. Hungarian socialism put an end to this sort of property inequality but, compared to other countries in the region, it made more concessions to market principles. In the later socialist decades high levels of growth and production were achieved in response to price incentives both by family labour farms (peasants) and by the collective sector. The two sectors were systematically integrated.

The economic climate for farmers has been much less favourable in the post-communist period. Many people, especially the younger generation, have expressed no interest in continuing as part-time peasants, let alone becoming private farmers. Why should they, if the economic prospects for the sector are very bleak? A formalist economic anthropologist would not be surprised at all. However, some older people have tried, for sentimental reasons and regardless of economic rationality, to re-establish private ownership rights over the specific plots associated with their families before the impact of collectivisation, some 30 years before. They were deeply disappointed when post-communist rulers did not (as happened in some other countries) return those plots, but instead offered more indirect forms of compensation. This was a more rational procedure, from the macro-economic point of view, than the complete break-up of integrated large-scale farming. Even so, the new ownership structure is very different from that of the precommunist period. Then it was common for one owner to employ large numbers of workers. Now it is common to find that a piece of land of similar size has many nominal owners but few of these actually farm what they own. If they are lucky they can find a large-scale concern, possibly a modified form of the old collective farm, willing to pay them some rent for their plots. The owner then usually has no say over the crops that are grown or the pesticides that are applied, even though these might be highly detrimental not only to the general environment but also to the long-term value of the privately owned asset. The additional paperwork required by the new structure of ownership is a nuisance to the big concern, but most *effective* property rights are exercised at this level, just as they were in communist days.

The case of Poland was a rather unusual one in the Eastern European context, since most farmland there was never collectivised, i.e. it was not confiscated from peasants in order to form large scale 'factories in the countryside', as pioneered by the Soviet Union under Stalin in the 1930s. Plans to do the same in Poland were abandoned after political turmoil in 1956. After that, the peasants were left to carry on more or less as they had in the past. The average size of their farms was far too small to be farmed efficiently using modern technology. As a consequence, the income levels of Polish peasants remained extremely low and the peasants were excluded from many of the social entitlements enjoyed by town and city dwellers. The peasants retained rights over their 'own' land, and you may say that this in itself was a source of satisfaction to them, that it raised their quality of life. However, many asked: what was the use of being the legal owner of a few fields if the state did not allow you to buy and sell land and did not create a framework conducive to profitable modern farming?

Polish peasants fought hard under communism to improve their property rights and they did make impressive gains as citizens, for example in gaining improved access to state welfare services. However, as elsewhere in the region they have been among the chief losers of the post-communist years. Most farms are simply much too small to be economically viable; but continued pride in private ownership inhibits the development of a land market and a more rational structure that would make Polish farming potentially competitive in the wider European markets.

New forms of property

Not all the things that people try to possess and to own have the physical qualities of a piece of land which, if one puts a fence around it, symbolises very concretely the *exclusionary* principle that lies at the basis of the dominant modern ideology of property. The economic arguments in favour of private property are underpinned by powerful psychological arguments, for who would deny that people take more care and expend more effort when given some sort of ownership incentive? In particular, without that mysterious property bond to the 'thing' in question, persons are less likely to invest in long-term improvement and the dynamism of the entire economy will suffer, as communism illustrated. You can even extend this logic to levels of community and state. Mach's study, noted in Chapter 3, showed that there were low levels of investment over decades in parts of western Poland. The explanation was that these lands had formerly belonged to Germany, and in the decades of the Cold War new settlers, and even their governments, could not feel absolutely secure in their property rights. There was always the possibility that further armed conflict could lead to the drawing of new boundaries. Only recently has this anxiety been dispelled, so that the younger generation of migrants can feel that this territory is truly theirs.

But can this sort of property logic be adapted to very different sorts of things that seem to matter in the economies of the modern world, such as the increasingly complex entitlements of modern citizenship based on a principle of *inclusion*? The old exclusionary model is still commonly applied to intellectual property, such as trademarks and patents. It has of course become increasingly difficult to enforce such property rights in the age of information technology. It has also become increasingly difficult to protect the names and symbols central to cultural identities from being expropriated by others. Some native peoples have gone to court and argued, in accordance with the dominant property ideology, that they have exclusive rights to their own cultural heritage. In some cases when local knowledge, for example of forest flora, has led to commercial profits for a capitalist enterprise, the natives concerned have negotiated a share in those profits.

These examples suggest that, whatever the technical difficulties, the dominant paradigm of exclusionary private property can often be adapted to meet changing conditions. Whether this is true in all fields is doubtful. For example, following rapid progress in new reproductive technologies, Strathern has suggested that property rights over artificially conceived embryos may be more amenable to study from a Melanesian perspective, where person and thing cannot be disentangled, than in terms of outmoded western notions of exclusive ownership.

9 | CONSUMPTION

Sumptuary laws

The last fundamental economic activity we shall explore in this part is consumption. This might seem intuitively to be the most important, the goal to which all other economic activities are subjected. As usual, however, we must be careful to avoid ethnocentricity in our definitions. Consumption takes pride of place if we define it in a formalist way, in terms of consuming that most mysterious and elusive of substances, utility. This has nothing to do with the acquisition of physical objects, for we have already noted other societies which place a premium on giving objects away for others to consume, or on minimising possessions for ease of movement. Consumption is not to be confused with *consumerism*, with distinctively modern attitudes to goods that approximate the economist's assumption of 'unlimited wants'. Rather, consumption can be explored anthropologically in all human societies. Even societies with simple technologies oriented primarily to ensuring subsistence have some scope to vary diet and their non-food consumption. These might include alterations in clothing and decoration of the human body, such as hair styling and tattooing. Some anthropologists expand the definition of consumption to include time spent singing and dancing, or praying, or watching television. This expanded approach makes the study of consumption as broad a field as the study of culture itself, and it can play a big role in understanding social identities.

Despite the potential interest of this topic in all societies, it has been neglected. Anthropologists have only recently begun to devote as much attention to consumption as they had previously given to exchange and production. A good deal of this recent work has been concerned with modern industrial societies, in which the range of goods available and the social pressures to consume are extremely great. First, however, let us consider consumption in some other types of society.

Hierarchical societies, including many agrarian civilisations, have attempted to enforce 'sumptuary laws', i.e. to *prescribe* specific forms of consumptions for specific social groups, and to *proscribe* them to others. For example, Aztec emperors tried hard to regulate the clothing worn by different groups in their highly stratified society. Certain items, such as sandals, and even certain types of material were theoretically banned for use by commoners. However, despite the serious sanctions which the emperor decreed for those who defied his sumptuary laws, plenty of people did so. The official dress codes were scrupulously observed on special ceremonial occasions, when élites paraded in the finery that it was their exclusive privilege to wear; but in everyday life ordinary people encroached on these rights and purchased the materials they wanted through unofficial (informal) channels. In other words, there seems to have been a constant process of status competition in this agrarian society that subverted, at least in part, its official hierarchical structure. In terms of the way in which consumption patterns contribute to the generation and reproduction of status, the differences between ancient empires and modern market economies may not be so great after all. This conclusion casts doubt on those paradigms (notably the neo-Marxist and the substantivist) which postulate a sharp divide at the onset of the modern industrial age.

Sumptuary laws do not have to be hierarchical and it is not only food collectors with 'immediate return' economies who have tried to enforce egalitarian consumption patterns. When Alfred Gell studied the Gonds, a tribal population in central India, he found that, although by the 1970s new sources of income had made some people rather wealthy, an older egalitarian tradition was strictly adhered to. The Gonds were 'newcomers to the world of goods' and they wished to avoid the sort of consumer differentiation typical of modern industrial societies. Similar collective moral resistance to relative inequalities has been reported for many other 'peasant' societies. People may oppose changes, such as the introduction of new techniques or new export crops, even if they make everyone better off, unless the improvements are equally shared. In practice this is seldom the case, and this creates a major dilemma for development planners. In Russia, for instance, an egalitarian tradition of this sort seems to be one of the factors inhibiting a smooth transition to a capitalistic system of farming. Villagers disapprove of the ostentatious display of wealth. So, if a new private farmer does become wealthy, he needs to think carefully about what to do with his money. A common solution, found all over the world, is to divert at least some of it to religious purposes, either for the collective consumption of the community (e.g. in renovating the village church) or for some more personal benefits in the anticipated afterlife.

Modern China illustrates both egalitarian and hierarchical forms of consumption. Until the end of the imperial era courtly fashion and dress codes were in theory strictly controlled but in practice, as under the Aztecs, the élites were imitated and emulated by other strata. In the early communist period the society was turned upside down by Mao's 'cultural revolution', when a radical egalitarianism was extended into all sectors of economic life. To distribute work equally, intellectuals were sent to the countryside to do manual labour. To enforce equality in consumption, everyone wore the same style of clothes and ate the same food. This extraordinary experiment is nowadays seen, even by the Chinese communists themselves, as an unmitigated disaster. As soon as political controls were relaxed, older patterns of differentiation reappeared, along with some new ones.

For the last few decades China has been open to new goods from all over the world. Current patterns of consumption can be seen as evidence of the force of globalisation, but it is significant that many foreign products have been modified in the Chinese context. Even if western drinks are consumed in large quantities, they are drunk in socially prescribed ways that follow traditional Chinese rules. Sometimes foreign products are utilised to give emphasis to important local social distinctions: In Chinese Central Asia during the 1998 World Cup competition straw hats, made in Thailand and carrying the World Cup text emblazoned around them, were very popular among the indigenous people of the region. They were not, however, worn by the Han Chinese. Clothing is not simply a matter of private consumption, it is a statement about one's cultural identity. In terms not only of clothing but also of the restaurants they patronise, the music they listen to and the dances they perform, China's Muslim minorities continue to emphasise how different they are from the dominant culture.

Consumption classes

Differing patterns of consumption can also be described in a culturalist manner in societies that are not, as modern China is, explicitly multiethnic or multicultural. In some cases the concept of class may also be useful. In the Marxist tradition class is determined by one's relation to the means of production, and the proletariat is defined by the fact that it does not own capital but only its labour power. This definitional basis seems inadequate in a world in which those who manage large enterprises seem at least as powerful as those who own their shares. The traditional approach is also unable to explain how some groups, notably intellectuals, may enjoy high status in society without the advantages of either material wealth or political power. The anthropologist Mary Douglas collaborated with the economist Baron Isherwood to develop a new approach to social inequalities that concentrated on consumption. Where most economists take consumer preferences as given, externally determined, in *The World of Goods* Douglas and Isherwood set out to explain the behaviour of consumers in modern Britain. They stressed collective determination: even apparently private pleasures, such as listening to music at home, were conditioned by the milieu of the listener. Douglas and Isherwood divided the British population into three 'consumption classes', which could be hierarchically ranked. At the bottom was the class which spent a high proportion of income on foodstuffs (necessities, as some economists might say, although most anthropologists find it impossible to maintain a sharp distinction between necessities and luxuries, even in technologically simple societies). In the middle there was a consumption class of people for whom status competition through the acquisition of relatively expensive consumer durables was a major preoccupation. The highest of Douglas and Isherwood's three classes was that comprising people for whom time and information were the most precious commodities. In a society like modern Britain, it is not enough to be wealthy and able to purchase expensive goods. It is also vital to know which goods to buy, which items of fashion are 'in' this year and which trappings of 'culture' attract high kudos in the circles in which you move. This is why the telephone, and means of communication generally, are so important to this class. In a world in which the criteria of good taste are frequently changing, it is essential to be able to network quickly, to obtain up-to-date information about the goods that maximise status.

Does status competition in the market conditions of contemporary capitalist societies differ in any fundamental way from the consumption patterns of other types of society, for example from the *potlatch* competition mentioned in Chaper 7? The key condition in our kind of society would seem to be that every individual is potentially eligible to purchase any commodity, using the standard medium of exchange. This condition of theoretically equal eligibility requires élites to shift the criteria away from wealth *per se* if their own position in the hierarchy is to be sustained. Pierre Bourdieu has shown in *Distinction* how the most highly educated achieve this goal in French society.

It is interesting to observe the changes in consumption patterns in communist and post-communist societies. Twenty years ago the opportunities for consumer differentiation in Poland were highly restricted, unless of course you had relatives in Chicago and a supply of dollars, or else very high political connections. The people in these categories were able to indulge in ostentatious consumption, but for the great majority of Poles this was impossible. This is one of the reasons why so many people, not only intellectuals but also ordinary workers, channelled their energies into political protests. The situation today is completely different. Nowadays the market economy of most post-communist countries provides virtually the same full range of consumer goods as any other modern European country. Successful private businessmen are able to build showy new villas without worrying about political reprisals and the popular media promote consumerism along lines that are familiar worldwide. Sometimes it appears that money is all that counts in the new societies but it is also the case, as in France and Britain, that people in intellectual and artistic circles engage in creative debates about quality and good taste; these may uphold values and consumer styles very different from those of the majority. It seems clear in cases such as Poland that, once the theoretical opportunities of capitalist consumerism are opened up to all, the class at the bottom of the hierarchy ceases to be a source of political instability, as it was under communism.

Note one feature of the consumer landscape in Eastern Europe which continues to diverge from the west. It is most conspicuous in the former East Germany, where many people whose relative or absolute position has declined since unification feel a certain nostalgia for the communist period and express this in their consumption habits as far as possible. For example, most people were only too happy to abandon the technologically primitive vehicle called a Trabant and join the mainstream West German market by purchasing a Volkswagen, BMW or whatever. But there are now clubs of Trabant enthusiasts who take enormous pride in their vehicles and are determined to keep them roadworthy for as long as possible. Even in Poland you will find some ordinary people who tell you that the products of communist industry (if you could get hold of them) were more reliable than the flimsy equivalents imported from the west, or that communist food production was more healthy than the chemically adulterated products of the modern multinationals.

Alienation and identities

Marxist approaches to modern consumerism tend to emphasise negative aspects. The accumulation of more and more goods for status display illustrates the 'fetishism of commodities' on which the capitalist mode of production depends. But of course not all our consumption is motivated by status competition and a very great deal of what people do in their 'leisure time' can be viewed more positively, as a celebration of identity. Culturalists argue that the Marxists have paid altogether too much attention to work and the question of whether or not one is 'alienated' from the product of one's labour. Virtually all modern workers are alienated in this sense, and even most peasants are involved in producing for a market. But human beings may be content to endure many hours of monotonous labour at the assembly line, at the computer terminal, or at the supermarket checkout, provided that the income they can earn in this part of their lives enables them to live pleasantly, perhaps fantastically, in another part of their lives. Even the routine activity of shopping may be a source of liberation and transcendence.

Of course not all of us realise our identities in the supermarket and some reached saturation point long ago. There are some people for whom work seems to be the principal means of achieving freedom from alienation. They are happiest when sitting in the library or at their computer. This brings us back once again to problems in the definition of work and consumption. We noted earlier that the distinction made little sense for many preindustrial societies but, if consumption is to be defined in terms of the pleasurable realisation of identity, then in our kind of society we should recognise that work must, for some lucky people, be seen as a consumption good.

Jonathan Friedman has pioneered a comparative approach to consumption strategies and their contribution to the expression of selfhood and social identity in the contemporary world. Sapeurs are young men from the People's Republic of the Congo, mainly from the Bakongo ethnic group, who go to enormous trouble and expense to purchase *haute couture* clothing when working as labour migrants in Paris. When they return to Brazzaville they display their exclusive designer labels in a kind of ritual, by sewing them into the lapels of their jackets. Friedman argues that these 'lumpenproletarian dandys' are doing something more than using clothing as a symbol of higher social status. They remain outsiders to the game of competitive status competition as it is played in advanced capitalist countries. Rather, as well as differentiating the Sapeurs from the 'peasant' majority of their fellow citizens, the expensive clothes connect those who wear them to the ultimate sources of power and 'life-force' in the world. The strategy only makes sense when one appreciates how completely the modern world has undermined traditional strategies of consumption and identity in these African societies.

In contrast to the 'third world hypermodernity' of this Congolese case, Friedman considers other examples in which cosmopolitan modernity is rejected. Traditional Hawaiian society largely disintegrated with the penetration of European production systems and European goods in the course of the nineteenth century. The twentieth century, however, has seen a revival of this 'traditional culture'. This cannot be an 'authentic' reconstruction of the culture as it was when Captain Cook visited these islands. The cultural revival has emerged from a denial of the values of modern consumerism, epitomised in the tourist industry that has dominated the local economy in recent generations. Friedman argues that the rejection of imported, manufactured food in favour of traditional, home-produced food is an example of a strategy of identity production which is 'not something intrinsically Hawaiian but a consequence of how the local society has been transformed by global forces.

Globalisation

Friedman's comparisons confirm the point already noted in the case of China, that an apparently uniform capitalist mode of production always undergoes local modifications. Even the consumption of Coca-Cola may have significant cultural variations, as in the Congo where to consume the expensive canned drink imported from Holland is to display a quite different identity from that transmitted by the locally produced bottled variant. In short, locality still matters and cultural diversity is constantly reaffirmed in ever-changing forms. Moreover the recent globalisation of consumption habits is not new. Luxury goods have spread systematically around the world over centuries, usually beginning with tiny élites but penetrating eventually to virtually all social classes. The globalisation of stimulants is only the most conspicuous example. The destruction wrought by alcohol on indigenous societies all over the world is well known. Other, less deleterious stimulants have been brought into European societies, notably tea and coffee. Stimulants more similar in their effects to alcohol have also become global commodities, although we find it culturally convenient to treat 'drugs' as belonging to a quite different category.

The best anthropological studies of these long-term changes in consumption patterns have connected them with developments in exchange and production. Sidney Mintz showed in *Sweetness and Power* how the demand for sugar in European societies was influenced by the new industrial systems of production in Europe.

Meeting the demand had far-reaching consequences for production systems in the Caribbean, where most of the sugar was initially produced, and also in Africa, where most of the slave labour for the sugar plantations was recruited. In *The Culture of Flowers*, Jack Goody examined virtually every conceivable aspect of the production, gifting, marketing and consumption of this 'natural' commodity. He showed that flowers flourished for many centuries in the differentiated societies of Eurasia, but noted the almost complete absence of a culture of flowers in the technologically simpler and more egalitarian societies of sub-Saharan Africa. In earlier work Goody contrasted the relative simplicity and uniformity of cooking in Africa to the more differentiated patterns found in Eurasia, where numerous cultures have established an *haute cuisine* tradition. Both Mintz and Goody show how anthropologists can integrate culturalist approaches to consumption issues, usually pursued in specific local communities or 'subcultures', with macro-level historical research.

SUMMARY OF PART II

All human societies have economies, but economic activities cannot be adequately understood by the modern discipline of neoclassical economies. Economic anthropologists move beyond universal assumptions about individual utility maximisers to show how economic activities are always embedded in social and political contexts. Anthropologists of the substantivist school suggested reciprocity and redistribution as key terms for analysing the sorts of economies least accessible to the economists. They devoted particular attention to aspects of exchange. More recently, adherents of the culturalist approach have pushed this sort of approach further, focusing on the 'local models' of economic actors and the cultural patterning of consumption.

Useful contributions of a different order have been made by those who favour political economy approaches. This school has been particularly concerned to analyse conflict between opposed classes in the realm of production, to explain long term historical changes, and to locate micro-analyses in wider regional even global political contexts. Analyses of changing property relations can also be illuminated from this perspective.

The various paradigms can be profitably combined, for each has its own field of validity. The formalist paradigm stands closest to mainstream neoclassical economies. It reminds us that human societies are composed of flesh and blood individuals who make choices. But much economic anthropology has been designed to challenge western stereotypes of 'economic man' and to illuminate those areas of the economy that the economists can never hope to penetrate – to describe and explain those preferences and cultural constraints that economists take as given. To most substantivists and culturalists the fundamental assumptions of the neoclassical economist are not so much wrong as unhelpful: they simply do not help to generate interesting information and understanding. However, in the hands of a sophisticated and culturally sensitive formalist such as Raymond Firth, concepts derived from modern market economics have been creatively used in the analysis of preindustrial economies. All markets, however, are full of 'imperfections'. The choice-making economic actors do not have perfect information. Anthropologists can explain some of the patterns in these distortions. They can show, for example, how social trust based on common ethnic or class allegiance may be vital to the extension of credit for successful trade, or how sentimental ties to the land may explain why some East European peasants wish to become landowners once again, even when this does not seem 'rational' from a narrow economic standpoint.

All economic activity, whether it takes place in a large organisation or within the family, has informal, culturally determined roots. Work in the 'hidden' or 'black' or 'underground' sector of the economy may be as exploitative and alienating as 'formal sector' factory work, but some forms of work can provide positive sources of identity, or at least the means to overcome alienation in the sphere of consumption. Advertising techniques can be viewed as tricks to deceive unwitting consumers into paying for more commodities than they really need, but culturalists attentive to the local models will reject this diagnosis because some people seem to find their liberation through consumption. The demand for goods is shaped not only by relative prices but by preferences that emerge from complex interactions of global and local processes.

Our external model distinguished between producing, exchanging, owning and consuming, but these are intimately bound up with one another in all societies. The exchange of labour between friendly households may be an important part of the peasant production process. The exclusive ownership of high status objects is a central goal of consumption strategies. All economic activities are concerned not only with the material business of survival and making a living but also with the establishment (we could even say production) of social identities.

Part III

CONTROLLING AND RESISTING

10 | POWER AND LEGITIMATION

The scope of political anthropology

Political anthropology is concerned with questions of social cohesion, order and violence, with the distribution and exercise of power, not only in modern states but in human groups of all types. Questions of power raise issues of consent as well as of mystification and coercion (force). When power is exercised with the consent of the people we may speak of legitimate authority. Max Weber, the German sociologist to whom we owe this vocabulary, also distinguished between authority grounded in tradition and authority grounded in rational, legal principles, as in a modern democracy. These are useful general models. The word politics derives from the Greek *polis*, referring to the public affairs of the city, but the basic questions of power may be pursued everywhere, from limiting cases such as egalitarian bands of hunter gatherers in Africa to hierarchical caste societies in India, from business corporations in Tokyo or New York to totalitarian states in Eastern Europe. In addition to looking at violence and warfare we shall also consider peaceful societies. We shall look at law in modern states, but also at less familiar mechanisms for settling disputes and conflicts. Anthropologists also investigate the contribution that symbols and rituals can make to the creation of consent, of the ideologies which legitimise powerholders. However anthropological research may also call into question the very concept of legitimacy: dominant ideologies may, on closer inspection of the kind that is only possible through fieldwork, turn out to be less effective than usually supposed.

Although the subdiscipline of political anthropology draws on earlier traditions, both inside and outside anthropology, a seminal volume was published in 1940 by M. Fortes and E. Evans-Pritchard,

African Political Systems. The editors' introduction was in effect a manifesto for this branch. It emphasised wider comparative aims (in line with the structural precepts of Radcliffe-Brown, who was closely associated with the volume) but also paid attention to historical conditions, including the impact of colonial rule, and to the grounding of authority in kinship and in notions of 'mystical' power. Above all the volume emphasised a dichotomy between *acephalous* ('without a head') and centralised political systems. The Nuer of the Southern Sudan, studied by Evans-Pritchard himself in the 1930s, became the most celebrated example of the former type. All the other societies represented in the volume had some forms of king or chief, although there were enormous differences between centralised kingdoms such as that of the Zulu and the loose forms of chiefdom found among groups such as the Tallensi of the Northern Gold Coast (Ghana).

Later researchers criticised the emphasis upon 'equilibrium' found in many of the analyses in *African Political Systems*. They paid more attention to individual actions and to contradictory forces that might lead away from stable equilibria. In *Political Systems of Highland Burma*, Edmund Leach argued that this region had been oscillating over a long period between relatively egalitarian forms of politics, known locally as *gumlao*, and more hierarchical forms known as *gumsa*, in which individual leaders attempted to consolidate a sort of chiefly, hierarchical structure. Leach provided detailed descriptions of the rituals practised in these communities and the marital arrangements which linked them. Politics in such a society was not a separate sphere from ritual and kinship. Leach was, however, criticised by later scholars for not paying enough attention to economic aspects. The inability of would-be chiefs to consolidate their power might have been a consequence of the fact that ecological conditions in the region were inadequate to generate a stable surplus to support a chiefly hierarchy. Moreover, although Leach paid more attention to history than was usual among Malinowski's students, he neglected the impact of the European colonial powers on the economies of this region. In short, a satisfactory explanation of the *gumlao/gumsa* oscillation requires consideration of various external factors, in addition to the internal factors analysed by Leach.

Fredrik Barth's study, *Political Leadership among Swat Pathans*, was another influential study of the 1950s that sought to break the mould of equilibrium analysis. Barth documented the ways in which individual Pathan chiefs competed with each other to secure followers and optimise their positions. He drew some of his inspiration from game theory, and many other anthropologists began around this time to approach politics in terms of the decisions taken by maximising individual actors. There is an affinity here to the paradigm that we identified as formalism in our earlier discussion of economic anthropology.

This affinity was recognised by critics, who developed positions that also had analogies in economic anthropology. Marxists argued that, instead of presenting Pathan politics as a game played by 'patron' chiefs and their 'client' followers, Barth should have recognised these groups as separate classes. The latter, according to the Marxists, were exploited by the former. The fact that, in some circumstances, a peasant farmer might be able to choose between patrons, did not alter the fact that part of his labour was continuously expropriated. The fact that peasants might not recognise this domination is neither here nor there, as far as the Marxist diagnosis is concerned. Other strands critical of Barth's analysis paid more attention to local views, and in particular to the importance of Islam. While Barth recognises that religious specialists ('saints') often played a role in dispute settlement in this society, he did not address the extent to which all acceptance of hierarchy was fundamentally grounded in an Islamic world view. Culturalist critique was sometimes linked to the complaint that Barth, like so many fieldworkers at the time, paid little attention to history. In this case, the original conquest of a peaceful society of peasant cultivators by a group of pastoral warriors seemed crucial to the inequalities documented by Barth some four centuries later.

As usual, these different approaches need not be mutually exclusive. Questions of a game-theoretical or formalist nature were prominent in the 1960s, Marxist agendas were prominent in the 1970s, while historical and culturalist approaches have gained in popularity over the last generation.

In related developments, F.G. Bailey and others extended political anthropology to include small group studies, such as the leadership dynamics of a religious faction or even the power relations of a university committee. The 'micropolitical' strategies pursued by individuals through the careful use of language in their everyday relationships were also scrutinised. Politics was a skilled craft and many noted the importance of 'informal' or 'backstage' interaction, where the right tactical rhetoric could be more important in determining political outcomes than the formal communication and ceremony that took place in the glare of a public arena. Later on, with the impact of the women's movement and feminism, researchers began to recognise that women might exercise influence in such informal ways, even when at first glance they seemed to be entirely excluded from positions of political influence.

One influential synthesis was that elaborated by Abner Cohen. Cohen accepted that a great deal in political behaviour could be explained in terms of utilitarian strategies to maximise or optimise political and economic outcomes for those involved. But, notably in his essay called *Two Dimensional Man*, he insisted that this dimension always be integrated with studies of what he termed the symbolic dimension. It was important to investigate how symbols and ideas were deployed to promote utilitarian interests. This has been far the most fertile area in the political subdiscipline in recent years. However, Cohen's framework is too restrictive for a comprehensive account of political behaviour. Instead of his 'two dimensions' we shall consider five sources of power: the economic, the democratic, the coercive, the legal, and finally the symbolic or ideological.

Sources of power

Economic

We have already seen that questions of political organisation are intimately related to economic conditions and constraints. You cannot organise a modern bureaucratic state on the basis of a hunter gatherer economy. Good economic performance usually bolsters the legitimacy of the rulers in hierarchical societies. The ethnographic record is full of examples where a chief or patron is praised for the security and prosperity that he confers upon his subordinates – often through ritual or magical activities.

Democratic

Competitive elections are the principal democratic source of power to establish the 'will of the people' in modern states. They normally provide leaders with a mandate to exercise power for a specified period and no longer. Many other forms of political system, including egalitarian and other non-centralised polities, also allow and indeed expect their 'citizens' to make their political preferences known, concerning both policies and personnel.

Coercive

Coercion refers to forms of power that involve the application of physical force, or at least the threat of its application. This power can be exercised in many ways and at many levels: the routine domestic brutality of a tyrannical husband towards his wife, the periodic depredations of well-armed pastoral nomads in the villages of sedentary peasants, the use of chemical weapons and of the nuclear deterrent by a state.

Legal

Every society has its notions of right and wrong, and every society has some system of 'customary law' which regulates aggression and violence. Legal institutions are highly varied and the connections between ideals of justice and the machinery of lawmaking and courtrooms are sometimes highly tenuous. Legal authority is backed up by some idea of *legitimate force*.

Ideological

Ideological sources of power, if they are strong enough, can outweigh all other sources. People can be reduced to a condition of abject subordination without force or even the direct threat of force. Some anthropologists have described such situations in terms of 'symbolic violence', but this metaphorical usage of violence is potentially confusing. Ideological power also implies an idea of legitimacy and it depends typically on representations of the past and the future, manipulated by means of symbols and rituals.

A Polish case study

This case study illustrates how the various sources of power may combine in a particular instance. All five sources were important in late communist Poland and, by tracing the balance between them, we gain insight into the final collapse of communist systems elsewhere as well.

The demotic and legal sources need not detain us long. It was very plain to all from the 1940s onwards that the Communist Party would never enjoy electoral legitimacy in Poland. Free political competition was therefore ruled out. Other parties were tolerated, but only under the condition that they posed no challenge to the leading role of the Communist Party. Virtually all political leaders were communists and accountable primarily to their party rather than to a wider electorate. The communists either ignored other demotic voices, such as those expressed in trade unions or in the church, or they tried to accommodate these through minor tactical concessions. As for the legal system, the slogan 'socialist legality' was meant to convey that political considerations such as pursuit of the class struggle always took priority over old-fashioned bourgeois notions like 'the rule of law'. In a purely formal sense the appropriation of private property in the early decades of communism might have been in accordance with new parliamentary laws, but since this parliament had no electoral legitimacy, neither could the laws it passed. In any case, in the early phase of communism legal process was often ignored altogether. Later on, legal institutions functioned more successfully across the fields that legal systems regulate in all societies, protecting the person from violence and also protecting personal property from theft. Nonetheless, late communist Poland still remained a long way removed from the ideal of the *Rechtsstaat*, the state in which law prevails, independent of political interference.

To compensate for their deficiencies in these dimensions Poland and all other communist states attached great importance to ideological sources of power. Marxism-Leninism was promoted as both science and morally uplifting ideology. It was inculcated not only in schools but, by virtue of the communists' control over the media, in virtually every zone of social life. The Polish case was modest in comparison with that of the Soviet Union, where every year the carefully choreographed parades held on May Day and 7 November (the anniversary of the Bolshevik Revolution of 1917) were the peaks of the new ritual calendar. The military hardware on display made these occasions demonstrations of state power, but participation in these and many other rituals, often compulsory for Soviet citizens, was also supposed to generate some of that elusive substance, legitimacy, for communist powerholders. In the case of the Soviet Union it would seem that at least some rituals did leave their mark, particularly those where communism was fused with nationalism in celebrations of victory in the Great Patriotic War. Cults of Lenin and Stalin, although engineered from above, did acquire genuine popular roots. Atheist rulers developed secular versions of lifecycle rituals which had previously had an exclusively religious character and these were taken up by millions of Soviet citizens (it may be significant that, although many people were happy enough to be married in a secular ceremony, fewer people were entirely comfortable to have their funeral celebrated by a Communist Party official in place of a priest).

In other parts of Eastern Europe the new secular rituals of communism were generally less well rooted and they faced vigorous competition. May Day was declared to be a public holiday in Poland, but patriotic Poles avoided the parade if they could and preferred to celebrate the old national holiday of 3 May, the anniversary of Poland's liberal Constitution of 1793. In the autumn there was no public holiday to mark the Bolshevik Revolution, but the state acknowledged the force of tradition in this overwhelmingly Roman Catholic country by allowing a public holiday on 1 November to mark All Souls' Day. In the later years of communist Poland there was intense competition between communists and Catholics to appropriate the most powerful symbols – the flag and other national insignia. Since the Roman Catholic Church could claim to have been indissolubly linked with the Polish state since its inception more than 1000 years ago, the contest was an unequal one. Lech

The Black Madonna

Walesa, leader of the Solidarity movement and later Poland's first post-communist president, was seldom seen without an image in his lapel of the Black Madonna of Częstochowa, a famous icon which had long been identified with the fate of the Polish nation. The Częstochowa Monastery is the most important pilgrimage site in Poland. This image of the Virgin Mary is known all over the country as the 'Queen of Poland'. It is believed to be miraculous, ever since it contributed to the defeat of the Swedes in 1655. Communists looked in vain for a comparable source of symbolic inspiration. Their main strategy was to try to wave the national flag themselves and to imply that Poland's national interest was best served by their remaining in power, since the alternative would be an intervention by the 'friendly' superpower next door.

More people might still have been prepared to put up with communist powerholders if the country's economic performance had been better. Unfortunately, for reasons that have a lot to do with their failure to solve the problem of the peasantry, the later communist years were marked by chronic shortages of most consumer goods, including food. These were the years in which all Poles had to develop their alternative, informal channels of supply, because the official economy functioned so badly.

Having lost the symbolic struggle for moral authority and failed to manage the economy successfully, the communists came under increasing pressure from the Solidarity opposition. Eventually they were left with no choice but to sustain their power by force and martial law was imposed at the end of 1981. In the years that followed the underground movements often represented their struggle as that of civil society, or the Polish nation, against an alien, oppressive state. Similar patterns developed in other communist states until the entire bloc collapsed a decade later. Unusually, rulers who lacked or had forfeited all other sources of power were not, in 1989–91, prepared to use all the instruments of coercion at their disposal.

11 | SOCIETIES AND STATES

Minimal politics

When Tony Blair became Prime Minister after the Labour Party won an overwhelming victory in the British General Election of 1997 he declared that he and his government would be the *servants* of the British people. Specialist political commentators paid close attention to the style of 'New Labour', but there were no dramatic changes in the relationship between government and governed. How could there be, in a country of Britain's size and complexity? But in many small-scale societies that anthropologists have documented the chief must act in a more substantive sense as the servant of the people. Some societies, those we term acephalous, have no formal leadership positions at all, yet they still have mechanisms to ensure social order. How have political systems evolved from egalitarian acephaly to the complex hierarchies that characterise all modern states?

The dichotomy drawn by Fortes and Evans-Pritchard in 1940 was basically one that they derived from their own European traditions: they distinguished societies that had some form of centralised political power, the state, from those lacking such a centre. They acknowledged the limitations of this dichotomy by recognising that hunter gatherer bands, although lacking a state, did not much resemble others in the acephalous type either. This chapter follows a slightly more complex typology. It starts with the forms of 'minimal politics' that Fortes and Evans-Pritchard were unable to document in their volume, because detailed studies of such societies had not yet taken place; and ends with debates about the scope of the state in post-communist countries.

James Woodburn used the term 'minimal politics' to describe the absence of anything resembling politics as we know it among the Hadza, hunter gatherers in western Tanzania. They had no leadership positions and, as we have already seen, their gambling was one of various mechanisms to ensure that no individual could accumulate possessions and establish any sort of base on which to exercise power over others. As among other groups, such as the !Kung, people resorted to techniques such as ostracism and avoidance in order to avoid relations of domination. Hadza society was extraordinarily flexible in consequence, although very poorly equipped for dealing with outside powers whenever these intruded. The main element of internal differentiation noted by Woodburn was the privilege enjoyed by a category of initiated men, who had first claim on particular parts of a slaughtered animal. The dominant principle was sharing.

Other hunter gatherers have been shown to form more structured 'bands' and to develop leadership positions such as that of the 'headman'. But this person does not have the power to command others. Rather, his job is to sound out the opinions of others, to work towards a consensus. Similarly, among small-scale horticultural societies it is also common to find persons who, although they may be styled 'leaders' or 'chiefs', are, in fact, simply respected elders. As Pierre Clastres argued in *Society against the State*, such chiefs were more 'servants' of their collectivities rather than rulers. The position was not necessarily sought after, since the duties it entailed could be very onerous. It very often happened under colonialism, however, that such figures were given formal positions as local leaders or mediators in the new administrative system. This placed them in an awkward position. Sometimes they disappointed the colonising power by refusing to play the new leadership role expected of them, because it was not in the interests of their constituency. If they did attempt to do so, for example by collecting a new tax, they often found themselves rejected by the local community. Their new power was not legitimate, not simply because they were being used by an external power for its own purposes, but also because the European assumption that such headmen or elders were the 'representatives' of their groups did not correspond to local ideas of accountability.

Segmentary lineages

This type of polity was well documented by Evans-Pritchard himself. The Nuer numbered some 200,000 when he worked among them in the 1930s – far larger than any hunter gatherer society. Evans-Pritchard described their condition as anarchic, since they lacked any form of central government. Yet this was an 'ordered anarchy'. The primary principle that brought order into the lives of the Nuer was grounded in kinship. Each Nuer was able to place himself in a system determined by kin relations. Evans-Pritchard's representation of the system is reproduced in Figure 11.1. At a low level of conflict, if people belonging to segment Z^1, a small group of relatives, come into conflict with any members of Y^1, they can expect members of Z^2 to support them. But Z^1 and Z^2 are also members of branch Y, and they would be expected to unite in opposition to the major branch X; but all members of major branches X and Y together form 'major segment' B, which

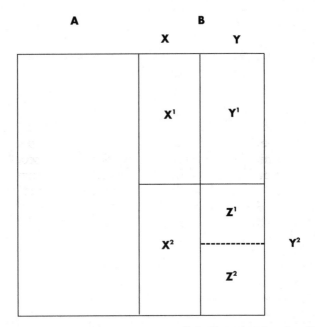

Figure 11.1   Nuer segmentary political organisation[17]

potentially unites against A, except when they fight together against the neighbouring tribe, the Dinka.

Conflicts between distantly related groups often escalated into long-lasting blood feuds. These could be resolved through the mediation of a ritual specialist, known as the 'leopard skin chief'. This figure, however, was not a source of political power, since he could only act when the parties involved allowed him to do so and he had no sanctions allowing him to impose his own views. Closer to our usual notions of powerful individuals were religious 'prophets', but these had appeared on the scene in the colonial period and had nothing to do with the traditional segmentary system.

Not all alliances among the Nuer were determined by kinship alone. The principle of age grading was also significant. So was residence, for in practice, as a result of the needs of their cattle, the people with whom one shared territory might not be close kin at all. In some cases it seems that the group of coresidents was an effective political entity in the pursuit and resolution of disputes. However, when more serious problems arose it seems likely that Nuer would follow the logic of their genealogies, even if this meant breaking up an established residential community. These ideas of segmentation are not simply the external imposition of the analyst, they are rooted in the 'local model' of how the system works.

Segmentary principles continue to operate in large regions of Africa. Ioan Lewis has shown how they underpinned a model of egalitarian democracy among the pastoral Somali in the late colonial period. Segmentary principles continued to operate under post-colonial regimes, even when the Somali state proclaimed itself socialist and tried to change the basic address term 'cousin' to 'comrade'. Finally, segmentary lineages plunged into a very 'disordered anarchy' with the collapse of the Somali state in the 1990s. All these recent changes have been traced by Lewis, who has also been among the pioneers of historical anthropology over longer time frames.

Big men

The model popularised by Evans-Pritchard was applied to many other tribal societies, but it soon became clear that, in regions such as

New Guinea, it was too far removed from the empirical realities to be of much use. (Even in the African context the model is still much debated.) Here ethnographers recognised the role of individual 'big men' who, unlike the passive, responsive chiefs and headmen noted so far, seemed to be the dynamic initiators of political action in their localities. Although the term originates in work on Melanesian societies, it can serve to define a general type that may be found in many other places. Indeed, it may be present in some form in all polities. The basic principle is that a position of leadership is *achieved* by the skills of an individual, rather than *ascribed* to him or her by virtue of birth. To the extent that modern democracies also proclaim that the highest positions in society should be filled by the most talented, rather than inherited by an aristocracy or a plutocracy, they resemble the horticulturalists of New Guinea. In the French expression, these societies are *ouvertes aux talents*.

The analogy cannot be pushed too far, for the links that bind a successful big man to the other men and women of his group are different from the sort of relationships cultivated by successful politicians and businessmen in our societies. Andrew Strathern wrote the classical account of how individuals in Highland New Guinea achieved higher positions through competitive exchanges of pigs in the ceremonial exchange system known as *moka*. Onka, the big man whose strategies Strathern explains in detail, built up his support through his rhetorical prowess. He was dependent on the women of his group, who raised the animals which he then exchanged with the big men of neighbouring groups. It was essential to give more pigs than one had received from these neighbours at an earlier stage in the cycle. The ceremonies established not only the reputation of the big man, but also the honour of his people as a whole. They served to promote both the internal integration of his group and the maintenance of peaceful relations with partners in the *moka* system.

Chiefdoms

Many tribal societies have a centralised position of power which, in contrast to the hunter gatherer headman and the big man, is inherited and gives the incumbent at least the potential to issue commands to others. These societies are usually known as chiefdoms, their leaders as chiefs, or 'paramount chiefs'. There is considerable range within this category. The Trobriand paramount had influence over a few thousand persons, but Malinowski saw this as a 'clear prototype of a politically organised state'. Many precolonial African polities were much larger and contained several culturally differentiated groups, but specifying the point at which chiefdoms become states is difficult. If the supreme leader and other 'aristocrats' live in basically the same way as their subjects, perhaps performing less manual labour but instead carrying out more ritual functions for the good of the group as a whole, and if they lack any means to enforce their power coercively, then it may be premature to speak of a state. If, however, the hierarchy persists over several generations and there is systematic transfer of surplus as 'tribute' to the ruler(s), then we should recognise an early form of the state. A further criterion is the presence of specialists whose job it is to enforce the will of the powerholders, if necessary by force. Collaboration with archaeologists may help in understanding the origins and evolution of the state over extended time frames.

Frederik Barth's study of the Swat Pathans, mentioned earlier, is a good example of the complexities we must deal with here. Barth described the complex interplay between the local chiefs as they compete, with a rather egalitarian ethos among themselves, to maintain the loyalty of their peasant supporters. Chiefly positions were inherited, yet individual skills, for example in the distribution of hospitality, were of great importance. Principles of kinship and segmentation also played a role, along with residence, caste and occupation.

The consolidation of state power in large agrarian empires did not necessarily mean that central power filtered down into the village communities and the kin groups that constituted the actual reality of most people's lives. In many regions of the Ottoman Empire, for example, a traditional 'tribal' pattern of segmentation proved to be compatible with the overarching structures of the Empire. The central power often played a key role in the emergence of the tribe, for example for some groups in pre-revolutionary Iran, as Richard Tapper has demonstrated in a magnificent study of the Shahsevan nomads. The prevalence of the tribal model should not, however, be exaggerated. Martha Mundy carried out fieldwork in Yemen in the 1970s and reported a complex system of 'domestic government', in which even villages located close to the capital had managed to preserve a high degree of self-regulation. A form of Islamic customary law, not state law, still resolved most marital and property conflicts. Women were active agents in this society, not the passive or totally excluded figures that stereotypes of the region commonly suggest.

These studies, like the work of Lewis that we mentioned earlier, all confirm the importance of combining fieldwork with historical research. Synchronic investigation may lead to an external model of the culture which the analyst can use to understand the group's history, alongside local models of the past held by group members. Where written sources are available, both these models can be tested, and corrected when necessary. It is important to avoid the implication, common in the way political scientists refer to culture, that this is homogenous and basically unchanging over generations and even centuries. Political anthropologists, provided they historicise their arguments, can differentiate between speeds of change of various socio-cultural phenomena. Just as early forms of the state grew out of chiefdoms, so even the most dramatic political revolutions of the twentieth century were inevitably built on pre-existing elements of culture. Anthropologists have commonly stressed *continuity*, but through closer co-operation with historians they can also achieve better explanations of *change*.

Modern states

Modern states, in comparison with the sort of agrarian state that we have just discussed, are usually defined in terms of their greater control over or penetration of society. State agencies are present at the local level, in the form of teachers, policemen and other officials. The type of domination is more 'rational-legal', in the terms of Max Weber, and no longer 'traditional'. But what does this actually mean for the people involved? Anthropologists can explore the state ethnographically at the local level, the level of everyday politics that other disciplines usually overlook. For example Mundy, in the study just mentioned, found that the consolidation of the Yemeni state led to a disintegration of many aspects of domestic government, but not to their replacement by an effective system of state law, impartially administered. The system was one of competing factions, something closer to stereotypical representations of tribal society in the region, although Yemeni communities had not in fact been regulated by such tribal-factional institutions previously.

In another rich study from the Islamic Middle East, John Davis investigated the Libya of Colonel Qaddafi. The Zuwaya were formerly a tribe enjoying a high degree of autonomy in their territory along a major trade route from the Mediterranean coast at Benghazi to Kufra, deep in the desert interior. They were not effectively incorporated into the Ottoman or any other empire that nominally claimed their territory. Davis considered how effectively they had been integrated into a Libyan state that claimed, rather paradoxically, not to be a state at all, but a revolutionary movement governed by a structure of popular committees. In reality, this version of Islam and socialism was a state as determined as any other to maintain its structures and to exercise influence over the life of all citizens, even those of remote oasis dwellers. Yet the system was by no means a crude dictatorship, for at the local level the revolutionary leaders were ordinary people, individuals who acknowledged their obligations to their kinsmen, and who were highly conscious of the old tribal ideas of equality and freedom from state interference. These local officials were mediators between diametrically opposed worlds, the stateless world of the tribe and the hierarchy of Qaddafi's state. One factor facilitating their balancing act in Libya, in comparison with the great majority of Africa's post-colonial states, was the country's oil wealth. Libya belongs to the category of 'hydrocarbon societies', defined by Davis as countries which obtain more than 90 per cent of their revenue through the sale of oil. Without this source of wealth, which was used to subsidise a high level of services that extended even to the remote rural population, it seems unlikely that Libya's revolutionary experiment would have lasted as long as it has.

One of the key tasks in studying the modern state is to see how its agents modify or adapt earlier forms of political power. For example, cultural continuities have been established in many parts of the Mediterranean between older systems of patron–client relations and the new party institutions, which establish themselves primarily by distributing state jobs in return for votes. Sometimes the transition is very smooth: the former landlord and patron now becomes a political boss. In other cases the attempt to maintain one's power by converting it into the new currency is disturbed by other, rival tendencies. We shall consider the case of *mafia* in the next chapter.

Anthropologists themselves tend to live in fairly strong and stable states and those who carry out studies in quite different conditions may react in various ways. Most were sympathetic to post-colonial governments in Africa and recognised the tremendous problems they had to deal with, given the often arbitrary determination of the state's boundaries and inadequate economic foundations. Later, however, when it became clear that some local communities experienced the power of the independent state as even more oppressive than its colonial predecessor, the anthropologist might again side with the underdog and become critical of the new regime. The policies previously praised as progressive nation-building were now condemned as suppressing minority rights and the ambitious projects of social as well as civil engineering were condemned as culturally destructive.

No doubt such negative evaluations are often justified, but they nonetheless reflect a privileged external point of view and may be founded on unrealistic estimations of the alternatives. In some cases the states that are, by external standards, guilty of human rights abuses may become sources of positive identification and pride for local citizens. Take the modern Turkish nation-state, which has maintained the strong statist traditions of the Ottoman Empire in Anatolia, but unlike its predecessor extended that power to reach down into even remote rural communities. It played a leading role over many decades in the transformation of a predominantly peasant economy, and it promoted mass literacy and a new nationalist ideology. This state has a poor image in the eyes of many of Turkey's European neighbours, and critical views are held by some Turks themselves, especially urban intellectuals; but anthropological research has uncovered more positive assessments among other segments of the population. The state is no longer a remote power centre but is present at the heart of society, where its agents are respected and its hospitals and schools much appreciated. Turks refer to their state as a 'father', clothing it in the intimate vocabulary of kinship.

Society against the state in Eastern Europe

It is nevertheless tempting, especially for those brought up in a liberal European tradition, to see the growth of the modern state in terms of a colonisation of society, of the diminution or destruction of the autonomy of human beings in the face of a dominant bureaucracy. The experiences of such binary thinking are especially vivid in Eastern Europe, with a long history of communism. However, an anthropological approach to politics at the local level may show that the differences between communist and democratic states were not as great as people imagined, and that all forms of state power are modified by local inter-personal relationships. This is not to say that there was no difference at all. Lenin's doctrine of 'democratic centralism' placed most emphasis on the imperative of obedience to instructions from the apex of the Communist Party, and much less on the obligation to channel the opinions of the population upwards in a democratic manner. The habits this doctrine induced were bound to be different from those of the British civil service. However, in both systems the ideals were necessarily modified by the personal contacts that flourished within the state bureaucracy and the way this penetrated society. Although western scholars were correct in not taking the 'democratic' component of Lenin's slogan very seriously, even the more repressive communist systems provided some flows of information from the citizens to the high level powerholders. The paths of influence and accountability are much harder to detect in the absence of a competitive party system, but they were certainly present under Polish communism. Without such channels it would be hard to explain, for example, the longevity of Communist Party rule in China.

The dichotomy between state and society, epitomised in Pierre Clastres' *Society against the State*, has been influential both as an external model and as a local model. But after Poland formed the eastern bloc's first post-communist government in 1989, it soon became clear that the rhetoric of state versus society conflict was a great simplification of the empirical realities. Lech Walesa, the head of the great social movement Solidarity, did indeed become President, but only at the second ballot and with a rather low turnout. When he sought a second term of office, an ex-communist was elected. Within a few years the Roman Catholic church, which enjoyed such moral authority before 1989, lost much of its popularity following what people thought were unwarranted interferences in political life (for example in connection with abortion legislation). Few Poles look back with much affection on the state that ruled under communism. But this was a state for which millions of ordinary people worked, it was thoroughly intertwined with social groups of all kinds. The rhetoric of 'state versus society conflict' was always an oversimplification, and its political effectiveness was short-lived. Yet this same rhetoric continues to pervade everyday life in many parts of the world. The political anthropologist must recognise that such discourse can itself have practical consequences: the concepts influence the ways in which people see their social world. However, rather like the case of informal and formal sectors in economic anthropology, it is important to point out that such dichotomies do not adequately reflect the empirical realities.

The concept of a 'civil society' that is opposed to the state seems in modern conditions to be promoted in an *ideological* way, by people who see states primarily as repressive and exploitative. Thus it has for a long time now been a part of the conceptual arsenal of organisations such as the World Bank and the European Union, that link the 'aid' they provide to developing countries to what they call 'civil society programmes' and 'democracy assistance'. In practise this understanding of democracy seems to mean that funds can be granted not to the state itself but to an organisation that is not formally a part of the state, a non-governmental organisation (NGO). Some poor countries have been clever enough to adapt to these requirements, and lots of NGOs have been established 'from above', by agencies or persons clearly tied to the state. This sort of subterfuge may only complicate the task of ensuring that aid funds are actually spent on the purposes intended, since it may be harder to check corruption in the bureaucracies of the rapidly expanding NGO sector than within the apparatus of the state itself.

12 CONFLICT AND VIOLENCE

The means of destruction

One of the main problems with Marxist explanations is that they tend to reduce all social and cultural processes to underlying changes in technology and production. It is preferable to be open to more complex possibilities. In the evolution of human communities the control over the means of destruction has often been as significant as control over the means of production. Of course the two may be closely related, for successful soldiers also require technology. But there are many cases in history of highly mobile nomadic people with a strong 'warrior' ethos conquering agricultural populations whose technologies were more complex and 'advanced' than those of their conquerors. Sophisticated empires such as that of the Chinese were vulnerable to the predations of 'barbarians' beyond the Great Wall who several times seized the central state power.

It seems impossible to identify ultimate causes for these patterns in evolutionary theory. Ethnographic evidence shows that there is a potential for aggression and violent behaviour in all known human communities. There are no grounds, however, for treating this impulse as the equivalent of the impulses to eating and to sex, which are essential to the survival of the community. The community can reproduce itself peacefully and all communities have some form of legal institutions and sanctions to keep aggressive behaviour under some sort of control. Where the boundaries are drawn and the forms which aggression may legitimately take are determined by culture, in our own societies as in so-called primitive communities. Let us turn to some examples.

It is a romantic delusion to imagine that people with simple technologies, such as the food collectors considered by Sahlins, with their 'Zen' economic orientations, are always peaceful. Homicide rates among some Bushmen, for example, seem to be high. But the environments these people inhabit make escalation into organised feuding and warfare extremely unlikely. It is easy enough to stay out of trouble by avoiding likely aggressors and if such behaviour is culturally censured, e.g. through ostracism, its incidence may be kept extremely rare. Colin Turnbull documented such a peaceful case, the Mbuti pygmies of the rainforest of Zaire.

But not all rainforest inhabitants are peaceful. Napoleon Chagnon titled one of his books about the Yanomamö Indians of Amazonia *The Fierce People*. He described how groups systematically raided their neighbours, slaughtering males and capturing and raping females. The brutality was entirely legitimate and it appeared to extend within groups as well, notably in the way that men treated their wives. Chagnon looked for explanations in terms of ecological and demographic adaptation, yet other Indian groups in similar conditions do not seem to have developed such fierceness. Moreover other accounts of Yanomamö present them as sensitive and generous people, with a behavioural repertoire not substantially different from the range we know in our own societies. It is possible, then, that Chagnon's accounts are unrepresentative. The Piaroa Indians studied by Joanna Overing in Venezuela are a basically peaceful society. Children here are socialised to avoid violence and, although this is a society without effective centralised controls, people do not attempt to exercise power over others by the use of physical force. The Piaroa do have a conception of violence, elaborated in their mythology; but this is a potential that they can and do resist, because they see it as a danger to their society.

Similar pictures emerge from other parts of the world. Many travellers and early anthropological studies of island societies in the Pacific paid great attention to head hunting and cannibalism. Some accounts of these 'exotic' forms of violence were so sensational that later anthropologists doubted their veracity. Yet these practices did exist and it is hard to explain them in terms of evolutionary necessity, since they did not develop everywhere. The explanation can only lie in culture. For example, the Buid of the Central Philippines, studied by Thomas Gibson, occupy an ecological niche in which some anthropologists would predict competition and violence in order to control scarce resources. Yet the Buid reject these options, emphasising in their culture the values of peace.

> All types of fighting are complex cultural responses due not to any direct dictates of an impulse but to collective forms of sentiment and value.[18]

Culturalist approaches to violence can also be pursued in societies closer to home. Spain, for example, has a distinctive form for the celebration of aggressive impulses in the bullfight. Villages in rural Poland used to offer a semi-formalised opportunity for regulated fighting every Sunday. Nowadays in this age of globalisation major sporting events seem to play a comparable role.

Weak states

The state was classically defined by Max Weber as a political entity claiming a 'monopoly of legitimate violence'. In other words, only agents of the state, its policemen and its courts, have the right to exercise violence for the common good. The principle cannot be taken for granted in all parts of the contemporary world and the strong states which we now have in Europe and North America did not always have the capacity to eliminate all challenges. Of course not all state violence is legitimate in the eyes of the population of that state, as, for example, many people in Poland with memories not only of communism but also of Nazi occupation know only too well. Those were strong states, at least in terms of their ability to coerce. But here we are interested in those circumstances in which the central power is not able to make its monopoly of force effective.

In pre-colonial and colonial chiefdoms, despite the existence of centralised institutions, the centre usually lacked the material resources to interfere in the political affairs of the periphery. Resistance was an ever-present danger, but Max Gluckman argued that it was bound to take the form of a *rebellion* rather than a *revolution*. In Gluckman's view, radical or revolutionary change was possible only in modern states, with their consolidated mechanisms of control and penetration throughout the society. The same argument could be made for peasant societies in other parts of the world. Riots and even large-scale insurrections by the downtrodden have been relatively common, but peasants have seldom been capable of organising themselves into a movement and developing a coherent set of policies. The bandits and 'primitive rebels' investigated by the historian Eric Hobsbawm were by and large the backward-looking leaders of communities threatened by new uncertainties. Anton Blok pointed out that, while 'social bandits' might begin their careers as the moral spokesmen of their communities, they could easily turn into the peasants' oppressors. Robin Hood and equivalent characters elsewhere, who took from the rich to give to the poor, were mythical figures, not the effective leaders of resistance. Even when peasant populations were successfully mobilised to bring about revolution in the twentieth century, above all by communists, it is doubtful whether the peasants were ever the main beneficiaries of these revolutions.

Anthropologists, often working closely with historians, have also explored the role that violence plays on a smaller scale in localised settings during the long period required to consolidate modern state power. One distinctive example is the emergence of the mafia in the context of Italian state consolidation. Anton Blok investigated the history of the Sicilian village of Gennuardo from the middle of the nineteenth century, when the old economic system of large estates began to disintegrate. It was replaced by new, more individualised and commercialised farming practices. There was a long period of uncertain transition, in which the older customs of the community no longer commanded respect but the state, with its distant capital, was unable to fill the gap. In particular, it was unable to police all of its territory, and so the way was open to alternative, private providers of security. The mafia emerged from intermediaries (*gabellotti*) between the peasant farmers and absentee landlords. Their practice was built on a code of absolute loyalty to the family, which no modern civil loyalty to the state had yet displaced. As a stronger Italian state emerged in the twentieth century, notably in the fascist period, the scope for private security systems dwindled. *Mafiosi* responded by expanding their activities into new sectors which even the strongest of modern states have difficulty in controlling, notably drugs and other realms of criminality.

Although the cultural details vary, the structural causes that gave rise to mafia in Sicily generated comparable types of organisation in other parts of Italy, such as the *comorra* in Naples. The comparisons can usefully be expanded to include criminal networks in many other parts of the world, such as the Chinese 'triads', or the mafia as it operates nowadays in many parts of the former Soviet Union, given the weakness of the state.

Another interesting form of non-state violence that may be of increasing importance in weak contemporary states is that of the vigilante. Unlike the *mafioso*, the modern vigilante defines himself as the representative of the will of the community, obliged to act on its behalf when the established legal institutions of the state are unable effectively to protect community interests. Ray Abrahams became interested in the phenomenon in his fieldwork in East Africa where, in the post-colonial period, states were unable adequately to control all of their vast territories. For example, where cattle were being stolen and no effective action was taken to catch and punish those responsible, some communities developed *Sungusungu* vigilante movements. These were an adaptation of cultural traditions concerning witchcraft accusations and some of the movements' activities were oriented internally, towards the control of women. Abrahams' sympathies for *Sungusungu* activities against cattle rustlers could not be extended to their witchcraft accusations, even though for some local people these were equally praiseworthy ways of 'cleaning up the neighbourhood'. The Tanzanian state deplored such action, but criticism conflicted with its own populist rhetoric, which proclaimed that power should be exercised 'from below', in the interests of the masses.

Such problems are not confined to the peripheral zones of weak post-colonial states. Similar dilemmas can be found in even the most advanced western democracies. Volunteer schemes such as that known as 'Neighbourhood Watch' in Britain, also set up 'from below' to improve standards of security for persons and property, operate in a grey area. They do not have the rights of a policeman to pursue suspected offenders, let alone the powers of a judge and jury to try and sentence. There is currently a growing demand for private security provision in many parts of Eastern Europe, and, for young men above a minimum size, taking a martial arts course is a sure way to escape the ranks of the unemployed.

Warfare

Malinowski distinguished warfare from less systematic forms of fighting and raiding, and from unilateral military expeditions and conquest. He attributed positive functions to all the latter. Warfare, in contrast, was best seen as an 'armed contest between two independent political units, by means of organised military force, in the pursuit of a tribal or national policy'. This was consistent with Clausewitz's famous claim that 'warfare is the continuation of politics by other means'. All forms of warfare are, on this view, driven by nationalism or by the aim of making the cultural unit, regardless of whether we term it a tribe or a nation, coincide with the political unit, the state. According to Malinowski, writing not long before his death in 1942, such political nationalism always had a strong tendency to imperialist expansion, and the world wars of the twentieth century were a 'pathological' threat to culture and civilisation.

Many more limited wars have taken place since Malinowski concluded his essay with the statement that 'Anthropological analysis supports those who believe that war must be abolished.'[19] Many post-colonial states, especially in Africa, have experienced more than the occasional riot or rebellion. They have declined into conditions of more or less open warfare, sometimes extending across state boundaries. It is important to address the causes of this violence and to ask to what extent its causes are new and to what extent it has roots in the history and traditions of the people concerned. Few post-colonial states had the material resources to impose effective control throughout their territories. In many, international aid provided the major sources of public finance. Even states able to avoid this sort of dependency, notably Nigeria, were unable to avoid attempts by some groups to secede, and the abuse of state offices by incumbents who viewed them only as instruments of personal aggrandisement. In some cases the anthropologist can relate the contours of state breakdown to older patterns of inter-group hostility, sometimes dating back to pre-colonial periods. The long-term history is important. The occurrence of violence may be directly related to new conditions, including above all the ready availability of lethal firearms in virtually all parts of the world. But the patterns that violence takes usually require a careful sifting of the historical record.

Similar approaches must be followed in those parts of Eurasia where the collapse of socialist power led to comparable disorientation and crisis. Consider, for example, the conflicts known as the Wars of Yugoslav Succession which in the course of the 1990s pitted Serbs against, successively, Croats, Bosnian Muslims and Kosovo Albanians. The precipitating causes of these wars were many. They included the power-seeking strategies of numerous politicians, the most notorious being Slobodan Milosovic, the Serb leader. They must also include mistakes made by external forces, who were accomplicies in the break-up of the former Yugoslav Federation before they had any idea of what to put in its place, and in particular, of what to do with Serbs who lived outside the boundaries of Serbia proper. But can these factors explain how villagers of different groups, who had over centuries lived alongside each other peacefully, could now be mobilised by external groups for violence against their neighbours? Behind the immediate causes of conflict, we need also to take into account a long history of religious and ethnic differences. The neighbours who lived peacefully alongside each other did not, by and large, intermarry. This group boundary was clear and it was old. It gave leaders such as Milosovic the possibility to manipulate Serbian public opinion, notably in his famous speech in 1987 when he claimed Kosovo for the Serbs by invoking the myth of their glorious defeat there in the fourteenth century. This representation of the past was largely a fabrication, but it built on assertions of Serbian identity that had been strong since their national movement was launched in the early nineteenth century. Moreover, Serbs and Croats had killed each other in large numbers in the Second World War years, within living memory for some and engraved into the social memory for all.

But it is not the case that long-term differences and tensions are forever bound to generate fresh violence. There is a long history of tension between Poles and Ukrainians, who also killed each other in large numbers in terrible circumstances during the Second World

War. This pattern was not repeated at the end of the twentieth century, because these states have remained basically stable and they have not been undermined by external forces. It is in the combination of historical traditions and proximate causes in the present that we need to look in order to explain why the Balkans has seen so much violence in recent years, while the regions of Central Europe have remained largely peaceful. It is completely wrong to argue that aggression is built into the 'national character' of the Serbs. But it is right to look carefully at their history and in particular, at the cultural effort that has gone into the construction of a strong nationalist ideology over the last two centuries.

There are plenty of other definitions of warfare and theories to explain it, but no single theory seems to work well in all cases. It is clear that humans are capable of fighting each other with appalling brutality, but even endemic warfare is marked by cultural constraints. Tribal warfare usually has something like an embryonic Geneva Convention, with provisions for the treatment of prisoners and civilians. Ritualisation of conflict often helps to restrict the numbers of casualties. But just as humans are capable of glorifying violence, so they are also capable of rejecting it altogether and working out alternative ways of regulating their social life.

This variation confirms the value of the culturalist approach. You might have supposed the application of physical force, or the threat of its use against another human being, to be patterns of behaviour that are understood in the same way everywhere. There are important common patterns, notably the fact that in so many societies violence is predominantly a male affair, driven by ideas about male pride, heroism and honour. Yet even here the cultural elaboration needs to be studied. Detailed attention to the aesthetics of violence may reveal much about a society's most basic values and norms. For some headhunters, the enemy's head is a trophy and it scarcely matters how it is obtained. For others, the style of the killing may make all the difference to the status of the perpetrator in his own group.

13 | LAW AND ORDER

The scope of law

The significance of law in the social life of human communities has been recognised since anthropology began. In fact many of the leading figures in the nineteenth century were themselves lawyers, and their work was much influenced by the legal traditions they inherited. One of the greatest was Sir Henry Maine, who became an expert on the legal history of India. He drew an influential dichotomy between traditional societies based on *status* distinctions and modern societies in which *contract* had become the dominant principle of social organisation. Maine was one of the first comparative lawyers to appreciate the problems of transplanting one legal system, in his case the English, to societies with quite different traditions, in his case to the Indian colonies. He recognised that law always developed in context, that the concepts on which it drew always depended upon deeper values and what we nowadays call culture. It follows that comparing legal systems requires more than a textual comparison of the laws themselves: it is also necessary to penetrate the institutional context in which the laws were implemented and, hardest of all, the subtleties of local meanings.

> A law is a social norm the infraction of which is sanctioned in threat or in fact by the application of physical force by a party possessing the socially recognised privilege of so acting.[20]

The anthropologist is more interested in the *pays réel* than in the *pays légal*, in other words in how societies actually manage and resolve situations of conflict, rather than in what the law books have to say. The difference can be considerable; to East Europeans, with memories of communist society, the distinction is particularly obvious. All East European countries had admirable constitutions, even the Soviet Union. Needless to say these were a rather poor guide to the way in which these societies actually functioned. Opponents of the regimes argued that law could not be 'socialist'. It was, by virtue of being law, above and beyond the realm of political ideologies, establishing norms and a framework of conduct for all citizens alike. The idea that the law could be made subservient to the implementation of party political programmes was anathema because it appeared to contradict the basic meaning of the term. For example, the word *Recht* means both 'law' and 'right', an association that is common in other languages as well. However, after the collapse of socialist rule many Eastern Europeans became more aware of the ways in which law and politics are inextricably entwined, in all forms of society. Phrases such as 'the rule of law' are themselves loaded with political significance. As always, we need to look behind such slogans and ask in whose interests are they being put forward, and what kinds of conflict and inequality they may obscure. This is not at all to argue that the law is unimportant. On the contrary, it plays a crucial legitimating role in modern states. The symbols and rituals of the law tend usually to reinforce the political *status quo*, but law may also offer channels to challenge powerholders. In the later years of communism this became possible for many in Eastern Europe. We shall give some examples from this region later, but let us turn first to some 'classical' materials from small-scale societies.

The first issue we need to discuss is whether or not all societies can be said to have 'law' at all. What about those small-scale societies like the Hadza, or even the Nuer, which lack centralising political institutions? Even chiefdoms are unlikely to develop specialised agencies comparable to the agencies of law and order in our own societies. Yet all of these societies have established means for resolving conflict, for preventing disputes from escalating into uncontrolled violence. We can term this customary law. Malinowski argued in the second of his Trobriand monographs, *Crime and Custom in Savage Society*, that transgression of a norm constituted a crime if met by a socially prescribed sanction, regardless of whether or not this was implemented by persons specially trained and equipped for the task.

To follow this definition is to make law identical with a broader field of dispute settlement or conflict resolution. Many societies have mechanisms for settling problems without a system of courts, or indeed any mediators or arbitrators, whose decisions can be backed up by the power of a state. Famous examples in the literature include the 'song duels' of certain Inuit (Eskimo) communities, in which the claims of the rival parties were elaborated in a song-like ritual, the result being determined by the applause received at the end of the performance. In this as in many other cases, there is little notion of judging alleged miscreants by a neutral, abstract standard of right and wrong. Like the members of any segmentary tribe, the Inuit rally to applaud their kinsman. Contrary to the modern ideal of equality before the law, the anthropological record is full of cases in which behaviour is judged by criteria specific to particular class or status groups. Observers or legal experts do not ask 'how would a reasonable man have behaved in the given situation' but 'how would a reasonable man *of that particular status or kinship group* have behaved?' The experts are likely to be political leaders or influential elders. If they have any specialist expertise at all, it is more likely to be in an area that we would more readily label religion than law. The outcomes of such 'judicial' processes are bound to vary from those found in a society operating with our notions of punishment and deterrence, and with a prison system at its disposal. In a small-scale society where such options are not available, the payment of compensation to the victim of a crime is likely to be more important than punishment. Reconciliation is especially important where the contesting parties have necessarily to continue sharing the same economic resources, to be part of a cooperative community in daily life.

The advantage of adopting a narrower definition of law is to draw attention to the changes caused by or linked to the emergence of specialised legal institutions. Typically there is a range of factors involved, including more generalised literacy and a stronger state, capable of enforcing the decisions of its legal officers. We might describe these societies as having Law, and not simply law. More of the vocabulary of our own system can be generalised in these cases: for example, tribal courts may be called upon to protect property rights. But just as there are many different ways of resolving disputes in societies that lack strong central institutions, so the existence of Law tells us nothing about its content or its importance. Even within Europe, historians of law are agreed in drawing a basic distinction to be drawn between the Anglo-Saxon common law tradition, in which the law is based largely on precedent, and the Roman Law tradition which has predominated in continental Europe, in which cases are determined primarily by reference to written precepts. Property in the Roman Law tradition is seen as 'a relation between persons and things', whereas the common law view is closer to the anthropological view and prefers to speak of 'relationships between persons in respect of things'.

In some societies, as in the contemporary USA, an enormous range of social conflicts is brought to court. This tendency seems to be increasing in European countries in recent years. Certainly the number of lawyers in Eastern Europe has increased enormously. By the same token, large countries such as Japan, despite the complexity of their social and economic systems, generate relatively much less business for lawyers. This does not entitle us to conclude that the Japanese have fewer conflicts than other people, only that they are less litigous. A fuller enquiry would probably indicate that many conflicts which in the USA would be dealt with in court are dealt with by quite different means in Japan. It is possible, of course, that equivalent conflicts simply do not develop. In either case, this is an argument for a culturalist approach to law, for it seems clear that the importance of the legal system and the definition of its tasks cannot be prescribed universally, but are necessarily tied to particular cultural traditions.

The unwritten law in Albania

To illustrate the richness of this field let us take the unwritten law in Albania, as described in the book of the same title by Margaret Hasluck, based on her extensive fieldwork in the northern districts of the country in the inter-war years. This mountainous terrain was never effectively controlled by the Ottoman Empire. When the Ottomans were pushed back shortly before the First World War new political divisions were imposed. The Albanians in Kosovo became part of a new Yugoslav state, while their neighbours to the west formed a new Albanian state. These new states attempted to impose modern systems of policing and justice, but with only limited success.

The 'laws' that Hasluck documented were founded on more than five centuries of legal tradition, dating back to the early fifteenth century and in particular to the semi-mythical figure of Lek Dukagjini. The laws associated with his name and with the Albanian national hero Skanderbeg resembled those of other European people in earlier times, including the Romans. They evidently underwent continuous evolution and could not have been the creative act of a single individual. Some of the principles were found much more widely, especially such norms as 'democratic' decision taking in public assemblies and hospitality rules which served to protect both host and guest alike. But alongside such general norms the system comprised highly detailed rules of a legal nature concerning property transmission, land use and road maintenance. Hasluck devoted ten pages to the 'law of the dog', of which Albanians distinguished four types, with rigorous penalties for damage they might cause to flocks.

The richest section of the book is that which deals with blood feuding, which was common. In the absence of any effective centralised power, it was *lawful* to punish certain acts, notably murder but also adultery and other crimes, by 'private' violence. There was much regional variation in the workings of this system. For example, the payment of blood money instead of a further killing was more institutionalised in North Albania, though it was not considered appropriate in all cases. Often, if the individual responsible could not be found it was considered right to kill any member of the family group or tribe responsible for the crime. Vengeance might be taken by any member of the victim's group, especially in the 24 hours following a crime, the period of 'boiling blood'. 'In such cases of inter-tribal aggression each tribe became temporarily a single family in which each member represented the whole.'[21] Women, old men and boys were, however, exempt from all calculations. Killing had much to do with pride and honour and so it was a disgrace to kill those not considered capable of bearing arms. The principle that 'women do not have rifles' afforded them a substantial measure of protection, even in cases where a murder had in fact been carried out by a woman. There was a very strong emphasis on 'blood' relationships in the patriline, though in some districts the avenger could be a maternal relative. People who belonged to another family but who had sworn 'blood brotherhood' with the victim were usually acceptable as avengers. These concepts have persisted in Albania and Kosovo down to the present day and the highest levels of identity in this region, now as then, are Albanian versus Slav. As Hasluck explains.

If an Albanian was killed by a Slav, any Albanian would kill any Slav in revenge. The crime, it was felt, had pitted the Albanian family against the Slav family. This national sentiment was so strong that though there has never been any love lost between Gegs (north Albanians) and Tosks (south Albanians), no Geg would allow a Slav to kill a Tosk without seeking in return to kill any Slav he could find. The less warlike Tosks did not feel a similar impulse. If one of their number were killed by their Bulgarian or Greek neighbours, they left vengeance to the victim's family.[22]

Even in the absence of the state, the law recognised a distinction between public and private interests. If a field guard was killed, he was publicly avenged. If the murderer was from another village, any of the field guard's fellow villagers could lawfully kill any man from the murderer's village during the first 24 hours, and afterwards he could kill the murderer or any other man in his household. If the field guard were killed by a fellow villager, the village expelled the murderer. Contrariwise if a miller were killed, the vengeance rested with his family. Only those who worked for the community enjoyed public protection. Feuds and all cases of conflict could be alleviated through the action of intermediaries. If peace were sought by the parties directly involved, this was interpreted as a sign of weakness, but if both sides agreed that a position of equivalence had been reached in the feud (which usually meant an equal number of deaths on each side) then a third party intervention could succeed. It does not seem that religious specialists were conspicuous in this role. Reconciliation was concluded through elaborate ceremonies over coffee and, ideally, a good meal.

Material property was not normally damaged in the case of feuds. When criminals were expelled from their villages, however, their animals were confiscated and consumed by the community. The offenders were required themselves to start the fire that burned down their house, making a return impossible. In less serious cases return was possible after a period of residence in exile; in these cases the offender's rights over his land and house were respected.

Law and politics in modern states

Whereas it would have made little sense to the members of most pre-literate societies to demarcate law as an area of activity separate from politics and the broader sphere of social control, since at least the time of the French Revolution this differentiation has become a central feature of Euro-American societies. Perhaps it is more accurate to say that there is an aspiration to differentiation, to insist that the law is the law and that it forms somehow a higher domain than the realms of politics and administration, which are more readily compromised by the need to strike deals and pragmatic compromises. The law, especially when enshrined in the constitution of a modern democracy, sets a normative framework for all citizens, irrespective of their social, religious or ethnic background. Or so we like to think.

The relationship between the legal and the political in a modern democracy differs from that which we used to find in African tribal societies, or in Eastern European communist societies, but law can never be entirely detached from politics. In Britain the head of the judiciary is a politically appointed member of the cabinet and appointments to the American Supreme Court have often been politically controversial. Even where a stricter separation is maintained, the laws that judges implement are regularly amended by politicians. The social background of the judiciary is often highly distinctive. In Britain it is sometimes difficult for judges, who mostly attend highly exclusive schools and universities, to comprehend fully the factors that motivate the crimes of their fellow citizens they are called upon to punish.

Let me develop an example from Germany which worked very hard in the second half of the twentieth century to promote an ideal of the law-governed democracy, or as it was known there, the *Rechtsstaat*. This tradition had strong historical roots, which, however, were not strong enough to prevent the crimes of the Nazi period. Hence the strong determination of the new Federal Republic to rebuild the *Rechtsstaat* after 1949. Some indication of its success is given in the fact that, proportionately, Germany has more judges than any other country in the world (whereas it is the USA which has the most lawyers).

Meanwhile, Eastern Germany became known as the German Democratic Republic and developed legal traditions closer to those of Poland and the rest of the Soviet bloc. With the collapse of that system in 1989–91, when the majority of East Germans (*Ossis*) voted in favour of reunification, the West German system was effectively imposed upon the East. However, West Germany had always refused to recognise the East as an equivalent *Rechtsstaat*. How could the constitutional principles of the west be applied to millions of new citizens who had formerly belonged to the Communist Party, served in the armed forces (where they might have been required to open fire as border guards), and accumulated personal property through their work at state owned firms? The old *Ossi* judges and prosecutors were mostly replaced by *Wessis*, but the most sensitive cases were tried according to the old eastern laws. Hence some top ex-Politburo members were sent to gaol because their actions, notably in authorising the shooting of those fleeing across the Berlin wall, was contrary to East German law – that 'socialist legality' that no one ever took seriously. Some of those believed to have collaborated with the secret services were spared prosecution on grounds of age, but many others were pursued through the courts. All the main political parties agreed that to 'draw a line' under communism by granting an amnesty would have been incompatible with ideals of the *Rechtsstaat*. Some *Ossis*, those who had always disapproved of communist power, were all in favour of these trials, but many were unpopular with the majority of the East German population, which saw in them not the rule of law but the 'rule of victors' (*Siegerjustiz*).

It is interesting to compare the German experience with the experience in Poland. There too, one finds the belief that recent changes have strengthened the rule of law, a rule which has good historical roots, not well respected during the communist period. But the end of communism did not bring anything like the sort of legal purification processes that occurred in Germany. In effect the Poles did draw a line and, compared to East Germany, many more former communists and their sympathisers have been able to hold on to their leadership positions. Of course the Polish experience of communism differed from the German in many ways, but the basic explanation for this legal contrast when the systems collapsed is simple enough and it is political. West German élites had everything to gain by sweeping aside as many senior figures in the east as they could, in order to promote colonisation by the west. If an equivalent situation had prevailed in Poland, the anti-communists could have been just as insistent on the need to implement rule of law, and hound every last member of the communist party into confessions and premature retirement from his or her post. In other words, the legal courses followed were very directly dependent on the political circumstances.

Transfer and legal pluralism

The imposition of West German law on the former German Democratic Republic is an extreme example of colonisation. Anthropologists are more familiar with less extreme cases, in which a new system is introduced by a colonial power, but it does not completely displace an older local system or systems. Malinowski thought that the British Empire of his day had developed a very reasonable and liberal practice, known usually as 'indirect rule'. While some branches of law, such as that governing export markets, were likely to replicate the codes of European countries, others, such as family law and inheritance, might follow local traditions. The codifying and consolidating of 'customary law' in reality marked a significant break with the way this law had evolved in the past. The colonial societies were not pluralist in the sense that choices were available as to which system to use: that was usually determined by your status and the nature of your problem.

Nonetheless, the outcomes produced a complexity that perhaps did less damage to local tradition than would have ensued from the wholesale import of foreign codes and the elimination of custom.

This can be appreciated if we consider the model developed by Turkey in the 1920s, when a secular republic took the place of the Ottoman Empire in Anatolia. The Turks decided at this point to import as much as they possibly could from the west, including the Swiss civil code more or less in its entirety. As a result, Turkey has long had law books that look extremely modern, e.g. in marriage law and in the provision of equal rights for females in inheritance. There is some anthropological evidence that, some time after this legislation was introduced, women were able to take advantage of it and pursue their interests through the courts. However this legal transplant did not succeed as intended. It did not seriously weaken the influence of long-established Muslim ideas about gender relations, including views about polygamy and inheritance. Thus, a woman who was unhappy at her husband's taking a second wife or unhappy that her father's land was allocated only to her brothers, could in theory take her complaints to court and win her case. In the *pays réel*, however, in this largely rural society there were overwhelming community pressures on women to prevent them from pursuing their 'legal rights'. Large areas of social life continued to be governed by customary law. The replacement of communist legal codes may lead to similar contrasts. Albania's post-socialist constitution was in large part drafted by a German law professor on the basis of German models and just a few short visits to Albania. He had no knowledge of the Albanian language or of the rich ethnographic literature on Albanian customary law from which I quoted earlier. No one familiar with this literature would have been surprised at the acts of vengeance committed by many Albanians when they re-entered Kosovo after the Serbian ethnic cleansing campaign and ensuing war of 1999. Again we are not arguing that this conflict was *caused* by the presence in this region of unruly tribes and primordial customs, only that these traditions of customary law, preserved until the very recent past, should be taken into account when external forces intervene and create new legal systems. The failure of the post-war tribunals to bring cases against the NATO officials who authorised the use of 'cluster' bombs in civilian-populated areas suggests that, as so often, the rhetoric of human rights is a disguise for *Siegerjustiz*.

Following the immigration of large numbers of Muslims and other immigrant groups, legal pluralism has recently become an issue in Europe as well. Some proponents of 'multiculturalism' argue that it is only right that religious minorities be allowed to follow their traditional customs, for example in matters of dress and marriage and practices. But what happens when, say, a female member of a minority group alleges that its customary law affords her rights and protection inferior to those enjoyed by members of the majority? In extreme cases, girls raised in Britain have been married against their wishes to relatives in Pakistan, sometimes before reaching the legal age for marriage according to British Law.

There is a further problem, in that the debates about legal pluralism presuppose a system of sovereign states with the power to control the legal systems applied on their territory. But what happens in conditions of accelerating globalisation, when people, goods and ideas are all in rapid motion between states? Should we be looking to identify legal pluralism on the global level? This would require some ultimate political authority, something like a world government. Until this happens international law is likely to remain a field in which decisions are taken according to political and commercial criteria, rather than criteria of cultural distinctiveness. Instead of global *Rechtsstaatlichkeit*, whether uniform or pluralist, ordered anarchy will prevail in the legal marketplace.

14 | SYMBOLS AND IDEOLOGIES

The politics of the past

Political behaviour, like other activities, can be motivated by the prospect of utilitarian advantage. It may also be motivated by fear of violence. But a very great deal that goes on in politics and in social life generally cannot be reduced either to an economic calculus or to coercion. Symbols and the rituals and myths in which they are expressed play an important role in all human societies. To understand what anthropologists term the symbolic dimension we need to enquire more carefully into the specific details of a culture. Malinowski, for example, made detailed analyses of Trobriand rituals and, in a memorable mixed metaphor, argued that they were the 'cement of the social fabric'. These were 'face to face' communities where everyone could map their relationship to everyone else on a grid of kinship and affinity. Nevertheless each subclan had a 'mythical charter' describing where the founding ancestor had emerged, as a way of explaining and legitimating the group's current location.

Contrary to the common assumption that symbols and myths become less important with the rise of large-scale bureaucratic states, it may be that they acquire greater significance in the anonymous conditions of mass industrial society, when they are the major instruments for binding far-flung communities together. Nationalists therefore often invent new rituals and mythologies. For example, Romanians have been taught over many years that they are the descendants of the Roman conquerors of a region known as Dacia. The antiquity of this claim is asserted in denying the claims of later arriving Hungarians and Germans to have a homeland in the territory known nowadays as Transylvania. Successive Romanian governments of very different political orientation have all helped to consolidate a powerful nationalist ideology. But constructions of the past play an important role in all political systems, not only among those we think of as 'extreme nationalist'. Think how important the American Revolution is for the continued legitimation of the political system of the USA, or the French Revolution for that of France. By virtue of their scale, all modern polities are necessarily 'imagined communities', to use the term of Benedict Anderson.There has to be some foundation beyond economic integration and political force if these are to persist over time and arguably it is provided by cultural symbols and by myths.

> The function of myth, briefly, is to strengthen tradition and endow it with a greater value and prestige by tracing it back to a higher, better, more supernatural reality of initial events. Myth is, therefore, an indispensable ingredient of all culture.[23]

For the anthropological student of politics it is more important to probe the emotive, imaginative appeal of myths and symbols than to assess their 'truth' according to rigorous scholarly criteria. Beliefs about the past that are demonstrably false can have very real effects, for example when ideas about a Greater Serbia help to mobilise people for ethnic cleansing in Bosnia and Kosovo. The past cannot be known directly and is always, up to a point, open to fabrication. History is always a selection of elements from the past, and the selection is often expected to conform to an ideal representation of collective identity. Often the selection will be determined by political leaders and textbook writers accountable to ministerial officials. Rewriting history may be a more complicated task in a literate society than in a society such as the Trobrianders, unconstrained by documentary evidence. Consider, however, the case of the Czech National Movement, whose leaders in the second half of the nineteenth century highlighted the phases in the history of Bohemia which suited their nationalist cause against Habsburg rule from Vienna. They did not hesitate to forge historical documents to back up their case.

But representations of the past, if they are to take firm root, must also have resonance in wider reaches of society. The study of 'collective memory' is almost always an important part of the symbolic dimension of politics. Memories of past violence are often especially significant, as we saw earlier in the case of Serbs and Croats. The mysteries of memory and myth were very important in the persistence of an idea of Poland during the long period between 1793 and 1918 when there was no Polish state. Paradoxically this was precisely the period in which Polish nationalism developed. Yet modern Poland is also a 'forged nation', in the sense that it is little more than a hundred years that most speakers of the language called Polish have acquired a clear national self-consciousness as Poles. As part of that consciousness they have come to accept a particular understanding of the past and internalised key dates, such as 966, the date when King Mieczko I embraced Catholic Christianity.

Malinowski himself was very much a cultural nationalist, although he tried to separate this from political nationalism. As we have noted one of the problems that faced the communists when they seized power was the difficulty they had in rooting their movement in the history of Poland. Their symbols and their jargon were necessarily international and oriented towards the future. They were officially allied to the Soviet Union and authorised historical accounts of the Second World War years tried to put the blame for every atrocity onto the Nazis. Their opponents, both religious and secular, could mine the Polish past for powerful symbols and meanings to sustain them in their resistance, and popular memories of Soviet violence between 1939 and 1945 could not be repressed.

Kingship

Some of the most famous examples of the use of ritual in the political process involve the institution of kingship, king being in effect a synonym for hereditary chief. The chief of the Ashanti of West Africa was installed in a ceremony which focused on his golden stool, a sacred symbol of his responsibilities as well as his powers. The chief who did not live up to his responsibilities was liable to be 'destooled'. The meaning of the stool was completely misunderstood by the British colonial governor in 1900 when he demanded that it be brought for him to sit on, as the new power in the land. The result was the last Ashanti war. Later the British, advised by the anthropologist Rattray, came to respect the significance of the stool, with its mystical power of *sunsum*, for Ashanti identity.

Evans-Pritchard's analysis of the succession of the king of the Shilluk (Western Sudan) provided a dramatic illustration of a principle which is well known in many other societies: 'the King is dead. Long live the King'. Individual incumbents might come and go, they might be good or bad, strong or weak (the latter seldom lasted very long), but the office of kingship endured. Through elaborate rituals, which in this case involve the slaying of an effigy of the old ruler, the king was treated as a god and raised far above comparison with possible mortal rivals.

The role of ritual in the creation of such ultimate values has been most elaborately demonstrated by the American Clifford Geertz in his analysis of the precolonial state in Bali. Geertz described this political system as a 'theatre state', built up entirely on lavish displays of pomp and ceremony. A very pronounced hierarchy had many brutal aspects, but it was rooted not in economic exploitation or in military domination but in cultural ideas about legitimate power, regularly reinforced in the performances of ritual. Geertz puts it as follows.

> The stupendous cremations, tooth filings, temple dedications, pilgrimages and blood sacrifices, mobilizing hundreds and even thousands of people and great quantities of wealth, were not means to political ends: they were the ends themselves, they were what the state was for. Court ceremonialism was the driving force of court politics; and mass ritual was not a device to shore up the state, but rather the state...was a device for the enactment of mass ritual. Power served pomp not pomp power.[24]

Geertz repeated the earlier call of Fortes and Evans-Pritchard for anthropologists to cease approaching non-western political systems in western terms. It was natural for *us* to assume that symbols and rituals were mere embellishments of a domination that has its roots elsewhere. But according to Geertz, in precolonial Bali the 'symbology' *was* the domination, ritual was in effect a form of warfare, and the state drew its force from its 'imaginative energies'. The anthropologist's task in such a setting was to provide a 'poetics of power'.

Not all anthropologists have been convinced by Geertz's elegant argument, based as it necessarily is on limited archival sources rather than direct fieldwork. One of the complaints is the same as that made against many more conventional anthropological studies of earlier generations: Geertz's analysis takes the Balinese Kingdoms out of any real historical time. It pays no attention to the changes that took place before the nineteenth century and the eventual intrusion of the Dutch colonial power. In this respect Maurice Bloch's examination of political rituals in Madegascar is an advance on that of Geertz. Bloch makes careful use of historical sources to show how the same rituals can be adapted in different periods to serve the interests of new powerholders. In the case of the circumcision ritual of the Merina, the level of political action shifted over time from the head of a kinship group to the king of an expansive, militaristic state, but the structure of the ritual remained the same. Malinowski, had he ever attempted such a historical analysis, might have argued that its *function* remained the same, namely to reinforce powerholders. Bloch, however, was critical of earlier functionalist theories and in their place developed a Marxist argument which viewed ritual as a special mode of communication for the establishment of a dominant *ideology*.

Can political anthropologists, by analysing symbols and rituals, shed light on the significance of 'constitutional' monarchies in modern European states? Britain is obviously the best example. Here the prime symbol of political legitimacy is ostensibly the ballot box. Since at least the mid-nineteenth century, the orthodox interpretation of the political system holds that the monarch has no significant 'practical' role. In fact, the monarch may on occasion exercise a very direct political role, for example in the event of a close election result and a 'hung' parliament. Of greater interest to the anthropologist is the sense in which the monarchy provides a focus for some sense of common belonging for all the people of Britain, transcending their many party-political, religious and ethnic divisions. Royal rituals, such as a coronation, the investiture of a prince, a wedding, or the funeral of a princess, establish a sort of national communion. That the British royal family retains its power to inspire strong emotions is evident almost every day in the tabloid newspapers. It may be that such coverage has weakened the foundations of royal mystique, in comparison with the more aloof sovereigns of other peoples and other periods. But it is also possible that such media coverage succeeds in generalising a novel sort of intimate identity, one which is not so different from that which people have felt towards their chiefs and divine kings in smaller scale societies throughout the ages. For the time being the royal family continues through its symbols and ritual performances to play a major role in sustaining a relatively stable and cohesive society in Britain.

Symbols and resistance

Most anthropologists, including Bloch, Geertz and their functionalist predecessors, present the role of symbols and rituals as inherently conservative. They represent the force of tradition and therefore reinforce the power of rulers. This link can, however, be questioned. In his analyses of certain harvest rituals in Southern Africa, Max Gluckman showed how they enabled subjects to act out and dramatise a rebellion against the authority of their king, which went unchallenged under normal circumstances. His argument was that relatively weak states in precolonial and colonial times lacked the resources to enforce the will of the centre throughout the society. Allowing opposition to be expressed in a formalised way at the 'first fruits' festival was a mechanism which functioned as a sort of safety vent for the society. By allowing people on this one occasion to express their opposition to the rule of the king, a real (perhaps military) rebellion was rendered less likely. It therefore helped to bind the society together. For Gluckman too, then, activity in the symbolic dimension still seemed at the end of the day to reinforce a *status quo*.

However, it is also possible that the symbolic domain may itself be a site of competition and rivalry. The same symbol may be appropriated by two or more parties. In most modern states the symbols of the nation seem to have the most intrinsic power, so it is not surprising to find that, in the case of Northern Italy, where

Catholics and communists have very different sets of symbols and messages, both deploy the national flag at their festivals and in their publicity materials.

Longstanding rituals may be taken over by new social groups and put to novel, even revolutionary uses. David Lan carried out fieldwork in Zimbabwe shortly after its liberation from white minority rule. He found that the power of traditional chiefs in Shona-speaking communities was legitimated by the ancestors through rituals conducted by *mhondoro*, spirit mediums. But the power of these chiefs had been compromised through their cooperation with white Europeans in the colonial period. When Marxist-Leninist guerillas arrived from neighbouring Mozambique in the late 1970s to pursue a struggle for independence, the *mhondoro* gave these strangers land, performed rituals to convert them into 'legitimate residents' of the territory, and blessed their campaign with the authority of the ancestors. Lan took the view that the guerillas would have won their struggle anyway, but the support of the spirit mediums had more than a merely practical, instrumental significance. The rituals of the *mhondoro* gave moral weight and dignity to the cause of the Shona black majority. Lan concluded that this was a case of 'revolution with continuity': the discredited chiefs were replaced by modern village committees as the main source of local authority, but this change was accomplished through ritual activity based on beliefs in the power of ancestors, beliefs which had barely changed at all over many generations.

This brings us back to the issue of whether it is ever possible to escape from the constraints of culture, or from dominant political ideologies as they have evolved over generations. Turkey, for example, recently celebrated three-quarters of a century of secular republicanism. It has a ritual calendar which in some respects resembles that of the old Soviet Union, with similar sorts of parades and statues of Atatürk as ubiquitous as statues of Lenin used to be in the USSR. Yet Turkey remains an overwhelmingly Muslim country and there is general agreement that its political structures are still marked by Ottoman history. A similar point can be made about all the countries that experienced socialist revolutions in the course of the twentieth century, though of course the precise mixture of continuity and change is variable.

Ideology and hidden transcripts

The continuities of culture are usually strongest in the micro-reaches of social life, inaccessible to other researchers. Here anthropologists can explore the extent to which a dominant ideology, i.e. a set of ideas, symbols and rituals justifying a particular way of organising society and politics, is actually 'internalised' by the population. If the masses resist their domination, are they nonetheless obliged to do so within the categories established by powerholders, with the consequence that any radical change is effectively ruled out? For example, we have already noted the tendency of protest movements among peasants to hark back to an earlier 'golden age' rather than to formulate programmes of revolutionary emancipation. On the other hand an ideology may be less dominant than it appears to be at first sight if subordinate groups are capable of adapting it to suit their own purposes, or alternatively, of showing, even in minor ways, that they reject their domination.

James Scott found, in the village that he studied in Malaysia, that poor peasants made a moral appeal to wealthy landlords to respect their community obligations and give employment to the poor, even when, following the Green Revolution, it became more economically rational for them to mechanise all their farming activities. The appeal was based on the Islamic ideology to which they all subscribed, so it could not easily be dismissed by the élites. Scott also documented what he termed 'weapons of the weak', techniques used by the poor to better their own situation or to express their disaffection, such as petty theft from the fields of the wealthy, or sabotage of their harvests. In conversations 'backstage', i.e. in private, with each other, when no landlord was present, the language of the poor might reveal an ability to 'see through' claims that rich and poor formed a single moral community. This recognition might be momentary. The 'hidden transcripts' of subordinate groups are seldom able to develop a rival ideology, they present no effective challenge to the power of the élites. Nonetheless, micro-level investigations such as that of Scott, which in principle can be undertaken by political anthropologists in any hierarchical system whatsoever, can help us to understand the limits of legitimacy. Poor people may consent to and even collude in their own exploitation, but they may also see through the dominant ideology. We may expect in most cases to find a distribution of opinions, indeed it is likely that the same individual will change his or her opinions from time to time, in different situations.

The idea of *legitimacy* is the beguiling concept that lies behind our interest in the symbolic dimension but we should not exaggerate its significance. Just how far Marxism-Leninism was 'internalised' through rituals is a matter for empirical anthropological investigation. It is fairly certain from the limited studies available that the picture varied considerable not only from one country to another but for different social groups within countries and for different historical periods. Fascists and Nazis also made considerable use of state-orchestrated rituals, on the whole with rather greater success. But we must be wary of assuming that all of the people all of the time are in fact taken in by symbolic performances, whether they be May Day parades in Moscow, Nazi rallies in Nuremberg, royal funerals in Bali or royal weddings in Westminster.

SUMMARY OF PART III

The sub-discipline of political anthropology is concerned with social order and the distribution of power in all forms of human society. Anthropologists have challenged the assumptions of western political theory by demonstrating that it is possible to achieve order and cohesion without any central apparatus (the state). Kinship is the basis of 'segmentary' organisation, which often persists even when some form of central power has been established. Many forms of chiefdom were inherently stable, but some modern states also lack the capacity for effective penetration of society. The export of western models of government to other parts of the world, and more recently the dissemination of western models of 'civil society', are often problematic because they diverge from local notions of governance and accountability.

Control over the means of destruction is an important element in all human societies and may have played as big a role in evolution as control over the means of production. Aggression and violence are a universal potential but they may be negated by culture and they are everywhere constrained by it. Warfare differs from the fighting and raiding found in technologically simpler societies, which are often highly ritualised and can be understood as part of 'customary law'. All societies have mechanisms for settling disputes and preventing the escalation of conflict, ranging from simple strategies of avoidance and 'self-help' to the complex court procedures of a modern state. When states do not command an effective monopoly of violence, private alternatives include networks such as mafia and vigilante groups.

Some anthropologists have approached politics in terms of very general assumptions about the maximising strategies of participating individuals, for example in terms of 'game theory'. It is always important, however, to explore the cultural contexts within which the individuals operate. Anthropologists have paid particular attention to the symbolic dimension of politics, sometimes as part of a neo-Marxist account of how powerholders maintain their dominant ideology. Nationalist ideologies lie behind the 'pathological' forms of modern warfare and the manipulation of beliefs and symbols to serve genocidal goals did not end with Auschwitz. But the symbolic dimension also helps us to explain benign forms of political coherence, as when the rituals of royalty provide people with a focus to celebrate a common identity. The full impact of political rituals is difficult to gauge and it is possible that some of the people who participate and spectate on these occasions remain essentially immune to the ideology, or they absorb only partial messages, which influence only a small part of their social and political behaviour.

The symbolic and pragmatic strands can be woven together. Political behaviour is governed both by the meanings of culturally specific symbols and by considerations of utilitarian advantage. Anthropologists' use of fieldwork methods gives them access to actors' informal social interaction and the covert discussions 'backstage', which are often more revealing than the formal performances of the public domain. The fieldworker who goes backstage to investigate the covert forms of practical activity may uncover alternative value systems and justifications for resisting domination. Subordinate groups cannot easily formulate alternatives and they may be unable to speak their minds openly for fear of the consequences; but, when given the opportunity, they may be perfectly capable of manipulating some elements of an ideology to their own advantage.

Part IV

BELIEVING AND CELEBRATING

15 | MAGIC, SCIENCE AND RELIGION

The subfield of cosmology

> We will call religion any collection of beliefs and practices referring to supernatural powers and bound into an organic system, which are expressed in social life by a series of acts of a cult which is systematic, public, obligatory and based on tradition...expressed by a series of norms of behaviour also defined by tradition, closely connected to the dogmas of the cult and possessing supernatural sanctions as well as social ones. The criteria for defining religion in this manner lie in social, objective facts, and therefore they are easily accessible to close observation, even among savage people.[25]

Religion and ritual are terms that anthropologists use constantly, without being able to agree on precise definitions. We can, if we wish, proceed from the sort of religions that anthropologists are familiar with in their home societies, which include complex bodies of codified doctrines and a hierarchical organisation. It would, however, be ethnocentric to investigate the beliefs and practices of other cultures by such a standard. Ethnocentrism persisted at the end of the twentieth century in Britain, where the Charity Commission defined religion as 'a belief in a supreme being and an expression of belief in that supreme being through worship'. The notion of single 'high god' is relatively rare in tribal societies, but that is not the only problem with this definition. The commissioners decided recently that the Church of Scientology did not qualify as a religion, because it did not organise worship on a public basis. Another possible drawback of the definition is that it prevents us from considering ideologies such as nationalism and communism as forms of religion. Yet these too establish transcendent values and promise a kind of salvation to their followers. We shall return to the theme of 'secular religions' later.

For the time being we shall accept the popular understanding that religion involves some sort of belief in one or more 'spirits' or 'godlike beings'. The term cosmology is also widely used by anthropologists. It derives from the Greek *kosmos*, which refers very generally to the order of the world. Cosmology may be preferable to religion if the latter always seems to tie us to the sort of faith and organisation we know in our own cultural traditions. If the ultimate purpose of a political ideology is the legitimation of political hierarchy, cosmology addresses more fundamental questions concerning the meaning of life, the place of humankind in the universe. But this distinction breaks down when the same symbols and rituals are involved in both, as we have already noted in the case of kings who are equated with gods.

Cosmologies are necessarily local models. In many societies they are fascinatingly elaborate and the sophistication of their discourses seems unrelated to economic or political complexity. A well known example is the Australian Aboriginal concept of 'dreamtime', a key idea in indigenous belief systems that seems richer and more complex than anything in the cosmologies of the peoples who colonised that continent. All cosmologies can be viewed as examples of human intellectual creativity, as attempts to *explain* the world, and this approach goes back to the discipline's foundations.

The intellectualist tradition

As in the formative phases of other sub-branches of anthropology, the questions asked in this field were influenced by deeply rooted ideas in European society. Early work in the anthropology of religion was much influenced by contemporaneous scientific progress, above all the insights of Darwin. Many attempted to apply an evolutionist perspective to religion. Tylor thought that 'animism' was the most primitive form of religion. By this he meant the idea that persons (but also animals, plants and even material objects) contained some sort of spirit or soul as their vital force. He thought that only later civilisations developed the idea of powerful supernatural beings that were independent of specific human beings and the things they could see in their environment.

In this field even more than other subdisciplines it is important to study the anthropologist, i.e. to be aware of how his or her bias may affect the work. Many anthropologists have been hostile to religion, especially in the early period before the Malinowskian revolution. Sir James Frazer recognised Christianity as a significant advance on the magical thought of primitive peoples, but for him it still fell a long way short of the rationality that he saw as the hallmark of modern science. In France at the same period Lucien Lévy-Bruhl argued that primitive societies had a basically different mentality from modern societies.

It is not merely the persistence of religious phenomena, even in the most technologically advanced societies, that casts doubt on the contrasts drawn by Frazer and Lévy-Bruhl. We also need to recognise the persistence of magical activities, for example in the millions of people who buy a daily newspaper in order to read their horoscopes. On the other hand, we must also recognise that yam farmers such as the Trobrianders carry out experiments in their environment with as much logic and rigour as any modern scientist.

> There are no peoples however primitive without religion and magic. Nor are there, it must be added at once, any savage races lacking either in the scientific attitude or in science, though this lack has been frequently attributed to them.[26]

Marx and Weber

The social anthropologist, unlike the theologian, is also interested in how mundane political and economic factors shape the beliefs that develop in human communities, the ways in which these are practised, and their consequences for other fields of activity. The nature of this interaction has been viewed very differently by the classical figures of modern social science. At one extreme stands Karl Marx, who rejected the Jewish traditions of his family and argued instead that 'the longing for a life of bliss in the beyond' could only be considered as part of an ideology that hindered workers from pursuing the possibility of a more just, non-exploitative social order in this world. Religion was therefore the 'opiate of the people', a set of beliefs which concealed the realities of class struggle and exploitation.

Dismissing religion as crudely as this does not help very much and leaves Marxists open to the criticism that they are themselves guilty of dogmatic assertions, that their own movement is in essence a kind of church, which substitutes communism, a utopian condition somehow to be realised in this world, for the afterlife that other religions prefer to locate in some form of supernatural world.

Although their emphasis upon material conditions is usually too narrow, the basic Marxist invitation to explore links between religion and patterns of domination and exploitation is important and has been productively taken up by many anthropologists. Peter Worsley, for example, related 'cargo cults' in various parts of the Pacific to the impact of capitalist economies on the region. These cults, in which significant quantities of material goods were destroyed or sacrificed, had a clear political dimension and can be seen as protest or liberation movements. In a very different context, Jean Comaroff's investigation of Pentecostalism as a form of cultural resistance in South Africa can also be read as a demonstration of the complex effects of expanding capitalism on traditional cosmologies. What these anthropologists do is combine the insight of political economy with a careful exploration of local cultural models.

Of greater value for the anthropological study of cosmology is the religious sociology developed by Max Weber. Weber's legacy is a rather bewildering mixture. On the one hand, his accounts of Hinduism, Confucianism and Islam are beset by many of the distortions that afflicted the work of other Europeans of his day. On the other, his study of the links between Protestantism and the rise of capitalism is a pioneering demonstration that economy and society are shaped not only by material factors but also by values and subjective dispositions that are determined by culture. In all his work on religion, Weber sought deeper understanding of the believer's perspective. His aim was essentially the same as

Malinowski's aspiration to understand the 'native point of view', or what we have termed the local model. Malinowski never wrote a full-length study of Trobriand religion, although we shall come back to his essays on magic and myth a little later, but several of his students and others in the school that he founded produced outstanding work. For example, Evans-Pritchard produced a sensitive and sympathetic account of Nuer cosmology, complementing his earlier work on the political, economic and kinship organisation of these people. The fact that Evans-Pritchard was himself a practising Roman Catholic does not seem to have been a handicap, indeed his own religious outlook may have helped him to appreciate the complexities of the very different outlook of the Nuer.

The American Clifford Geertz also belongs to this broad Weberian tradition and he has given it an explicit anthropological formulation. He approaches religion as a 'cultural system' and sees all religions as serving two basic functions. They must provide believers with a 'model of' the world, in other words, with an explanation of how it works and of man's place in it, and simultaneously, with a 'model for' living in this world, with a guide to action, and with solace in times of misfortune. In his empirical studies of Indonesia and Morocco Geertz showed how one and the same world religion (Islam) could assume very different local characteristics.

A religion is a system of symbols which acts to establish powerful, pervasive and long-lasting moods and motivations in men by formulating conceptions of a general order of existence and clothing these conceptions with such an aura of factuality that the moods and motivations seem uniquely realistic.[27]

Two kinds of functionalism

In *The Elementary Forms of the Religious Life*, drawing particularly on then recently published ethnographic work concerning Australia, Émile Durkheim defined religion not in terms of the supernatural but in terms of an opposition between *sacred* and *profane* that he thought all human societies had in one form or another. He saw religion as a direct expression of the organisation of the society and argued that, in the 'collective effervescence' of its rituals, primitive society was in effect worshipping itself and celebrating its existence as a moral community. Extending the ideas of Tylor and Robertson Smith, Durkheim argued that the origins of religion lay in *totemism*, the notion that the human group had a special link to some plant or animal. For this group, but not for others, that plant or animal was a sacred symbol, since both were believed to descend from the same spiritual origin. Durkheim stressed the functionality of totemism for the maintenance of the cohesion and collective identity of the group. In principle the argument developed for Australian Aboriginals could be extended to more complex, larger scale societies. All religions, all models of the cosmos, of the ordering of human society, of time itself, were socially determined. Where Marx emphasised social conflict, the general model put forward by Durkheim stressed cohesion, the ultimate source of which lay in a common definition of what was sacred to the group.

The second type of functionalism that we must note is that of Malinowski. On the basis of his years of Trobriand fieldwork he criticised the intellectualist bias of virtually all previous writers. They had failed to appreciate that magic was more than a primitive form of religious belief. For Malinowski, in contrast to Durkheim and Frazer, magic was an inseparable part of religion. It was extensively used in the Trobriands to ward off evil spirits and considered an indispensable, routine part of gardening activities. He saw this not as evidence of irrationality or a 'pre-logical mentality', for the magical practices did not inhibit the Trobrianders from the careful performance of all the other actions necessary for their crops to grow. Magic functioned to provide people with additional psychological and emotional reassurance, to help them cope with trials and tribulations. It was especially important in deep-sea expeditions which were more dangerous than fishing in local lagoons. More generally, beliefs about the supernatural gave human individuals comfort and strength, particularly in the face of death. In short, Malinowski's functionalism differed from that of Durkheim in emphasising not the social cohesion of the group but the needs of individual human beings.

Shamanism

Since the work of Malinowski and Durkheim most anthropolgists have recognised that, while the world contains an extraordinary variety of belief systems, they are the products of human minds which work in basically the same way everywhere. The actual experience of religion, however, is culturally specific and remarkably diverse. Neither functionalist approach does justice to the emotional content of religion, to the charisma of prophetic leaders, the sanctity of ascetic monks, or the inspirational qualities of the shaman. Perhaps because these qualities were not much in evidence among Trobrianders at the time of his fieldwork, Malinowski emphasises the pragmatic aspects. Many others have been attracted to the study of other cosmologies precisely because of their emotional and aesthetic power, in comparison with the 'routinised' prayers of organised churches in complex industrial societies. Shamanism is a good case in point.

First of all note you cannot hope to pin down shamanism with a tidy definition in the way that you can define Roman Catholicism. There is no shared body of doctrine, and no agreement among anthropologists as to where shamanism ends and some other -ism begins. Most would probably see it as one among many forms of spirit possession, associated particularly with technologically simple societies in Siberia. The archetypical shaman is a man or woman thought to have exceptional characteristics, often inherited, often expressed in everyday life by minor forms of deviance and eccentricity, sometimes considered a form of madness. The shaman's main talent is to be able to enter a trance when 'called' by a spirit in a public performance, often accompanied by a drum or other monotonous rhythm. Detailed studies suggest that some shamans do genuinely achieve another state of consciousness in these performances, perhaps with the aid of hallucinogenic drugs. He or she then uses the shaman's power to control the spirits and answer questions that address urgent needs of the individuals present or of the group as a whole.

Few forms of shamanism involve elaborate cosmologies. This is a religious practice that seems compatible with almost any set of beliefs and it has certainly persisted long after the impact of Buddhism and other 'world religions'. In some parts of Asia, notably in Korea, shamans are now licensed by the state and the activity has been partially 'folklorised' for tourism purposes; but deeply rooted beliefs have not been eradicated. Shamanism seems also to have survived several generations of communist rule, though the patterns documented in recent years may differ significantly from those of the pre-Soviet past. Post-communist shamans may be selected in much the same way as their predecessors, primarily on the basis of their special talent, but city shamans, instead of giving public performances, tend nowadays to work privately for paying customers. The reputation of a shaman spreads informally, in much the same way as people pass on information about the quality of a doctor; and indeed the functions of the two may overlap.

This suggests that even exotic and inspirational forms of religion can be illuminated by attention to social context. In this case, it seems clear that the activation of this traditional cultural form is shaped by the sudden uncertainties of post-communism. It is possible that closer inspection would show more systematic patterns, of the kind uncovered by Ioan Lewis in his investigations of 'ecstatic religion' in Africa. Here, for example, women and other subordinated groups may find a way through spirit possession to articulate protest.

16 | MODES OF THOUGHT

African witchcraft

Anthropologists have paid a good deal of attention to issues of causation, for example, in comparing how different peoples explain misfortune. Both Malinowski and later his student Evans-Pritchard reacted to the work of Lévy-Bruhl, who was primarily a philosopher, not a fieldworking anthropologist. Lévy-Bruhl argued that the primitive mind was somehow 'pre-logical', incapable of reasoning as we do, but permanently under the sway of mystical associations. Malinowski and Evans-Pritchard emphasised the opposite.

The latter's research among the central African Azande was the most rigorous ethnographic analysis of the problem. The Azande followed standardised procedures when looking to identify the witch responsible for someone's misfortune. One procedure involved feeding poison to a chicken and then asking a series of questions, the answer to which was given by the fate of the bird: would it die, or would it recover? Superstitious nonsense, you might say. But after living among them for some years, Evans-Pritchard himself came to find the Azande procedures straightforward enough. Their beliefs did not prevent them from recognising that some problems had entirely obvious pragmatic causes. If a granary collapsed after its foundations had been eaten away by termites, there was no doubt that the termites were a cause of this misfortune. But the Azande might wish to ask the further question: why have the termites chosen to undermine this particular granary? Evans-Pritchard's point is that Azande behaved consistently, logically (or we might wish to say rationally) within the limits of their knowledge, the traditions that had been handed down in a hierarchical but technologically unsophisticated and non-literate society. He did not classify these people as 'pre-logical'.

Their environment did not present them with good reason for rejecting their inherited beliefs, since their knowledge was certainly not readily falsifiable. That said, however, Evans-Pritchard was not an extreme relativist, the sort who takes the view that Azande knowledge of the world is just as valid as that of modern science. He took it for granted that modern scientific thought is more accurate and powerful.

Evans-Pritchard provided rich detail on the Azande case, which helped to inspire much further resarch into the social significance of witchcraft in Africa and elsewhere. The Azande made a distinction between witchcraft and sorcery. The latter was the deliberate use of magic to cause misfortune to others. Witches, however, might not know that they had inherited dangerous powers. In this, by African tribal standards markedly hierarchical society, the pattern of accusations respected the hierarchy and it was not permitted to challenge your social superiors of witchcraft. Elsewhere accusations usually reflected the kinship organisation. For example, the Cewa of Zambia are a matrilineal societiy, i.e. they trace descent in the female line. The most common pattern of witchcraft accusation discovered by their ethnographer Marwick was for a man to accuse his mother's brother, the man whose authority over the kin group he stood to inherit. (We say more about kin groups in Part V.) More generally, research has shown how witchcraft functions as a form of social control and accusations indicate persons or relationships experiencing particular pressures, often for quite mundane, non-magical reasons. For example, persons who have become suddenly wealthier than their neighbours may be accused, especially if others seem to have become simultaneously worse off. This is, of course, a major disincentive to economic innovation.

Witchcraft was a central element in the cosmology of many African societies. It has been much less central, at least in recent centuries, in European societies. Nevertheless in times of acute economic and political tensions witchcraft played an important role. In early modern England Alan Macfarlane showed that accusations were not directed against the major beneficiaries of economic transformation but against the poor and marginal, notably elderly women.

The same basic issues raised by beliefs in witchcraft can be explored in many other contexts. Robin Horton studied the

Kalabari, a coastal Nigerian people whose world view he found to be as complex as the theology of any of the world religions, with supernatural beings existing at three levels. There was a rich spirit world, that included the spirits of ancestors, who were thought to punish deviant behaviour by their successors. Beyond this spirit world, each individual had a personal creator, and the cosmos in its entirety was thought to have a 'Great Creator', a being comparable to the monotheistic god of larger scale religious systems. Like the Azande, the Kalabari proceeded in a logical way within the confines of their belief system. Misfortune was commonly attributed to a spirit. If it continued after appropriate rituals and sacrifices had been carried out, then it would ultimately be ascribed to the Great Creator. At no point did the Kalabari have any good reason to doubt the existence of their spirits.

This ethnography led Horton to compare and contrast western scientific knowledge and 'African traditional thought'. Horton argued that the former was an 'open' system of knowledge, but he rather ignored the fact that professional scientists are but a small minority in our own societies, and even they take a very great deal of cultural information for granted as they go about their everyday lives. His characterisation of traditional African thought as 'closed' is similarly dubious, since there is abundant evidence that new ideas have been disseminated in Africa, even before the subversion of so many indigenous cosmologies by Christianity and Islam. It is possible to express *doubt*, even scepticism, concerning the existence of spirits and witches. Jack Goody has argued that a 'kernel of doubt' is to be found in all societies.

In short, it is not modes of thought that differ, but the technological and cultural context. Horton may have overdrawn his contrast slightly, but he is surely right to distinguish some basic characteristics of African belief systems from those of modern science. One key aspect is a greater emphasis on personal relations and on emotions. Another is the paradoxical fact that it is the belief systems of the less technologically advanced societies that explain *more*. Both the Azande and Kalabari seek and provide specific answers to questions where most modern Europeans would be content to recognise accident or coincidence.

Millenarian movements

Millenarian movements are religious movements that promise a paradise on this earth, usually to be achieved through dramatic magical-ritual performances. They are typically products of periods of economic dislocation and political uncertainty. Often they develop among people who have been exposed to colonisation and conquest, one of the most famous examples being the Ghost Dance movement among North American Indians in the late nineteenth century. The cult promised its members magical protection against the white man's guns and the return of the exterminated buffalo herds as well as deceased ancestors.

The cargo cults mentioned in the last chapter are another example. In the 'Vailala Madness', which broke out in New Guinea in 1919, normal economic activities were abandoned and people destroyed many traditional ritual artefacts and proclaimed that their ancestors would return and bring with them a wealth of European cargo, i.e. goods which these Melanesians had seen in their contacts with foreigners and work on plantations, but which they were effectively prevented from acquiring. Many later cults in this region followed similar patterns. Some were galvanised by charismatic individuals who might have more intimate knowledge of the white man's society. For example, in the Madang movement studied by Lawrence, the leader had spent some time in Australia. This movement did not collapse when his prophecies failed to materialise, for the same reason that people did not lose their beliefs in the magical powers of spirits and witches when these did not bring the results desired and bring an end to suffering and misfortune. Instead people often persuaded themselves that the cause of failure lay in the fact that some element of the ritual had been performed badly, and a further variant could be developed in order to bring about the desired goal.

These cults were considered by some colonial observers as irrational. Some anthropologists reached the same conclusion, since this behaviour deviated dramatically from the norms of tribal behaviour. Yet the cults made cultural sense within the established cosmologies of the people concerned. They were an attempt to re-establish coherence in a situation when the assumptions of the old cosmology had been swept away by a new political system and by the introduction of money and work for wages. In short the cults were a pragmatic way of trying to cope with the new conditions of relative deprivation and exploitation. We could say that they were *contextually* rational.

Some relativists would object to the qualification contextual here and argue that the modes of thought at work in these cults were absolutely as reasonable and rational as anything in the organised religion of our own societies or any secular actions. Other anthropologists insist that modern science has a superior standard of rationality. Cargo cults were – indeed are, for they still continue in some parts of the Pacific – rational in terms of local cultural models, but it is futile, given the information available to us, to put a local model on a par with the external model of the comparative analyst of millenarian movements.

Classification and pollution

Questions of rationality and modes of thought can be pursued in many other contexts. One of the most fruitful has been work on classification, which derives from the essay *Primitive Classification* which Durkheim and Marcel Mauss published in 1902 and continued in Durkheim's *The Elementary Forms of Religious Life* (1912). A totem was a species of animal or plant with which a human community asserted a close identification and towards which particular respect had to be shown. If the totem was an animal, consumption of its flesh might be strictly prohibited. This latter step came to be understood as a taboo, the Polynesian term first recorded by Captain Cook coming to serve in anthropology as the general term for a ritual prohibition. Such beliefs and practices were seen by Europeans as examples of that mystical bond between humans and their natural environment that Lévy-Bruhl saw as typical of the primitive mentality.

Durkheim insisted on the functionality of totemism and taboo for the maintenance of the cohesion and collective identity of the group. Much later, Claude Lévi-Strauss was concerned not so much with sociological cohesion as with the potential that natural species afforded human groups to classify and bring conceptual order into the world around them. He pointed out that the cross-cultural literature on totemism was full of inconsistencies; for example, in some cases it was not in fact forbidden to eat the meat of the totemic animal. But such details did not invalidate his claim that totems were always 'good to think with'. They were interesting to him as examples of the patterned ways in which the human mind works in 'savage society'. Lévi-Strauss made similar points in his many investigations of the myths told by the native peoples of the Americas. Whereas Malinowski had been interested in myths as 'charters' that functioned to raise certain ideas to a higher level of cultural authority, and Durkheim too was committed to a sociological functionalism, Lévi-Strauss's structuralist approach to myth and totemism emphasised the logical mental processes that underpinned all human creativity.

Lévi-Strauss, however, confined his investigations to societies that had not yet entered the 'historical time' of modern European societies. Underlying his work is an opposition between the savage and ourselves, between 'cold' unchanging societies and 'hot' dynamic societies like our own. This is not quite the dichotomy drawn by Lévy-Bruhl and other predecessors, but it has nevertheless exposed Lévi-Strauss to much criticism.

Others have been less cautious and extended their enquiries into 'primitive classification' to Christian and Jewish traditions. Both Edmund Leach and Mary Douglas have applied structuralist techniques to the Christian Bible. For example, Douglas has explored the logic underpinning the food prohibitions of the ancient Israelites, as recorded in Leviticus. Her general hypothesis is an ingenious modification of the Durkheimian tradition, which leads her to focus attention on items that fall outside the standardised boundaries of a classificatory scheme.

> If uncleanness is matter out of place, we must approach it through order. Uncleanness or dirt is that which must not be included if a pattern is to be maintained.[28]

Thus, in a well known example from her fieldwork among the Lele of Central Africa, the pangolin is singled out for a special role in the mediation between spirit and human worlds because of its peculiar, anomalous characteristics: it is fishlike but it burrows, and in certain respects even shows affinities to human beings. In her work on the body as a symbol of society, Douglas suggests that concern with purity will lead 'naturally' to a tabooing of dangerous places, orifices where the body is in contact with the external environment. A structuralist explanation can thus be given for widespread perceptions of menstrual blood as polluting. Some feminist anthropologists have found this example exceptionally stimulating, since many unrelated societies all over the world classify substances and activities relating to fertility and reproduction as dangerous and polluting. The relation between men and women is modelled on or analogous to the relation between culture and nature, an ideological reflection of women's subordination.

Further research has cast doubt on this interpretation. First, the pattern is not universal, and there are societies where men are considered to be just as close to nature as women. Second, and more significant, strong representations of male and female differences may not primarily concern relations between men and women at all, but may serve other purposes within the society. In his demonstration of this possibility, Michael Stewart shows how notions of shame among Roma (Gypsies) in Hungary serve to differentiate this minority from the dominant Hungarian population. The Roma are aware that they themselves are viewed as dirty and polluting by many Hungarians. In their own representations the disadvantaged turn the tables by emphasising the 'shameless' character of Hungarian women, in contrast to the Roma. For Stewart, the anomalies or 'dirt' are an integral part of the pattern, rather than excluded from it, as Douglas tended to argue.

This example is a reminder that modes of classification function in particular social contexts. Structuralist approaches such as that of Douglas have generated many insights, but problems arise with structuralist explanations when their elegant and stimulating patterns do not fit the empirical sociological evidence. Even Douglas's interpretation of the pangolin is unconvincing in other parts of Africa.

17 | MODES OF ACTION

Symbols and rituals

> Solidarity is produced by people acting together, not by people thinking together.[29]

In this chapter we leave behind intellectual approaches to religion that focus on how it explains the world philosophically and enquiries into the rationality of modes of thought. We turn now to action rather than thought, to religion's practical role in helping individuals to cope with trials and tribulations and its symbolic significance in generating social cohesion. The former was stressed especially by Malinowski and the latter by Durkheim. Both recognised the central importance of symbols and rituals for human social life. We have already drawn attention to them in our discussion of politics, where we noted that 'ritual symbolism' often plays an important role in legitimating powerholders, in persuading some people to accept the authority of others to define the goals and the values to which they should aspire.

Durkheim's original theory was powerful in its simplicity. He paid special attention to the large-scale collective rituals in which, as he phrased it, 'society worshipped itself'. These need not necessarily be religious rituals in our conventional usage of the term religion. Take the case of coronation rituals in Britain, which have a strong religious component to them, since the monarch is also the head of the Church of England. But for most observers this ritual is a celebration of national unity, not a religious service.

But there are many other kinds of ritual and definitional approaches. For Edmund Leach all practical actions had a ritual aspect, which he defined as the aspect that was not technically necessary for achieving the desired goal. Of course the people themselves, in their local model, would not make the same distinction. As Malinowski always stressed, the Trobrianders believed their ritual practices to be just as technically necessary as their other activities in their gardens. Leach came later to argue that ritual is best understood as part of a system of communication, the meanings of which always had to be teased out by the analyst. He applied this approach to many types of ritual, including those known (following Arnold van Gennep) as *rites de passage*, or lifecycle rituals (see Figure 17.1). Each individual human life is marked by a series of transitions, the more important of which are marked in most societies by some form of ritual. The forms of ritual are infinitely diverse, but Leach followed van Gennep in seeing a common threefold structure. This can be summarised briefly as follows: the subject enters a phase of separation, which is followed by a phase of liminality, in which many aspects of normal life are likely to be distorted, inverted or otherwise altered, and finally a phase of reintegration into the community.

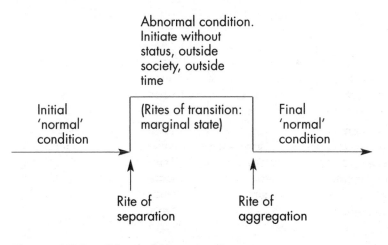

Figure 17.1   Rites of passage[30]

This theory complements to the Durkheimian focus on social cohesion. By structuring individual lives, rituals of passage promote the stability of the social structure, in ways that reinforce the effects achieved by more spectacular collective rituals. Sometimes the two types may merge, as when initiation rites are organised not on an individual basis but for all the members of a given age set. The model has also been extended by Leach to explain sacrifice, and by others to death rituals.

Initiation

It is characteristic of Leach and of structuralist approaches in general that they see the local model as a code to be deciphered. An alternative view, one that has been increasingly favoured by anthropologists in recent decades, is to pay more attention to what the actors themselves say about their symbols and the rituals in which they engage. The anthropologist often faces a dilemma: to what extent should the people themselves be the privileged interpreters of their symbols and rituals, and to what extent is the anthropologist entitled to interpret for them? Structuralists are by no means the only group who tend to silence the local views. The 'interpretive anthropology' of Clifford Geertz aims at a 'thick description' of what the anthropologist observes, for example Geertz himself in the case of a Balinese cock-fight. But Geertz's account of this ritual, it has often been pointed out, is one that few Balinese would reach for themselves or endorse at all.

A good balance is struck by Gilbert Lewis in his study of the puberty rites of a small population in New Guinea, the Gnau. The Gnau considered their rituals to be an expression of their distinctive identity, and to have a quality of permanence. Yet they were aware that the detail of the performance changed over time. When he completed his fieldwork in the 1970s a whole class of rituals was falling into disuse. Lewis suggested that the *tambin* rituals, which glorified traditions of heroism and violence, were not appropriate to the increasingly pacific circumstances in which the Gnau found themselves. For young men at this time, plantation labour was a quasi-substitute for these initiation rituals. It would seem that the Gnau themselves saw the analogy, to judge from details such as the fact that they drew blood from their penises when they arrived at the coastal plantation, in the same way that they had formerly begun the *tambin* rituals. Yet they did not make this analogy explicit to the anthropologist, indeed Lewis says they would surely have rejected the notion of a substitution.

The puberty rites themselves, however, were still practiced. Lewis suggested this was because the values that they expressed, the importance of the lifecycle, growing up, marrying and producing children, had not changed so much under the impact of new economic and political institutions. The symbols used in the ritual helped the Gnau to grasp and internalise values that were still important to their society. Previous anthropologists, including Evans-Pritchard, had considered this to be the territory of the psychologist, by definition out of bounds to anthropologists. Nonetheless Lewis argued that an essential aspect of ritual has to do with emotion and the inculcation of deep personal feelings:

Human ideals and values and counter-values are pre-eminently the sort of things for which people require symbols, because they are insubstantial and abstract. They are hard to grasp and apprehend. But the values and ideals are felt as real; they have personal validity for the people who hold them.[31]

Lewis's post-structuralist approach focused not so much on the meaning of an act of communication, understood intellectually, but on aesthetic and emotional aspects, on what he termed 'that seriousness of real life' which no amount of detailed observation by an outsider can grasp adequately. He is sensitive to the considerable variation that may exist within a society concerning the interpretation of rites, and to historical change. Ritual, as we noted when discussing its political efficacy in an earlier chapter, achieves much of its effect because it is seen as embodying tradition, the way things have always been done. It aims to standardise and fix something. But in actual fact, rituals can evolve, in content, in form and in both. Sometimes (as we noted in the example of circumcision among the Merina) the significance may change despite a lot of continuity in the form of the ritual. Sometimes it is possible to invent new rituals, but it is hard to find examples that do not somehow, however fraudulently, establish a connection to what people consider venerable through some form of tradition. It follows that anthropologists always stand to learn something new from paying serious attention to the interpretations and commentaries of the participants, even though there may be some circumstances in which the observer (listener) may doubt whether people really believe what they practise and say. The complexity and inherent ambivalences in cases like that of the Gnau suggest that a structuralist approach which aims to decode an unambiguous intellectual message communicated by ritual is bound to be inadequate.

Multivocal symbols

Gilbert Lewis was more interested in interpreting the moods and emotions of the participants than in plotting a sociological function of which they themselves were unaware. However, his account of the differential impact of social change on lifecycle rituals suggests that a Weberian concern to enter into the world view of the participants and understand their own experiences in their own terms can be reconciled with a Durkheimian concern to relate ritual to the social order. Victor Turner's detailed studies of symbolism among the Zambian Ndembu are built on a comparable synthesis.

The Ndembu were a small matrilineal society for whom ritual was important in preserving some modicum of social order. In this respect Turner's analysis was fully in line with functionalist traditions. He went further, however, in exploring the emotional power of symbols, and their tremendous complexity. Most of the symbols emphasised by earlier functionalists were unambiguous in their meaning: for example, we have already mentioned the Golden Stool, a symbol of royal power among the Ashanti. Turner recognised that ambivalence could itself be a source of strength, allowing individual participants to extract a message appropriate to their circumstances and conditions. Colour symbolism was important in the Ndembu case, but the same colour could have different interpretations. Such symbols are ambiguous and multivocal.

Multivocal symbols are significant in many kinds of ritual. For example, the texts of national anthems show a high degree of uniformity, a good tune or rhythm may matter more than the content, but different people may make different associations and even committed anti-monarchists may enjoy the communal singing of 'God Save the Queen' before, say, an international rugby match. The Welsh dragon is also prominent on such occasions. For older people it may be a powerful symbol of a national heritage, for younger people it may also be a symbol of progressive pop music originating in the principality. Few realise that this symbol, along with the anthem and other symbols of contemporary Welsh identity, are in fact nineteenth century inventions.

Recent East European history is full of attempts to exploit the multivocality of symbols. For example, in Hungary the reburial in June 1989 of Imre Nagy, executed by communist powerholders in 1957 and placed in an unmarked grave, was an important moment in the collapse of communist power. Nagy was appropriated as a symbol not only by dissident opposition leaders and by a wider Christian public but also by 'reform communists'. In her analysis of this and many other reburials, Katherine Verdery has demonstrated the importance of 'dead body politics' in the political contestation of the post-communist years. The materiality of the human body creates an illusion that people are communicating about the same thing, even when their interpretations are in fact very different. Reburials, whether of national heroes, or of ordinary co-ethnics murdered by members of another group, are especially effective symbolic performances because they connect up with ultimate, 'cosmic' questions and have an intrinsic emotional power.

Pilgrimage

Victor Turner followed his exhaustive studies of Ndembu ritual and symbolism by turning to the rituals of a world religion, namely pilgrimage in the Roman Catholic tradition to which he himself converted. He and Edith Turner showed how religiously inspired travel could establish a special form of solidarity that he termed *communitas*, outside and opposed to the usual forms of social structure. Where Durkheim saw the activity of ritual as a celebration of society, in Turner's emphasis ritual was a celebration of how the conventions of society can be left behind or transcended; and this element certainly contributed to the popularity of his books in the years of the 'counterculture' in Western Europe and North America.

Turner's approach can be tested outside the Christian tradition for which he developed it. It does not fit the Islamic case quite so well. The model works well for visits to local shrines, but the pilgrimage to Mecca, far from being opposed to orthodox beliefs and practices, is the prescribed duty of every Muslim who is in a position physically and financially to make the journey. Millions of Muslims complete the *haj* every year. Their experience can be schematised according to the van Gennep model. First, there is a phase of separation, when pilgrims are taken apart from their community and required to wear distinctive white clothing on their journey (which nowadays tends to be a relatively rapid plane flight). The time spent in Mecca is liminal (Turner himself preferred the term *liminoid*). The peak of *communitas* is celebrated at the most sacred site, the Kaba stone, where no unbeliever is ever allowed. After the journey home the pilgrims are reintegrated into the community, but their status is forever changed and they will be addressed respectfully as *haji*.

In addition to the impact that a pilgrimage has on the individual participants at the time, it also has significant long-term social consequences. Above all the modern *haj* reveals the global character of the Islamic community. Pakistani migrants to northern England may encounter Communist Party members from Chinese Turkestan, West African pastoralists rub shoulders with Indonesian rice producers, and so on. The details of the languages and even the religious practices of these groups are highly varied, but they share a common faith and the pilgrimage demonstrates unity. The social effects spill over to all the different communities from which the pilgrims come and to which they return. Often, since the number of places is limited, the decision as to who should attend is one taken by the community. Even in cases where the process seems more individualistic and dependent upon ability to pay, the potential pilgrim's behaviour is carefully vetted and scrutinised by the religious authorities. After his return he is obliged to follow an exemplary lifestyle. Actions such as drunkenness that, in the case of other men, might lead to rebuke, would in his case lead to ostracism or even more serious sanctions. Thus the pilgrimage plays a role in upholding the moral standards to which the entire community is urged to aspire.

18 | WORLD RELIGIONS

The means of communication

The evolution of anthropological discussions of religion, or cosmology, could lead us to draw the conclusion that no evolutionary account of religion itself is possible. In other words, all human societies have religion, but they all have magic and science as well. This conclusion, however, is unsatisfactory. Few comtemporary anthropologists defend the sort of theories advanced by Lévy-Bruhl concerning a 'pre-logical mentality'. However, it may still be possible to examine changes in religion over long time frames. It is problematic to apply an evolutionary perspective to the complexity of the beliefs themselves, for as the case of Australian Aboriginals shows, technologically simple societies can develop extremely complex beliefs. Moreover we see that rather simple forms of cult and even shamanistic practices can become popular even in highly developed, post-industrial societies. If anything, it may be that the technologically sophisticated societies evolve *simpler* religious ideas.

Drawing a dichotomy between 'primitive' and modern is rejected by most modern anthropologists, and it certainly cannot be supported by claims that we are more rational than our predecessors. However, a possible basis for a weaker form of dichotomy is to be found in the 'means of communication' and in particular, in the expansion of literacy. For most of human history language could only be used orally. The impact of writing is seldom sudden and dramatic, since pictorial representations usually precede the emergence of characters and a fully fledged alphabetical system, and in any case knowledge of the new techniques is usually restricted to a small élite. Nonetheless, Jack Goody has argued that even this restricted literacy had far-reaching consequences by allowing for systematic reflection and standardisation of knowledge. It enabled the codification of sacred knowledge and the rise of 'world religions' based on a sacred text, including the three that have common origins in the Middle East, Judaism, Christianity and Islam. Expanded literacy, thanks above all to the invention of printing, may in the end have been conducive to the rise of science and to secularisation, because by opening texts to systematic scrutiny and debate it increased the scope for what Goody terms the 'kernel of doubt', the scepticism that he believes is present in all societies, but which is able to achieve much greater prominence in the modern world.

Theology versus practice

The religions that have been consolidated into powerful international faiths, among them Judaism, Christianity, Islam, Buddhism and Hinduism, have all had a textual basis of some sort. First, let us stress the features they have in common and how these can be illuminated by anthropologists. Then we shall look a little more closely at Islam, the youngest and in many ways the most remarkable world religion. Finally, we shall discuss processes of missionisation and syncretism, and connect up again with the discussion of globalisation. In religion, as in most other fields, there are powerful forces that operate to reduce diversity, but there are also continuous trends in the opposite direction.

We shall ignore differences in doctrine and theology, except to note that beliefs about the forgiveness of sins, redemption, and some sort of future reward for good behaviour in this world are recurrent elements in these world religions. The anthropologist is interested primarily in how the faith is lived and experienced in a social context. In the case of a world religion this is certainly influenced by the doctrines, as these are set down in texts and disseminated by priests and other specialists, whose dress and lifestyles (for example celibacy) mark them as distinctive. Edmund Leach spoke of a 'dialectic', a continuous process of interaction between doctrines and practice. Religious knowledge is seldom equally distributed and some world religions have specialists whom we call monks, who ideally cut themselves away from ordinary secular society in order to be closer to god or to attain greater enlightenment. Both Christianity and Buddhism have strong monastic traditions. What interests the anthropologist most is how these institutions fit in to the wider societies, how even ascetic monks must maintain sufficient interest in this-worldly affairs to obtain a food supply of some sort. In reality monasteries such as those developed by Buddhism in Tibet and other parts of Inner Asia became dominant political institutions and a substantial proportion of the entire population became lamas. Some of them worked on the land, but some were supported by the work of other believers. Chinese communist governments have condemned such traditions as 'feudal', and indeed in parts of China conditions were not so radically different from sixteenth century England, when Protestants criticised the abuses of the monasteries and proceeded to dissolve them. Then too, as in China in more recent times, there were some who felt that any attack on the monasteries was an affront to a vital cultural tradition.

In other respects, Christianity and Buddhism could hardly be more different. The latter is based on the teachings of a human being, who made no claim to supernatural powers but achieved enlightenment at the age of 35 after years of intensive study and meditation. His teachings were written down and spread by disciples, but Buddhism does not have a sacred book equivalent to the Bible. It does not emphasise collective worship, as the Christians do in their churches, and Buddhism has never had a hierarchical organisation comparable to that of 'universal Catholicism', headed by a Pope.

Yet as a practical religion, the similarities are impressive. Like all religions, Christianity and Buddhism provide their faithful with a wide range of rituals, both collective and personal. The timing of some of the most important festivals, marking stages in the life of the founder, is still determined by the lunar calendar (*Asala Puja* in Buddhism, Easter in Christianity). Each has developed rich supplementary social teaching and practices designed to maintain cohesion and a high degree of equality in the communities of peasant cultivators where they took root. In Mexico, for example, Cancian has shown how Catholicism developed a hierarchy of 'cargo' festivals that brought ritual prestige and respect in the community. They were, however, very expensive and often drove the sponsor deeply into debt. But debtors might become creditors in a later phase and the constant channeling of resources into non-productive religious activities was an effective device for preventing the emergence of new class inequalities. It was an innovation of certain strands of Protestantism, according to the theory of Max Weber, which we noted earlier, that material differentiation in this-world might itself be viewed as a sign of merit.

Spiro and others have argued that 'merit making' had a similar levelling function among Buddhist peasants in Southeast Asia. This does not mean that the religion is a basis for organised resistance to new forms of economy. It can, however, provide some resources for those subtle strategies of resistance that James Scott, in the Malaysian example that we mentioned earlier calls the 'weapons of the weak'. In the long run the hierarchical notions based on merit, although working against material accumulation in the traditional system, may have been conducive to new forms of capitalist entrepreneurship. Grant Evans has shown in his work in Laos that Buddhist peasants were unreceptive to the very different style of egalitarianism imposed upon them in the name of socialism, which was explicitly antagonistic to their religion in a way that capitalism was not.

A cyclical model of Islam

The dichotomy between text and practice can also be formulated in terms of 'great' and 'little' traditions, that may coexist harmoniously for centuries but occasionally come into conflict with each other. In addition to its central gods and goddesses, Hinduism has many regionally specific minor deities and many thousands of festivals and fairs. Some anthropologists have doubted the value of distinguishing a 'great tradition', since for some believers the locally specific forms are not distinguished from the common, 'universal' forms. It is clear, however, that for at least some Hindus the existence of a great tradition, outside and above their local practices, is itself a part of their local model.

A similar distinction between orthodox faith and popular adaptations, has been well developed in anthropological work on Islam. The Koran is the unchallenged sacred text of this religion, and there is general agreement that Islam in principle dispenses with figures that mediate between the faithful and their God in the way that Mary and the saints mediate for Catholics. In this sense Islam has more common ground with Protestantism. It is more modern, in presupposing that at least some of the faithful are capable of reading the sacred text themselves of reading the sacred text and appealing to their God directly. Of course Islam does not dispense altogether with religious specialists. It is the job of the local *imam* to organise the prayers of the community, and it is the job of the scholarly *ulema* to implement Islamic law and make rulings on theological and legal points when necessary.

But behind this orthodoxy, the spread of Islam was accompanied almost everywhere by a wide range of popular practices. Some were a fairly direct continuation of earlier practises, for example forms of shamanism. Some were innovations, such as the various movements usually described as Sufi. Dervish orders provided a more mystical experience of spirituality than the puritanical orthodoxy espoused by the *ulema*, and some of these currents have retained their popularity to the present day. It is a mistake to confuse these with religious fundamentalists, which we shall consider in Chapter 19. Most so-called fundamentalists insist on strict orthodoxy and are therefore opposed to the deviations associated with Sufi currents, for which no legitimation is given in the Koran.

Ernest Gellner has argued, following the analysis of the medieval Arab scholar Ibn Khaldun, that orthodox and popular forms of Islam were connected by a simple cyclical relationship. This model located orthodoxy firmly in the towns, where the literate *ulema* were the ultimate arbiters. But social control over illiterate tribesmen in the hinterland required different political structures and a different form of Islam. Gellner found that mediation via sheikhs or 'saints' was important not only for religious practice but also for resolving political disputes in regions that were governed by segmentary lineage systems rather than effective centralised states. The countryside was a source of violent energies which every so often erupted and led the tribesmen to conquer the stagnating towns. But the new rulers would acknowledge the supremacy of orthodox teaching as they consolidated their power; eventually they in turn were replaced, and so the cycles continued.

Gellner gives an elegant model. It is, however, very much the model of an external analyst and many critics have doubted its usefulness, even for those regions of the Moroccan High Atlas where Gellner carried out his original fieldwork among Berbers. The studies of Clifford Geertz, such as *Islam Observed*, in which he shows how very differently Islam is experienced in Morocco from his earlier encounter with the same world religion in Indonesia, have been rather more influential. Whether Geertz is any more successful than Gellner in conveying a local model of this faith is, however, open to question.

Missionaries and syncretism

The world religions all had modest origins in small cults or sectarian groupings. Their very existence over thousands of years is a reminder that globalisation cannot be entirely new and, still more importantly, that the romantic image of the world as divided up into a host of separate and autonomous cultures is seriously deficient. It is certainly possible to argue that processes of conversion accelerated and became more organised in the age when European powers built up their colonial empires, when missionaries and traders were usually active on the scene well before anthropologists appeared. But unequal competition between religions is nothing new.

Explaining the patterns of religious expansion and contraction is a challenging task. The explanatory task is simplest in cases where a new religion is forcibly imposed on a conquered population, and these cases have been common enough in modern history. At the other extreme, in contemporary Central Asia various missionary groups, most of them Protestant and based in North America, engage in peaceful battle to recruit new followers. They fight this battle with reference to their theology and their moral teaching, of course, and they have to take big risks in some countries, where the import of Bibles or other foreign religious literature is forbidden. But the competition for souls is also fought with cash. Some groups are willing to pay substantial sums (by local standards) to persons who commit themselves to attending regular prayer meetings and perhaps to spreading the religious message among family and friends.

This type of activity can readily be interpreted as undermining an indigenous religious culture. In Central Asia the dominant tradition nowadays is Islam, but Islam too, of course, undermined earlier traditions, including variants of Buddhism, Christianity, and Shamanism. Conversion, or even merely experimenting with a foreign religion can lead to enormous personal difficulties in terms of relations with family members, marriage prospects and so on.

Material incentives have often played a part in religious expansion. This was one of the factors that made Christianity attractive when it was little more than a minor cult in Palestine: the abolition of expensive animal sacrifices made it cheaper than its pagan competitors. Similar economic arguments may explain why some world religions have succeeded better than others in those parts of the world where they have competed on more or less equal terms.

However, no one would claim that the rise and fall of religions can be explained solely or even primarily by an economic calculus of this narrow sort. A more refined evolutionist model is called for. Unless force is a major constraint, religions are selected, like other aspects of culture, for the advantages that they confer, which may include emotional and psycological advantages. The rise of Christianity to become the state religion of the later Roman Empire must have had something to do with the simplicity and attractiveness of its theological reworking of the older Jewish traditions, as well as with the dynamic organisation of the early Christian communities and explicitly material factors. On the whole Protestant missionaries have not been very successful in Central Asia, because even when they can provide financial incentives, these have not been sufficient to outweigh the advantages that most people derive from continuing to adhere to their established faith. It still attracts much more support than atheism, although in the recent past, when communism was able to provide good incentives for rejecting faith, in terms of better educational and employment opportunities, many people in Central Asia did indeed cease to observe the rituals of Islam. Whether they ceased to *believe* is another matter.

In many cases of religious contact, even those where people are ostensibly required to make clear choices between alternatives, the post-conversion reality is some form of fusion or synthesis. Syncretism is usually defined as a mixing of elements from more than one religious tradition. It is commonly applied when a local religion encounters a world religion, where it may lead to a distinctive 'little tradition'. It is evident in practises such as *voodoo* cults that combine African rites involving spirit possession with elements of Roman Catholicism. Some cargo cults could be viewed as syncretistic forms which linked millenarian elements in the Christian tradition to a local belief system in some part of the Pacific. Shamanistic and other 'unorthodox' forms of ritual have persisted in many Buddhist and Islamic environments.

The accelerated decoupling of culture from place led to a new surge of interest in religious syncretism in the late twentieth century. It was sometimes implied that, in some Golden Age before the processes of missionisation and globalisation, religions were coherent and pure. It seems preferable to assume that there has always been an evolving process, in which beliefs and practices were never pure but always syncretist. Having said that, when a religion like Christianity is exported around the world as it has been in recent centuries, the term syncretism may still be a useful one to characterise the mixtures that then ensue.

19 | CIVIL AND UNCIVIL RELIGION

Secularisation and sects

The 'great tradition' of the social sciences, including social anthropology, developed in the nineteenth century when Darwinism and the rapid progess of industrial and scientific revolutions seemed to many likely to lead to the complete disintegration of religion as traditionally defined. Strong versions of the 'secularisation' thesis have clearly not come to fruition. At the end of the twentieth century the richest and most technologically advanced country in the world, the USA, was also, according to some measures, the most religious: the proportion of the population participating regularly in religious worship was high.

Whether or not secularisation is a helpful term, it is undeniable that major changes have taken place. In France, for example, since the Revolution the major public symbols have been secular and religion has been treated primarily as a matter of private conscience and commitment. Congregations may, of course, worship collectively but, in contrast to Poland and Italy, France has no special agreement with the Vatican guaranteeing Catholicism a place in public life, for example in the state's education system. When French Catholics sought in the nineteenth century to elevate Joan of Arc into a more powerful symbol, so that her Feast Day might rival the modern secular rituals of Bastille Day, the move encountered strong opposition and eventually failed. The French case is exceptional in many ways but there is a more general sense in most economically developed countries that religion has been largely 'privatised'. For example, this has also been the goal of republican governments in Turkey for most of the twentieth century. Atatürk abolished the Islamic traditions that had underpinned the Ottoman state and implemented 'laicism'. Religion and state were separated, and religious affairs were brought under the control of a ministry, controlled ultimately by politicians. The population of Turkey remains overwhelmingly Muslim, but modern Turkey cannot be regarded as a Muslim state.

This privatising of religion creates difficulties for those anthropological approaches to religion that seek to explain it as a symbolic projection of society. For the tradition of Durkheim, a church is a community of believers whose boundaries coincide with that of the society. This model was fruitful in studying totemism in Aboriginal Australia but it needs some adaptation if it is to work in situations of religious pluralism, for example where a world religion is aggressively supplanting a local tradition, or where several religions, each drawing its clientele from different social groups, are competing. Even in Poland there has been, since the collapse of communism, an upsurge of minority religions. Many of these are Protestant or evangelical groups well known in other countries, although Poland also has a flourishing branch of the Friends of the Western Buddhist Order. The dominant Roman Catholic church does not like to experience competition from such sources, but it has little trouble in recognising them as legitimate forms of religion. The situation is quite different with other forms of religious activity, such as the so-called New Age movements. These are not seen as valid forms of religion by the Roman Catholic leaders, although many students find them extremely interesting. They pose a problem to the secular authorities who, because they endorse documents such as the International Declaration of Human Rights, are committed to respecting the citizens' freedom of belief and freedom of worship. Does this also mean unconditional freedom to spread new beliefs, such as those held by Scientologists? Opponents often allege that such groups are 'sects' or 'cults', rather than churches, and accuse members of using 'brainwashing' techniques.

It is by no means only the ex-communist countries that have a problem with these new religious movements. States with a strong commitment to secularism, such as France, also tend to take a harsh view of 'cultic' activities. Although Islam is the second largest religion in France, it has little public recognition. External signs of religious affiliation, notably the headscarf, are not allowed in the 'public sphere', for example in schools. Critics of these policies, not only from the religious groups affected but also from international human rights organisations, point out that many groups that we label, negatively, as sects or cults, are likely, if the past is anything to go by, to become respectable, established churches.

Some countries suppress new churches because one church occupies a privileged position in the religious life of the nation. Greece, for example, with a dominant Christian Orthodox tradition, sees foreign religious groups as a threat to the integrity of its culture. Given the behaviour of many missionaries, this stance is also one that attracts some anthropological support. As already noted, some of the new churches compete for followers as fiercely as capitalist enterprises in the marketplace. Does it follow that much of their behaviour can be analysed with formalist techniques, as used in economic anthropology, to explain the rational choices made both by the purveyors of new religions and by their consumers?

Some scholars have argued that we need to extend the concept of a church beyond the usual definition of religion, i.e. to contexts not concerning beliefs about spirits and an afterlife. For example, when Ernest Gellner had finished his fieldwork on Islamic saints in Morocco he made plans to carry out a comparable empirical study of Freudian psychoanalysts in England. His supposition that the practitioners and their clients could be considered as a new form of church was confirmed when they refused to allow him any access to their activities. In the book that Gellner managed to write in any case, he demonstrated that psychoanalysis was a closed system of beliefs, not subject to testing and verification by conventional principles of scientific enquiry. Here we come back once again to the debates about rationality; some might counter that the scientists themselves also form a kind of church.

Fundamentalism

Fundamentalism is a distinctive feature of the contemporary religious landscape in many parts of the world and the term can be applied to many of the sects just noted, jostling with each other on the religious marketplace. The term fundamentalism was first used in the 1920s to refer to American Protestants who insisted on the literal truth of the Bible and resisted Darwinian teaching in schools. Christian fundamentalists are among the most energetic of contemporary missionaries.

Other types of fundamentalism have had a greater impact on their communities of origin, and some have come to pose threats to civility and democratic government. The rise of Jewish extremism in Israel is one case in point. The Islamic fundamentalism that led to revolution in Iran in 1979 is another. Like their Christian equivalents, the fundamentalists in these traditions emphasise a return to scriptures. They go further in insisting that the entirety of community life be built on religious foundations, i.e. in rejecting the confinement of religion to a private sphere, while public affairs are regulated by secular laws. Gellner viewed Islamic fundamentalism as a strong assertion of the original orthodox foundations of the faith. The challenge facing the anthropologist is to explain the attraction of such a message and the mechanisms by which it has been disseminated. Most explanations have included a range of social, political and economic factors pertaining to the impact of external forces, including the 'secularising' impact of increasingly global cultural forms. In other words, the Islamic movement that toppled the Shah in Teheran was triggered by external forces in much the same way as cargo cults in Melanesia were triggered by the inequalities of colonialism. In both cases the religious response can be interpreted as an attempt to reassert the validity and the dignity of one's own cultural traditions. There were, however, differences in the mechanisms. Although the personal qualities of some *mullahs* were important, just as charisma was vital to the success of prophets in the Pacific, Islamic fundamentalism has also relied on the textual interpretations of intellectuals, of scholars who did not reject science but argued that their religion was fully compatible with the modern world.

The case of Hindu nationalism in India has also attracted anthropological attention, although it has not yet achieved comparable success in the transformation of the polity. Hindus are India's largest religious community, but the number of Muslims is also very large. Antagonistic relationships between these faiths have old roots but are nevertheless very largely a product of modern political circumstances. At the time of Indian Independence few would have predicted that half a century later a political party that based its appeal on religion would triumph at parliamentary elections. In the absence of linguistic and other sources of unity, it seems that religion provided the most suitable vehicle for political mobilisation at the national level. Peter van der Veer has shown that transnational migrants were especially active in the new religious nationalism. In addition, charismatic leaders were able to tap into the resentment of many Hindus over what they considered to be the excessive privileges accorded in post-colonial India to some minority communities (the lower castes and also so-called 'tribal' peoples). The consequences have included tragic incidents of 'communal' violence, such as that which took place at Ayodhya in 1992, when several thousand Muslims were killed at a site that had come to be considered as sacred by both communities.

Nationalism as religion

What we see in cases like Ayodhya can be termed the nationalisation of religion. Glen Bowmann has described similar processes at a pilgrimage centre in Palestine. Where once Muslims and Christians could practise their faiths alongside each other, as a result of the Palestinian people's struggle against the Israeli state the local relationships became strongly politicised and complementarities turned into antagonisms. With cases like these we return to a more classical Durkheimian model, in which the political and the ritual communities have identical boundaries. *Nation* is the most important form of church in our time, the prime object of worship, and nationalist ideologies the leading example of a religious creed.

Of course there are many kinds of nationalism and all are of potential interest to anthropologists. The myths and symbols of American nationalism include not only the flag that flies outside public buildings but also Hollywood film images and Disney characters. This has been termed the 'banal' dimension of nationalism, on a par perhaps with many collective rituals in modern society that seem to be quite unconnected to the sacred, even though they may be capable of generating powerful emotions and identities. Examples might be the fan clubs of big football teams, or the 'fan worship' of celebrities in popular culture. Of course, for the people who obtain some part of their identities through these practices and symbols, they are rather more than banal.

The concept of a 'civil religion' was developed by Robert Bellah as an application of Durkheim's central idea to a modern pluralistic society, the USA. Bellah recognised the continued force of the Judeo-Christian tradition in this society, but pointed to a range of secular rituals and versions of past events which add up to a sacred order of a somewhat different kind. It was the interplay between traditional forms of religion and modern national identity that interested him. Christian symbols remain of prime importance in many other western democracies which, like the USA, are far from being made up entirely of Christians. This synthesis seems, however, to express a tradition and thereby to play an important role in the maintenance of a national identity.

The US situation is quite different from one in which a national identity is intimately tied to one religious denomination in the way that, for example, the overwhelming majority of Poles belong to the Roman Catholic Church. What this means to the contemporary Polish population varies enormously, from pious old ladies who attend church every day to hard-nosed youngsters who are unimpressed when a frail Polish-born Pope makes emotional speeches in the course of a pilgrimage tour of his homeland. The great majority are significantly touched by such occasions, and there seems little doubt that this Pope has done much to strengthen the historic association between Polishness and Roman Catholicism. However, some citizens of Poland are not Roman Catholics, and there have been times when these minorities, most of them also Christian, have resented the power of the dominant church, just as the pervasive influence of the Judeo-Christian tradition in the USA may be resented by minorities.

The case of American 'civil religion' shows that nationalism can combine with conventional forms of religion in peaceful, civil ways, quite different from the aggressive combinations that sometimes occur when nationalism intersects with fundamentalism. But plenty of modern nationalisms have become 'hot' and antagonistic towards neighbouring groups without such a link. The question arises in such cases: how far can the nationalism itself be understood as a religion? This is a form of collectivity that seems to provide the citizens of modern societies with a kind of secular transcendence, a 'sacred' experience that is no longer tied to spiritual beings. Nationalism may not explain man's place in the universe, but it can serve nonetheless to establish moods and values that seem so strong that it is reasonable to desribe them as having a religious character. Katherine Verdery showed how intellectuals helped to disseminate a 'nation-centred' view of the past in communist Romania, where control over the production of knowledge was a vital part of social control in general. Republican Turkey has also been predicated on a strong nationalist ideology, in which the mythical founder Mustafa Kemal assumed a new name, Atatürk, 'Father of the Turks', in much the same way that the central figures of other cosmologies assumed new names and became the focus of worship.

Nationalism has specific historical origins in Europe, but the modern state system has generalised it to most parts of the world. Many anthropologists have taken up Benedict Anderson's phrase and investigated ethnic groups and nations as 'imagined communities'. The modern nation is imagined in the sense that one cannot ever hope personally to know more than a tiny fraction of one's fellow nationals, yet one feels somehow tied to them. The bonds are created above all, in Anderson's view, by new forms of communication, including a standardised literary language and a national press. He is careful not to claim that the imagined community of the nation is a substitute for earlier forms of religious community. Yet Anderson does seem to recognise a sense in which it is the nation that provides most people with their most basic form of integration in the modern world; it is the nation which has become their church. We shall return to these questions again in Chapter 24, when we shall address more comprehensively the subject of 'identity'.

Communism as religion

Let us conclude this chapter by taking a look at another cosmology which has had a bigger impact on the eastern region of Europe over the twentieth century than any other, the church of communism. You may object to classifying communism as a religion. The founders of the movement did not see themselves as prophets but as rational men concerned to unmask the superstition that lay behind all traditional forms of religion. Yet they too developed a system of beliefs and practices showing many affinities with those traditional forms.

First, it had a basic doctrine of salvation, promising relief from suffering and inequalities. What distinguished communism from the other world religions was its promise that salvation could be achieved in this life, if the appropriate actions were taken. In this respect it was paradoxically closer to movements such as cargo cults than to the theologies of Christianity or Buddhism.

Like these earlier 'great traditions', communism developed on a textual basis. The doctrines of Marxism-Leninism were developed over many years and left much scope to specialists for flexible interpretation and implementation. The detail was intricate, but it supported a main message that was stark in its simplicity and conveyed with considerable rhetorical and symbolic skill.

Above all, this movement developed disciplined forms of organisation that brought it a stream of successes in the first half of the twentieth century. Admittedly these did not come in the most advanced countries, as the evolutionism of the nineteenth-century prophets had led them to predict. It was in backward agrarian societies that socialist programmes had to be implemented, and this was arguably one of the major causes of their failure.

Like other world religions, communism was obliged to adapt and it developed distinctive 'little traditions'. Syncretism with traditional religions proved difficult to realise, but syncretism with various forms of nationalist ideology was common enough. On the whole, however, one is struck by the similarities one finds in communist rituals all over the world, to the extent that even poor agricultural countries also organised parades on May Day and inscribed the Russian Revolution of 1917 into their own ritual calendars. In certain parts of Central Asia it is still possible to see statues of Lenin in virtually every town. The people regard him as a part of their tradition and are quite shocked at the summary way his image has disappeared from most other parts of the former Soviet Union.

It seems clear that this cosmology achieved a very wide measure of acceptance in many countries, although success was extremely uneven. In Poland, as already noted, all the circumstances were unfavourable. In Russia itself, however, Lenin's mausoleum developed into a sort of pilgrimage centre and certainly had a mass impact, probably greater than that of Atatürk in Ankara. Collective rituals also seem to been efficiacious, at least in cases where a communist message was reinforced by patriotism, as in the ceremonies to commemorate Stalin's victory in the 'Great Patriotic War'. Christel Lane has also suggested that one should not underestimate the significance of personal lifecycle rituals either, such as the ceremonies performed with young adults at the moment of transition from school to the workplace. Communists had no difficulty in adapting wedding customs from earlier traditions to suit their own legitimating purposes.

It seems, however, that even in the Soviet Union secular funerals did not gain such a ready acceptance. The reasons are obvious. At the end of human life one is comforted by the promise of redemption and rebirth. Communism, however, promised goods here in this world and, when its backward and cumbersome collectivised economies failed to deliver and its political hierarchy moved beyond the phase of inspired mobilisation into a stage of corrupt routinisation, then the whole basis of legitimation was exposed.

SUMMARY OF PART IV

Ideas about the nature of the cosmos, which usually include beliefs concerning spirits and ancestors, and very often some forms of prayer and sacrifice, are found in all human communities. Anthropological approaches to religion have moved from ethnocentric considerations of the 'magical' and 'primitive mentality' toward better understanding of the complexity of the belief systems of non-literate peoples and of the difficulties which beset all attempts to rank and to compare them.

A good deal of discussion has been 'intellectualist' in orientation, focused on questions of 'rationality' and explanations of the world. Witchcraft and cargo cults make sense in their cultural context, even though the external analyst knows these beliefs to be false. Accusations and millenarian movements often reflect specific social tensions or cataclysmic changes, such as the emergence of capitalism or the imposition of colonialism.

An equally important element in the anthropological contribution has emphasised the needs that religion fulfills in all human communities. Rituals and symbols have emotional effects that seem to be vital in helping individuals to cope, and also for binding the person to the group and maintaining social cohesion. Émile Durkheim argued that all societies employed some version of the sacred/profane dichotomy and the structure of the religion or church necessarily reflected that of society itself. His work has been consistently influential, for example in structuralist work on myth and totemism and in modern approaches to ritual.

One way to sustain a cautious evolutionism is to focus attention on the role of literacy in the rise and spread of world religions, which also had their origins as local cults. Here it is important to consider the relationships between text-based theological orthodoxy and popular practice, and between the 'great' and 'little' traditions. Pilgrimages are sacred journeys with far-reaching implications both for the individual and for the collectivity.

The current trend towards a world market in religions raises controversial issues: the right of each individual to freedom of belief and of every religious group to prosyletise its beliefs may be resisted by people fearful that full implementation of these principles will erode the distinctive elements in their own traditions. Some anthropologists feel uncomfortable when they see a weaker faith overwhelmed by aggressive missionary activity. Others argue that religious beliefs have always been diffused in essentially the same ways, so recent globalisation is not really new. Major contributions to the anthropology of religion have been made by scholars who were themselves committed members of a church, including missionaries.

Nations can be conceived as churches in Durkheim's sense and nationalist ideologies seem to provide the most powerful principle of sacredness in the modern world, perhaps especially when they combine with an older form of religion. The case of communism, too, suggests that the distinction between a modern secular ideology and a traditional church is by no means straightforward. For some people it succeeded in fulfilling the key functions of a conventional religion, but the more *particularist* claims of nationalists have been more persuasive up to now than the *universalist* models of the communists.

Part V
RELATING AND BELONGING

20 | INTRODUCTION TO KINSHIP

The scope of kinship

Kinship is often perceived by non-anthropologists as the most technical branch of the discipline and somehow the most fundamental. When anthropologists study economic systems, politics, law and religion, they are addressing fields that are the main concern of other disciplines. The anthropological perspective is distinctive, but it can usually be elaborated without a very complicated specialist vocabulary. With kinship, things are a little different. However, the jargon which anthropologists have developed in this field is not really complicated. The study of kinship can become arcane, but the most important points are not mysterious at all. Kinship plays a greater role in the structuring of social life in most pre-capitalist societies than it does in modern capitalist societies, with their highly developed specialist institutions. However, the family remains basic to the socialisation process and networks based on interpersonal relations, rather than formal institutions, are indispensable in our own societies as well. These networks often adapt the idiom of kinship.

Some argue for confining kinship to the study of close genealogical, 'biological' relations. This would seem consistent with the Greek origin of the term *genos* (cf. Latin *genus*). But the anthropological study of kinship reveals that the biological capacities and relations that are common to all humans are represented culturally in astoundingly different ways. People use kinship as a metaphor and these metaphorical usages vary from culture to culture. Beliefs about relatedness that are in some sense modelled on understandings of biological relatedness play an important role and in most societies extend well outside one's immediate 'blood' relatives inside a family or descent group. Think of the way that in-laws (*affines* is the more technical term) are assimilated to kin in Euro-American societies. Less familiar to most of you will be the case of 'milk siblings', children who are not genetically speaking siblings but who are given milk by the same woman. This is considered to be such a strong relationship in many Islamic societies that a boy and girl who are milk siblings are prevented from marrying each other, just as if they were brother and sister. Other extensions of the idiom of kinship have been termed 'fictive'. The relationship of godparenthood in the Christian tradition establishes binding ties that complement those of kinship in the ordinary sense. In some communities relatively poor peasants cement a relationship of patronage and dependency by asking a wealthy family to assume this position. If, in modern social conditions, a wealthy protector is no longer so important, then people may dispense with this fiction and nominate ordinary kin to be godparents to their children.

Our ideas about kinship underpin personal relations for all of us and determine the domestic groups in which most of us live. Furthermore, kinship relations play a much greater role in the larger structures of contemporary societies than most people appreciate; ethnicity and nationalism can be regarded as extensions of kinship, as 'primordial relations' that seem important to many people in the contemporary world. Ultimately, we shall argue that the study of kinship is an essential component of anthropology's more general concern with social identities. This is why it lies at the very core of the discipline and seems likely to remain there.

Origins and key terms

The study of variation in the ways in which people classify their relatives, trace their descent, and organise their domestic groups was a major theme in anthropological work of the nineteenth century. Given the evolutionist orientation of virtually all scholars in this period, attention naturally focused on how these arrangements had changed over the long term. It was common to speculate about an early human condition of promiscuity, speculation that has not been confirmed in later ethnographic research. In fact all human societies have devised ways of limiting sexual access and of uniting men and women in marriage. These are by no means the same thing, and there is tremendous variety in the detail of these arrangements around the world. Nonetheless, early European fantasies about primitive promiscuity can be dismissed as exactly that.

Another long-standing issue was the question of which came first, *patriliny* or *matriliny*. A patrilineal society is one in which descent is traced through the male line only. Think in terms of your own family tree, and imagine that the names and origins of all the women in this genealogy are irrelevant to the collective identity of the group as it persists through time. In the simplest case, just assume that they arrive from outside, and that your own sisters will also marry outside the group. Sisters count as members of the descent group, but their children do not (see Figure 20.1). Assume further that your brothers will continue to reside with or very close to your father. This, then, can be described as a *patrilineal* society, with a *patrilocal* (sometimes *virilocal*) residence pattern.

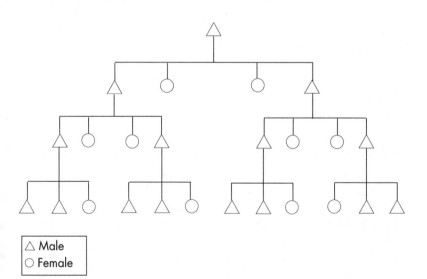

△ Male
○ Female

Figure 20.1   A patrilineal descent group

The term *patriarchal* is usually applied to societies in which *power* lies unambiguously with men. Indeed, most patrilineal societies can also be described as patriarchal. The usefulness of this distinction becomes apparent when we come to consider *matrilineal* societies, those in which people trace their descent althrough the female line. Many such societies have been documented by anthropologists, though they are less numerous than patrilineal societies. But the number of societies that can be described as *matriarchal* is very small – in fact, it is probably zero, although a moderately compelling argument can be made in the case of the Iroquois Indians. We shall consider this problem, sometimes known as the matrilineal puzzle, in more detail in Chapter 21.

Several scholars, notably the Swiss legal scholar Bachofen in 1861, speculated that matriliny (*das Mutterrecht*) must everywhere have preceded patriliny, on the grounds that early humans would have found it much easier to identify their mothers than their fathers. This argument was closely linked to the argument about primitive promiscuity and it has been deservedly ignored by the great majority of later researchers. Twentieth century research has shown that hunter gatherers, the people with the simplest forms of technology, do not have descent groups at all. Their kinship is, like ours, *bilateral* (sometimes also *cognatic*).

Five styles

Lewis Henry Morgan

Lewis Henry Morgan was the most influential of the nineteenth century evolutionists and his *Systems of Consanguinity and Affinity of the Human Family* (1871) is usually taken as the starting point of systematic investigations into kinship. Morgan was especially interested in kinship terminologies, following his field researches among North American Indians. He made a distinction between *descriptive* and *classificatory* kin. A descriptive term was one which gave a precise reckoning of a person's relationship to another, in terms of a genealogical grid that he presumed to have universal validity. A classificatory term is one which allows many other persons to be assimilated to this category. For example,

Morgan thought we should speak of a classificatory relation if the term for 'brother' was used not only for male children who share the same parents but also for all other males of approximately the same age considered to be descendants of a common ancestor.

Modern scholarship has not confirmed Morgan's attempts to correlate terminologies by reference to a general model of evolution. The fact that the modern Euro-American pattern is basically the same as that of many simple hunter gatherer groups shows the futility of attempting to plot terminologies onto an evolutionary map. Anthropologists have continued, however, to pay close attention to kin terms. Let us give an example of the sort of detail which interests us, the terminology with which most English speakers are familiar does not have a separate word to distinguish between cousins on the female side and cousins on the male side, but many other people can make precise distinctions. English and Polish do not distinguish the sister of a father from the sister of a mother: both are called 'aunt'. But Polish does, unlike English, have separate terms for the uncle who is a father's brother (*stryj*) and the uncle who is a mother's brother (*wuj*). Growing up familiar with this difference may have helped Bronislaw Malinowski grasp more quickly the complexities of the matrilineal Trobriand system, in which the social position of the mother's brother was radically different from that of the father's brother.

George Peter Murdock

Twentieth-century anthropologists have by and large rejected evolutionist hypotheses, with Malinowski leading the way. As the quantity of ethnographic data increased rapidly, non-evolutionist tabulation and comparison seemed to offer the most potential for developing the subject further. Murdock established the human relations area files at Yale University to work towards this goal and analysed some of these data in his major study *Social Structure* (1949). Similar aspirations underpinned some of the work of British structural-functionalists, such as those who sought correlations in Africa between the strength of the principle of patriliny and low divorce rates.

Most contemporary scholars see such efforts as futile, because the details of kinship and other elements of social organisation only make sense in their particular cultural contexts. There are also problems in defining the units and problems of scale: it makes little sense to compare the kinship practices of hundreds of millions of Chinese with those of tiny tribal societies. Despite these difficulties, it is possible to argue through correlational analysis of Murdock's materials that the major direction of change has indeed been from matrilineal to patrilineal, though not for the reasons presumed by nineteenth century scholars. Jack Goody has made statistical use of Murdock's archives in his comparative analyses of what he calls 'the domestic domain'. Unlike Murdock, who saw his datasets as basically timeless, Goody has also sought specific historical and even evolutionist explanations for cross-cultural differences. For example, he has shown that marriage with first cousins in Europe, previously allowed and even encouraged, was discouraged and forbidden by the early Christian church because of the church's own desire to accumulate property. On a larger scale, he has contrasted the kinship systems of Europe and Asia with those found in Africa and related this contrast to divergent economic systems over the last several thousand years.

Meyer Fortes

British ethnographic work in the late colonial period, especially those investigations into non-centralised African societies whose importance we have already noted when discussing political anthropology, set aside evolutionism and systematic comparisons in favour of meticulous descriptive accounts of kinship in action. They paid particular attention to the principle of descent. Meyer Fortes, a Jew from South Africa who studied with Malinowski, emphasised the overwhelming social strength of kinship ties among the Tallensi of the Northern Gold Coast (now Ghana). A rule of patrilineal descent established the group, called by Fortes a lineage, which was fundamental in shaping social life. Land was collectively held and it was by virtue of lineage membership that the individual acquired his or her social rights. The elders of the group resolved disputes and took political decisions as and when necessary. Their authority was buttressed by religious beliefs and rituals grounded in ancestor worship. The origin of wives was of only minor interest in societies of this type, since they were of no importance in the perpetuation of the descent line. The 'web of kinship' had moral as well as practical significance, since it established standards of conduct throughout social life.

So powerful did the descent models seem that many were tempted to generalise them outside the African contexts for which they were originally developed. When anthropologists were beginning to document tribal societies in Highland New Guinea, John Barnes warned against the unthinking transfer of the African descent models to people who thought in quite different terms, and for whom the skills of a 'big man' could be more important for determining the pattern of residential and cooperating groups than any notion of descent.

Claude Lévi-Strauss

We have already come across Lévi-Strauss as the founder and most distinguished practitioner of structuralism in social anthropology. In *The Elementary Structures of Kinship* (1949) he aimed to address underlying issues of structure, rather than plot statistical correlations in the style of Murdock. Rather than emphasise a principle of descent as the basis for the persistence of a group through time, he stressed the relationship formed between groups by marriage. In the very simplest form of relationship, group A would give wives to group B and receive wives in return. In systems of asymmetrical exchange, group B would give wives not to group A but to group C, and group C to group D, and so on. Such sytems, whether symmetrical or asymmetrical, provided a basis for social integration. The groups concerned might think of themselves as village communities, rather than as descent groups (*lineages* or, on a larger scale, *clans*) whose members were bound together by 'blood'. This approach became known as 'alliance theory'.

There was a vigorous debate between alliance and descent theorists in the 1960s. Both were valid ways of approaching kinship, although in some ethnographic contexts the one was usually more plausible than the other. It was gradually recognised that both were rather abstract models, and not necessarily of much help in understanding how people actually married and the relationships they maintained with their kin and in-laws. At about the same time some scholars began to question whether there was really any such thing as kinship. For example, Peter Worsley reanalysed the Tallensi case from a Marxist angle and argued that the crucial relationship between father and son could better be understood as a relation of production. Similarly (but without endorsing Marxism), Edmund Leach claimed on the basis of his fieldwork in Sri Lanka in the 1950s that kinship was really just a way of talking about property relationships. In the village he studied, based on irrigated rice production, people would regularly distort or invent genealogies, if they had a good economic motivation for doing so. The 'rules' were regularly broken in practice. This was not to say that the rules, in this case mixed up with an ideology of subcaste purity, were of no significance at all. But Leach did show that a preoccupation with this level, for a long time typical of the descent school, gave only a partial understanding of what was really taking place on the ground.

David Schneider

More radical attempts to undermine or dissolve the category of kinship emphasised that kinship relationships were constructed differently all over the world and could have no universal basis in biology. Schneider saw American notions of 'blood relations' as metaphorical ideas, just as culturally specific as the ideas he had previously investigated among the tribal Yapp. Ideas about the constitution of persons, their 'substance', and how they were related to other persons, were ultimately shaped by each separate culture. Hence it was a mistake to see kinship as grounded in biological relationships. For Schneider, the meaning of kinship was not a matter to be understood in relation to the sociological significance of descent groups and their role in politics and the transmission of property, but rather as a symbolic understanding of the person and ordering of the world. This approach is another manifestation of the 'culturalist' paradigm that we identified early on in our discussion of economic anthropology, which gives priority to the local model.

Some critics have rebuked Schneider for seeking completely to detach the concepts and symbols found in American kinship from human biology. Ernest Gellner, for example, insisted that it was only against the background of our common knowledge of biological universals that we could have a comparative discussion about the meaning of terms such as 'father(hood)'. However, the symbolic approach advocated by Schneider proved to be an extremely fertile way of opening up alternative ways of understanding human social relationships. Biological universals are irrelevant to this task. What matters instead is the 'folk biology' and the use to which this is put in each different culture.

Gender studies

The tendency to shift discussion away from biological constraints is also apparent in the enormous increase in recent years in work on gender, often swamping or substituting for more traditional investigations of kinship. Gender can be defined as the cultural construction of sex. While the sex of an individual is determined by biology, anthropologists usually find it much more interesting to enquire into what different societies consider to be appropriate roles and behaviour for men and women. We have touched briefly on gendered divisions of labour, but gender may permeate society much more deeply, extending for example to ideas about the nation and even the cosmos. Gender is evident in such commonplace assertions as 'a woman's place is in the home', but such convictions can have far-reaching effects and contribute to the exclusion of women from the society's most prestigious positions and from public decision taking.

Interest in gender began with the recognition, linked to the wider social impact of the women's movement in many western societies, that the position of women had been seriously neglected. It was soon realised, however, that generalisations such as 'the position of women' would not be very helpful, since women were seldom a homogenous group, and even where they were fairly homogenous, the resources at their disposal varied with age and with changing social conditions. One feminist school looked back to the theories of Morgan and Engels in efforts to explain women's subordination in relation to the rise of agriculture and the state. Others drew on sociological theories that contrasted the public domain to the private and argued that it was women's close identification with the private or domestic domain and their exclusion from the public domain which explained their domination by men. Later, however, it came to be recognised that women could exercise considerable power from their domestic base.

Still other approaches, as we have noted already, picked up a structuralist dichotomy and argued that women's closer identification with nature placed them at a disadvantage, since culture was assumed to dominate nature. General models of this sort have been explored in many detailed case analyses of how gender is constructed in different times and places. Culturalist investigation of the use of metaphor can expose the insidious effects of gender, often impinging on the most basic categories in our social lives. For example, Polish people speak with pride of 'a fatherland' (*ojczyzna*), in a way suggestive of the patriarchal ethos that permeates throughout the society.

These gender ideologies can of course have tangible consequences Frances Pine has shown how in Poland deeply rooted notions about women and their place in the family helped to ensure that they would be the first to lose their jobs when factories had to shed labour in the early post-communist years. Women continue to bear the brunt of domestic responsibilities and it is culturally understood that the woman has responsibility for all the expenses of the children and the collective household. Therefore she can seldom allocate any extra cash she earns from her own activities to her individual use, in the way that a man is able to retain a portion of his income for personal expenditure.

21 | DESCENT AND PROCREATION

What are descent groups?

The first part of this chapter looks at descent groups in more detail, emphasising their importance for social organisation in tribal societies. The second part of the chapter illustrates a very different approach.

> Two persons who are kin are related in one or other of two ways: either one is descended from the other, or they are both descended from a common ancestor. It is to be remembered that descent here refers to the social relationship of parents and children, not to the physical relation. Kinship is thus based on descent, and what first determines the character of a kinship system is the way in which decent is recognised and reckoned.[32]

The fullest elaboration of descent theory was given by Meyer Fortes in his studies of the West African Tallensi but we also came across this principle in our discussion of how political order is maintained among the non-centralised Nuer. The idea of descent is simple, perhaps deceptively so. It refers to *ancestry*, to the tracing of parents, grandparents and so on, which we can represent in a genealogy. But diagrams such as the one we introduced in Chapter 20 tell us nothing about the social significance of the relationships they depict. If you were to draw your own you could probably chart your great grandparents and include some second or third cousins in your *kindred*. But it is unlikely that you know them all. And even if you do, it is doubtful that this kindred has any social significance as a group. It does not mobilise itself for any political purposes and it is not through the kindred that children are socialised.The kindred of every individual is different, except for those of full siblings (brothers or sisters who share the same parents). Our principle of bilateral descent does not play a major role in our social organisation. In this respect our societies have much in common with hunter gatherers in many parts of the world who emphasise the flexibility of their groups and have no need to assert exclusive rights to the land on which they hunt and gather their food supply.

It seems that people begin to take more interest in the principle of descent when they have economic and political reasons for wishing to assert exclusive rights to a particular territory, for example because it is now being used in a more intensive way to produce crops. Descent is used to specify the groups that hold those rights. However, some cases are inconsistent with this broad evolutionary hypothesis. Many Australian peoples, for example, have a strong interest in descent that does not seem to fit with their hunter gatherer economies. Besides, the assertion of a principle of descent need not make any difference to the readiness with which strangers are incorporated into a group as honorary or 'fictional' members. It is characteristic of African descent groups that even slaves can be easily integrated; and even if they themselves are not, their children certainly will be.

But how is a descent group actually formed? The main reason why it is difficult to imagine our personal kindreds as effective groups is because bilateral descent can only generate effective groups if some further criteria of selection are introduced. The task is simplified if descent is traced on one side only, either patrilineal or matrilineal. Since patrilineal systems seem to be a good deal more common let us take them first and look a little more carefully at the case of the Tallensi. When Meyer Fortes worked among them in the 1930s they were an agricultural society not effectively integrated by a centralised state. They had a few prestigious political offices, and social integration was also promoted by priestly offices and an elaborate ritual system. From Fortes' accounts, however, it is clear that the most important principle of social integration was patrilineal descent. The lineage was a clearly defined group associated with a particular territory, which recruited its members through the father's line. Sisters left the lineage when they married. Authority lay with the male elders. The entire system was reinforced by ancestor worship, in the sense that the spirits of deceased males were thought to follow the affairs of the group and to punish miscreants.

Fortes made it clear that, in reality, the composition of Tallensi patrilineages allowed for some flexibility: for the integration of strangers and for the formation of new groups from time to time. He also took pains to show that people also acknowledge their relations on the female side They might even have detailed knowledge of their maternal ancestry. Fortes coined the term 'complementary filiation' to denote the links that individuals might have on their mother's side. Links with the mother's brothers might be emotionally closer and warmer than descent ties within the patrilineage. Some property of a personal nature might be inherited from the mother. However, the male side had clear priority when people conceptualised the group to which they belong. This group, the patrilineage, was an effective *corporation* when it came to managing land rights and resolving disputes and there was no equivalent matrilineal corporation.

In a small number of cases, the most famous being the Yakö of Nigeria, studied in the 1940s by Daryll Forde, matrilineal and patrilineal descent principles exist side by side. In these so-called 'double descent' systems a clear distinction is maintained between the tasks and the property controlled patrilineally and those regulated by matrilineal groups.

The matrilineal puzzle

Matrilineal descent is not quite the inverse or mirror image of patrilineal systems. If we continue to suppose that the primary purpose of the unilineal descent group is to function as an effective social group with respect to a specific territory, the matrilineage would be a mirror image of the patrilineage if men were recruited into the group and authority were exercised by its female elders. As noted in Chapter 20, there is little evidence for such matriarchal societies. Authority in matrilineal systems is normally exercised by a woman's brothers. Now, to exercise this authority effectively the brothers should reside together on the territory with which their matrilineage is associated. They can only do that if their wives join them there, which implies that their own sisters, the women through whom the matrilineage will be reproduced, must move elsewhere. This 'matrilineal puzzle' arises directly from the fact that, although descent is traced through females, day to day power in the group is in male hands.

The puzzle can be solved in a variety of ways. Among the Hopi Indians the brothers did move away at marriage, but they did not move very far away and so there was no difficulty in practice in their continuing to meet and manage the affairs of their matrilineage. Among the Melanesians of Dobu the solution was to alternate residence, allowing everyone in theory to spend every other year back in the hamlet associated with the matrilineage. The neighbouring Trobrianders solved the puzzle in yet another way. When they married, women moved to live with their husbands on land controlled by his group. Her sons, the heirs to the authority of the matrilineal corporation, moved back when they reached adolescence to live with their mother's brother. Her daughters would remain with her until marriage, and the sons of these daughters would also eventually join her brothers in the location identified with their matrilineage.

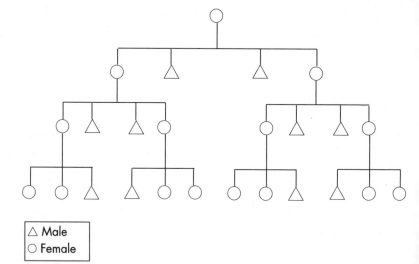

△ Male
○ Female

Figure 21.1   A matrilineal descent group

Similar qualifications can be added at this point to those noted already for the patrilineal Tallensi. The reality on the ground always deviates significantly from the ideal pattern of residence and descent, which leads critics to question whether we are right to attach much weight to descent after all. If, however, people continue to assert the ideal and to reconcile exceptions, such as voluntary adoptions or forced incorporation as in certain types of slave raiding, by eventually incorporating them into the genealogy, then it seems reasonable to see descent as the leading principle of social organisation. If, however, groups are increasingly formed on some other basis, then even if some people continue to stress their descent ties we would have to say that the descent principle has weakened. In some cases we might conclude that a principle of 'alliance' with another group is more significant than the principle of descent.

Both descent and alliance theories presuppose that all peoples have essentially the same understanding, based on the universals of human reproduction, of what it means to stand in a certain genealogical relationship to someone else. It is precisely this assumption that has been challenged by Schneider and others, who argue that the entire field of kinship studies has suffered from a biologising ethnocentrism. In the case of the Trobrianders, for example, Schneider would see no justification for considering the father's brother as in any way comparable to the mother's brother: for us, both are uncles, with the same genetic closeness to ego, but for the matrilineal Trobrianders they are simply incommensurable.

Procreation beliefs

Let us illustrate the point by turning to a very different type of society. There is no sharp dividing line between 'tribal' societies in which anthropologists routinely speak of descent groups as the most basic social units and 'peasant' societies in which the household or the village is typically taken as basic. For example, it would theoretically be possible to look at contemporary rural Turkey in terms of descent group, household or village. The first might be most convincing in some of the Kurdish regions of the southeast. Elsewhere much depends on local settlement pattern. But it may be a mistake to insist on prioritising one or the other. The members of households are also members of village communities and of descent groups. In many parts of Turkey the significance of the patrilineal descent groups seems to have declined in recent centuries. But this has no particular significance for a feminist interested in studying the continued strength of a patriarchal ideology throughout Turkish society. Carol Delaney has recently carried out such an investigation, paying particular attention to procreation beliefs.

The details of how human reproductive biology is represented culturally have fascinated anthropologists since the nineteenth century. In 1895 two ethnographers of Australian Aboriginals reported that these groups were unaware of the male contribution to procreation. The Trobriand case as documented by Malinowski seemed at first glance to be similar. The natives did admittedly recognise a connection between sexual intercourse and having babies, but they denied that semen had any direct role in generating the child. According to Trobrianders, penetration by the penis was necessary in order to allow a baby to exit through the vagina, but the baby was actually created by a spirit that entered through the woman's ear.

This was what the Trobrianders told Malinowski. More careful analysis suggests that this 'ignorance of paternity' is better seen as a part of Trobriand matrilineal ideology. There is good linguistic and other evidence to suggest that Trobrianders were not in fact as ignorant as Malinowski first thought. The more interesting question, it seemed to Edmund Leach when he commented on the issue half a century later, was why so many anthropologists seemed determined to believe that 'primitive people' really were ignorant. Leach's own recommendation was to set Trobriand stories of conception in the same structuralist context as the no less strange stories of people whom we do not think to classify as primitive, such as Christians with their myth of Mary's 'virgin birth'.

Anthropologists have long recognised that social paternity need not coincide with biological paternity. In many societies the details of biological fatherhood are not significant, provided the mother has a husband ready to assume the social role of the father. John Barnes introduced a further distinction when he pointed out that the local notion of 'biological father' might not be the same as an external scientific assessment of parentage. Barnes, too, viewed motherhood as something self-evident in nature, whereas fatherhood, both in its social and its physical aspects, was not self-evident, but has developed historically and culturally.

For the modern cultural anthropologist, this external scientific account must itself to be approached as a folk conception and rather few non-scientists in modern western societies have any precise knowledge of the complex genetics involved in the fertilisation of human eggs. New reproductive technologies and practices such as commercial surrogacy have further complicated these issues in modern western societies where definitions of 'parenthood' are undergoing major changes. Carol Delaney, a student of David Schneider's, has argued that all the earlier commentators failed to address the key issue, which in her view was the *meaning* of the concept of paternity. She argued that Malinowski was unable to rid himself of the dominant western 'folk model' according to which procreation is the outcome of a male seed being inseminated in a female 'field'. Delaney explored the far-reaching significance of this metaphor of 'the seed and the soil' in the Turkish village where she did fieldwork in the early 1980s. It is clear in this case that the nature and essence of the new human were thought to derive entirely from the contribution of the man: the woman was merely a passive receptacle for his seed. Delaney terms this a *monogenetic* theory of procreation. The Trobrianders also held a monogenetic theory, but for them, as a matrilineal people, the creative source was the mother, through the agency of an ancestral spirit. Hence they did not need a theory of paternity and the question as to whether or not the Trobrianders were ignorant of the male biological contribution only shows up the ignorance of the anthropologists, for asking inappropriate questions.

> The views held about the function of sex and procreation, about the relative share of the father and mother in the procreation of a child, play a considerable part in the formation of kinship ideas.[33]

Their theory of procreation was reflected in the way in which Turkish villagers separated tasks according to gender in the domestic sphere and it filtered through to infect all areas of life. Women were not capable of political decisions. They had a lesser claim to be educated. They could not inherit land. Once they reached sexual maturity their hair and other parts of the body that could potentially arouse men had to be covered. In Delaney's account the modern Turkish state, with its semi-mythical founder Atatürk, reinforced the prevailing patriarchal ideology. The ultimate underpinning of this world view came, however, from cosmology. Islam was, in Delaney's view, a world religion in which all power was concentrated in a single dominant figure of male gender. There was an intimate link between the *monogenetic* theory of procreation and this *monotheistic* religion.

Delaney had rather little to say about kinship in the traditional sense. Her gender analysis was, like earlier paradigms in the study of kinship, open to the criticism that it did not pay sufficient attention to subtle ways in which, in practice, the rules and ideals could be contravened, for example by resourceful women in the domestic sphere. She was not actually very interested in the sociological complexities because, as a culturalist, her priority was to give a clear account of the ultimate concepts through which people understood their social world. In this respect she succeeds and her analysis provides a good example of how, taking gender as the basis of a world view or cosmology, one can move from the study of a particular metaphor of procreation to build up a comprehensive critique of patriarchy throughout a society.

22 | SEX AND MARRIAGE

The incest taboo

It is self-evident that sexuality is an important element in all human societies. Variations in sexual ideas and practices have been documented by many ethnographers including Malinowski, who titled one of his Trobriand monographs *The Sexual Life of Savages* (1929). This book is in fact a rigorous exploration of relations between men and women which includes discussion of their erotic imagination and of how sexuality changes over the lifecourse of both men and women. Our first theme in this chapter is addressed by Malinowski in the closing chapters of this book: incest. Why do the Trobrianders prohibit sexual relations with certain close kin? Why do we find this taboo in one form or another in all human societies? How far is it determined by our common human biology?

It seems clear that this is one of those problems where we cannot afford to ignore the evidence concerning our closest primate relatives. There is a tendency to avoid sexual relations with parents and between siblings among chimpanzees and some other primates. Is there, then, a clear Darwinian argument that can adequately explain the incest taboo? It is commonly assumed that close interbreeding is genetically deleterious. The high incidence of many unpleasant diseases and deformities among people who practise and even encourage first cousin marriage suggests that the incest taboo could well be seen as an evolutionary adaptation to avert the negative consequences of even closer unions. However, societies which allow or enourage first cousin marriage do not show lower rates of fertility than other societies and it is by no means obvious that an argument in terms of evolutionary 'fitness' can explain the taboo.

Social anthropologists have advanced a quite different kind of evolutionism. Developing an idea put forward by Tylor in the nineteenth century, Lévi-Strauss viewed *exogamy*, i.e. marrying outside one's group, as the basis of human society. Groups that did not form alliances with other groups by exchanging women would not survive: it was 'marry out or be killed out'. This view attracted the criticism that Lévi-Strauss did not seem to be familiar with a distinction well known to every teenager, namely that sex and marriage are quite different things. Even supposing that marrying out brings long-term evolutionary advantages (which is not proven), why should this require such a strong taboo on sexual relations within one's own group?

A possible answer would be that the taboo is needed precisely because exogamy might otherwise be hard to achieve, because humans in fact feel strong attractions to their close kin, which only a strong taboo can overcome. This Freudian approach was rejected by those who prefer the more sociological argument that sexual relations between family members would undermine the basis for group integration. The importance of considering power relations within the group becomes apparent when we consider what type of incest occurs most commonly. In modern western societies it seems clear that father–daughter incest is a good deal more common than mother–son or brother–sister relationships. To understand such patterns we need to understand not just the deviant psychology of an individual but the dominant ideologies of the society, as Jean Lafontaine has shown in her research on child abuse in Britain.

Data from Israeli *kibbutzim* have often been used to support the argument that close familiarity throughout the years of childhood leads young people who are not biologically close kin at all to seek their sexual and marital partners elsewhere. It seems that the fact of close proximity in their rearing is sufficient to 'trigger' the mechanism that, in most cases, applies to close biological kin. The *kibbutz* evidence is not, however, conclusive. The reason why few marriages take place probably has more to do with the movement of members away from the *kibbutz* in the years when they are most likely to consider marriage. More persuasive are the data which show a high rate of failure in marriages in China that take place between a son and an adopted daughter. The strategy of adopting a baby girl and raising her in the same household as the boy she will marry is an attractive one for poorer families. However, although the two may be unrelated genetically, many seem to have difficulty in consummating the marriage.

The argument from biology cannot explain the variation that we find in precisely which categories of relationship are sexually prohibited. Jack Goody compared the rules of patrilineal and matrilineal peoples in West Africa. Sexual relations with the wife of a brother are treated in the former case as incest, but in the latter as a (substantially less reprehensible) form of adultery. Some societies regard sexual relations with a parallel cousin (i.e. in the case of a man, the daughter of his father's brother or of his mother's sister) as incestuous, while they positively recommend marriage with a cross-cousin (the daughter of a father's sister or a mother's brother). Yet in strictly genetic terms the cross-cousins are, of course, equally close.

Despite this variation, some category of prohibition strong enough to justify the term incest taboo seems almost universal. The most powerful evidence to the contrary is that from Roman Egypt, where it seems that the practice of brother–sister marriage was common, not only among royal élites but also in wider social circles. This seems to be genuinely exceptional, and there is no evidence that parent–child relationships were similarly tolerated.

Defining marriage

Similarly complex debates have raged over many years concerning the universality of marriage. In considering the incest taboo we are dealing with physical relationships and must pay attention to possible explanations from the biological side. In the case of marriage we are dealing only with a social relationship. But what exactly is this relationship? It may seem obvious enough to us, given the kind of society in which we live. Marriage is a union between a man and woman, who will thereafter live together and produce legitimate children. However, the marital arrangements of many non-western societies are not as simple as this. Moreover, such a definition does not really fit modern western societies either, since in recent decades we have all heard of homosexual marriages, we know of married couples who have no wish to produce children, and we know of many children without married parents.

Consider the famous case of the Nayars of South India, as documented from the early years of British colonialism. This society was matrilineal. The men were frequently absent for long periods. When a girl reached sexual maturity she was ritually 'married' in the *tali*-tying ceremony. She was unlikely to see this man ever again, but this rite of passage qualified her, as a mature woman, to receive lovers. A physical relationship with a particular individual over an extended period was marked by the transfer of gifts to the woman and her group. When a woman became pregnant it was usual for the presumed biological father (*genitor*) to send further gifts, but he had no long-term relationship with the child or the mother's group in which the child was raised. In this case we can hardly speak of social fatherhood at all; yet it was not acceptable to have children without going through the *tali*-tying cermony, and the death of this 'husband' was mourned by the wife's group.

Social fatherhood takes different forms in other societies. Among the patrilineal Nuer, Evans-Pritchard documented the practice of 'ghost marriage'. This took place in circumstances where a man died, but his lineage had paid over a certain number of cattle for his wife in the socially approved way of recruiting her to their group. The widow was expected to remarry within this lineage, or she might simply take lovers. In either case, further children were classified as children of the deceased first husband. The identity of the *genitor* was not socially relevant. It was equally irrelevant in cases, much less common, when an influential woman took a 'wife', by making the usual payments of cattle. The ensuing children acknowledged this senior woman as their *pater*, and they grew up as members of her patrilineage.

After discussing the Nuer case and five others, selected to establish the diversity of forms of marriage, Edmund Leach concluded as follows.

> Words like 'marriage', 'family' and 'religion' do not mean very much when viewed in a cross-cultural framework. But the patterns of relationship which turn up in the institutions

that get allocated to these categories are important patterns which always invite the anthropologist's close attention. 'Marital' relations in particular, in providing a bridge between the biological and the social, serve to illuminate in a very special way the manner in which the local population has resolved the paradoxes which arise from our attempts to fit the continuity of nature to the discontinuities of social categories.[34]

Prescribed and arranged marriages

Exogamy, the injunction to 'marry out', is often modified in practice. One may be expected to marry *outside* the kin group (lineage or clan) but *inside* some larger tribal or ethnic grouping. Many societies have more restrictive rules that specify particular categories of kin as prescribed partners. One relatively common prescription is that a man should marry his matrilateral cross-cousin, the daughter of his mother's brother. Such a pattern of marriages through time would help to maintain close relationships between the groups. It is not necessary that all marriages should strictly conform to the 'prescription' for people to continue to assert this pattern as their norm. It is more accurate to call such rules preferential rather than prescriptive.

In some societies the principle of exogamy is not stressed at all and most marriages are *endogamous*. For example Carol Delaney noted, in the course of her fieldwork in rural Turkey, that all marital partners were found within the boundary of the village. Most of these marriages were between relatives, often first cousins. There is a traditional preference in many Islamic societies for a man to marry his father's brother's daughter (his patrilateral parallel cousin). Explanations for this preference have varied. The most common have seen this form of marriage as a way of preventing the loss of property to strangers. This is not entirely convincing since land, the most important form of property, is, despite the injunctions of the Koran, in Turkey as in most other Islamic societies, not in practice inherited by women. The fact that all types of first cousin marriage seem to be equally popular suggests that there is a preference in these communities for marrying someone who is 'close', a person who can be trusted, because their family is already intimately known. The preference for marrying 'close' in this way is by no means restricted to remote villages. There is evidence which suggests that the proportion of cousin marriages may even increase among the first generation of migrants. In the context of a huge anonymous urban population it is even more important to ensure that one's children do not marry a partner whose family reputation or 'honour' cannot readily be verified. The same principle is followed among Turkish migrants in Germany: there is a preference for marrying within the Turkish community, and the proportion of first cousin marriages remains very high.

It should be evident from this brief discussion that marriage in many human societies is very far from what it probably is for most readers of this book, namely the result of an individual decision based on a mutual emotional attachment that we call 'love'. This freedom to choose and the emotional attachment are not necessarily unique to the modern west. Malinowski's Trobrianders, for example, allowed their children greater sexual freedom than is usual in Europe or the USA today and marriages were based for the most part on the preferences of the parties involved. This is much less true in Turkish villages. The disposition to 'love' is definitely present. There is an increasing tendency for young people to succeed in persuading their parents to allow them to marry the individual of their choice. The decision, however, remains a prerogative of the families. It is considered too important to be left to the young.

Arranged marriages do not, in general, have a good press in modern western societies. We have noted the example of young Pakistani girls, brought up in, say, Britain or Norway, who feel themselves in many ways part of the society of those countries, but who, as a result of decisions made by their families, must marry a man they have never seen, usually a relative of some sort from the home village in Pakistan. But is it necessary to generalise from such tragedies to condemn the institution of arranged marriage altogether? Many arranged marriages are extremely successful. The emotional bond that is not present at the outset may be formed quickly enough, and it may turn out to be as strong or even stronger than romantic love as this has developed in western societies. The children of such marriages are more likely to grow up in stable environments, supported not just by having both of their parents resident in their domestic group but also by a strong network of kin on both sides outside this group.

Much the same sort of point may be made with regard to plural marriages or *polygyny*. *Polyandrous* marriages are those in which, as in some parts of Tibet, a woman may simultaneously have several husbands. *Polygamous* marriages, the more common type, are those in which a man is allowed more than one wife. It should be stressed that, even in societies which allow polygyny, it is not practised by everyone – this would usually be a demographic impossibility. It is strongly associated with the wealthy and the more powerful. It is also, as in the contemporary Turkish village, associated with the desire to produce sons. A man is much more likely to take a second wife when his first wife has failed to produce a male heir. This confirms Delaney's diagnosis of Turkey as a patriarchal society. The position of the first wife and of any existing children is negatively affected, while the second wife normally enjoys no legal security in the eyes of the state. Yet some people in Turkey, both men and women, defend the practice. They point out that it may reduce the incidence of prostitution and provide a home and an economic future for some women who might not otherwise be able to marry at all. And they may ask how it can be considered worse in any moral sense to allow a man to take several wives (whom he is required by customary law to treat equally) than to allow, as most western societies do, repeated changes of partner in 'serial monogamy', particularly when this is more likely to have destabilising consequences for children.

Marital payments

In virtually all human societies marriage is accompanied by significant material transactions. These may, as among the Trobrianders, take the form of gifts made by the groom, or the groom's kin, to the bride and her kin group. Alternatively or additionally, the groom may be obliged to work for a stipulated period for his new father-in-law. This is known as *brideservice*.

Bridewealth refers to the transfer made between two groups in exchange for the bride. We have already noted that cattle are the most important medium for making this payment among the Nuer. In many parts of the Islamic world and China the payment has long been made in cash, or in a combination of cash and other goods. Some anthropologists have seen these transactions as somehow reducing the bride herself to the status of a commodity. This is not a helpful approach, even though it may seem well justified in cases where a higher sum is paid for a bride who is considered especially attractive, or exceptionally hard working and therefore a more valuable economic asset to the group that she will join. It is more important to see these payments as marking the relationship between two groups. The goods involved are not paid to an individual but to her group. They are normally used as a 'circulating fund' in order to obtain brides for the young men of that group, the brothers of the bride.

Dowry is a quitě different type of transfer, involving the bestowal of a part of her future inheritance onto a daughter at her marriage. This is not a payment to a group, but to an individual woman whose ownership of this property gives her an important element of economic security in the event of problems in her marriage. The bestowal of an appropriate dowry is also a sign of a family's status or 'honour'. Generous provision can help to ensure that the bride finds a partner of higher status than she might otherwise, as Nur Yalman described in detail for Sinhalese marriages in Sri Lanka. The bride often receives gifts from the groom and his family, while the groom may receive similar gifts from the bride's side. All these details and others, such as who is to bear the costs of the wedding and of furnishing rooms, possibly a house, for the new couple, must be carefully discussed in the negotiations which precede engagement and marriage.

Bridewealth is a 'horizontal' transaction between kin groups that control property on a supra-household basis. In an important essay, Jack Goody showed that bridewealth systems were associated with the more egalitarian tribal societies of sub-Saharan Africa, where agricultural technology was based largely on a simple digging stick. Dowry systems transmit property vertically, i.e. between generations, and they predominate in the plough-based societies of

Eurasia, where inter-household inequalities and status competition are significant. These are, however, only ideal types. Many parts of China and the Islamic world, including Turkish villages, have combined elements of both bridewealth and dowry.

Divorce

The quality and strength of marital bonds are rather hard to measure. What can be measured more readily is the frequency with which marriages end in divorce. There is no doubt that divorce rates in countries such as Turkey and Pakistan are far lower than they are in the USA. They are much lower even than they are in Poland, despite the strong anti-divorce teaching of the Roman Catholic Church. Yet it is a mistake to associate high divorce rates only with modern industrialised societies. There is considerable variety in the pre-industrial world. As might be expected, where bridewealth is relatively high the incidence of divorce tends to be low: the issues of returning the payment and reintegrating the woman into her natal group provide strong disincentives. Divorce rates seem to be higher in matrilineal societies and in patrilineal societies where bridewealth payments are relatively low.

The high divorce rates of contemporary industrial societies have different social consequences from divorce in a tribal society. The woman is less likely to move back to her natal group and more likely to retain custody of her children, instead of having to hand them over to the husband's group. But the divorced mother who heads an independent household is, like the unmarried mother, often obliged to live in difficult material circumstances compared to the children's father, who is much more free to pursue his career and to remarry if it suits him. Attempts to explain these patterns must address the structure of the labour market, where in some sectors women find it almost impossible to combine motherhood with a career. Culturally oriented anthropologists explore how the construction of masculine and female identities is not simply an outcome of changing technologies and working patterns, but helps to *constitute* these patterns in the first place.

23 | FAMILIES AND HOUSEHOLDS

The nuclear family

In Chapter 22 we saw how, after a good deal of stretching to cover cases very different from those familiar to us, it is just about possible to hold on to the idea of a universal notion of marriage. Marriage is universal in the sense that all human societies have some socially standardised means for regulating sexual contact and legitimating children. The rules may be very strict or they may be extremely lax. There is so much variation that one may well end up concluding that it makes no sense to describe the unions entered into by a Nayar woman with the same term that we use in rural Turkey or urban Poland.

The same basic issues can be posed with regard to the family. Is it possible, as George Peter Murdock thought it was, to define the family universally? Does it follow automatically that wherever we have marriage we also have families? How large does a family have to be before we call it something else, such as a lineage or a clan? How do families renew themselves through time? Can the functions of the family be carried out by alternative institutions? Everyone has a family and we tend to take the term for granted. Yet this institution is nowadays the subject of a lot of public discourse in many countries, especially by politicians and church leaders who believe that the family is at the heart of the value system of our society, and that it is under threat.

If the marital bond is the basis for the constitution of a family then we must recognise the family even in cases such as the Nayar, where neither the biological nor the social father of the child is a resident member of the matrilineage, but the child does grow up with the mother. But there are other cases, including numerous

South American Indian societies, where men are segregated from women so rigorously that male children are not left in the care of the mother after a very early age. Here the raising of these children is a group responsibility, not that of individual parents. In these cases, although we may still find formal ceremonies to mark marriage, we cannot speak of families in the usual sense at all.

In the great majority of societies, however, children do grow up in the direct care of at least one parent. This does not mean that they grow up in families just like those that predominate in contemporary western societies. The child can often call on a larger number of kin, for example because her 'classificatory sisters' are not just those girls who have the same mother but all the girls in her neighbourhood whose mothers are related to her own mother. Socialisation in larger groups may have various consequences but the interest of the anthropologist lies in the social aspects rather than the psychological. The man who can call many hundreds of members of his lineage 'brother' may find it easier than his typical counterpart inside a small western family to mobilise family members for economic or political purposes. This seems borne out in the history of countless migrant communities, where without the ties of family people might never have felt able to take the risks that led them to new places, or to take up previously untried economic options. An external analyst might call the groups mobilised here lineages or clans, rather than families; but the people themselves may speak only of family.

Networks

It would be a mistake, however, to suppose that families in our sort of society are incapable of providing support functions on a larger scale. In the past a great deal depended on close residence. When aunts, uncles and cousins all live close by, as used to be the norm for working class families in British cities, then you can expect ties to be very close. Michael Young and Peter Wilmott examined family life in the East End of London in the 1950s. They found that members of extended families would routinely cook for each other, share information about jobs and negotiate childcare on a reciprocal basis. This may have declined in recent decades but at the same time greater personal mobility enables close links to be maintained. A high proportion of the weekend traffic around London's orbital motorway is motivated by family ties.

Similar patterns are meticulously described in Donald Pitkin's microhistorical study of how one Italian family, originating in an area of the south where nuclear families were the norm, developed a form of extended family household based on intense co-operation. Culturally it was the man's duty to provide for his wife and children and Giacomo, the hero of Pitkin's account, behaves at times like a patriarch. Yet control over the family purse, including his own allocation from it, lay with his wife Maria. Theirs was a true partnership, in which the identities of the individuals were at least partially submerged. Later in her life and after the first edition of Pitkin's book, when money was seriously short in their family Maria did go out to work, despite the strong cultural idea that she should not.

Close relationships also persist in Poland. The economic shortages of the communist period were a major factor in promoting close contacts between urban migrants and their relatives in the countryside, able to produce their own food. The improved market conditions of post-communist years have put an end to some of these patterns, but there is no evidence that interaction with extended families has declined in other respects. In some post-communist countries we know that, following the disruption of the old collectivised systems, rural-urban networks have gained in economic significance.

But suppose that all these families in England, Italy and Poland were less and less inclined to trust each other and to interact within their own circles of kin. Suppose that, instead, people build up their personal networks in a variety of other ways, including neighbours, workmates, fellow members of a sports club, church, or whatever. Is the mobilisation of such a network any different from the equivalent mobilisation by a member of a unilineal descent group in Africa ? On the surface it might seem completely diffferent, since in the one case it is a matter of a corporate group on which many other members can equally draw, and in the other it is a network built up by a single individual, which would not function together as a group except at the behest of this individual. Yet the substantive ties of reciprocity and sentiment involved may not differ much at all. Again we should question the conventional western privileging of close biological relations when we talk about the family. It is more important to ask about the work that families do. If we consider a wider range of interpersonal relations as forms of kinship, then the importance of kinship for social organisation has hardly declined at all. Of course there are some people who prefer not to cultivate such ties,who prefer to buy all the services they want on the market. But the market can seldom provide all the goods that people want, and to acquire the information one needs to use the market one is often again thrown back on to family and personal networks. For this reason, maintaining these ties is a highly rational strategy for most people, everywhere.

A further example from Turkey is especially instructive. In recent decades there has been very high rates of rural-urban migration in this country, particularly to the metropolis of Istanbul. The migrants draw assistance above all from their close kin. They may be helped by others as well, and they may join associations that are open to all migrants from their home district, or to all members of their religious or ethnic group, but it is primarily with kin that most people have the closest contacts. Jenny White has studied such contacts among women and noted the ways in which the idiom of kinship can be extended when people develop close economic relationships. In particular, women who undertake piecework by sewing in their homes are addressed by kin terms by the men who buy the products of the labour. These women say that 'money makes us relatives' and they attach some value to being treated in this personalised way. An external observer of the situation might say that the language of kinship and reciprocity is here being used to paper over relationships of economic exploitation.

Households and the developmental cycle

The household is usually taken for granted in contemporary western societies in much the same way as the family, but the cases already presented should lead you to question your familiar assumptions. If household is defined as the basic residential unit of society, then it must – unlike family – be universal. But what do we really mean by residential unit? The people who sleep under the same roof may not eat at the same table. They may not pool their finances at all, or they may do so only in part. Depending on what precisely one chooses to look at, household may diverge significantly from family. It may include extensions of families, such as widowed parents or unmarried siblings; but it can also include servants, apprentices or other 'strangers'. The household may contain more than one family, for example when brothers continue to reside on the same premises after marriage. In fact the fastest growing type of household in most industrialised countries, including Poland, is that which contains no family at all but only a solitary individual.

The most important point to bear in mind when subjecting households to this sort of classification is that such data reveal little about change over time or about how that change is experienced. It may be that, at the moment when a census is taken, or indeed at any other moment, the proportion of multiple-family households is small. This might lead the analyst to see the pattern of nuclear families as dominant. Yet the people might think of their society as one of extended or multiple families, and it is possible that most individuals will spend some time living in such a household – typically, for a short period only, before it breaks up or *fissions*. We have already noted how changes in household and residence patterns enable the Trobrianders to resolve the 'matrilineal puzzle'. A well documented case from Eastern Europe is the Balkan *zadruga*, a multiple-family household which in the age of nationalism came to be mythologised as the 'natural' ancient custom of peoples such as the Serbs. In reality it seems that very few people lived for more than a few years of their lives in a household containing more than one family. When a son married and his wife joined him in the household of her father-in-law, tensions almost always ensued between the older conjugal pair and the new pair. They typically increased with the birth of children, and with the marriage of a brother and the arrival of a second young wife into the household. In short, pressure built up on the father to allow his sons to build their own houses and live apart. This was normally accompanied by a division of the land, draught animals and other assets. The youngest son might receive a larger share in return for supporting his parents in their old age when they were no longer capable of working themselves. In most societies the details of how and when land and other property are transmitted vary considerably. There has to be a certain amount of flexibility in household structure and property transmission, even within each particular culture, in order to allow adaptations to the pattern of births and other variables. For example, the structure of households is affected by the opportunities available to household members outside the family farm, via education or migrant labour, which may detach the main 'breadwinners' from their family and long-term household for years of or even decades.

House societies

It is not only over the successive generations of its developmental cycle that we need to view households dynamically. To close let us note a very different sort of temporality, the evolutionism implicit in the argument put forward by Lévi-Strauss about 'house societies'. The argument in brief is that these form an intermediate stage between 'elementary' systems of kinship and societies with more developed economic bases that are structured by new forms of political hierarchy. The house then mediates between the principles of alliance and descent, between attachment to territory and to 'blood'.

This argument can be admired for the imaginative way in which it directs attention to an institution that is undoubtedly of central importance in many human societies, but whose importance has been neglected in most studies of kinship and the family. By the same token, the evolutionary argument, although not fully developed by Lévi-Strauss himself, has been criticised by some of his contemporaries, who feel that this is too reminiscent of nineteenth century speculative hypotheses. He has also been criticised for continuing to assume that houses are composed primarily of biological families. But the notion of 'house societies' can provide us with a useful means of ordering the variety of ways in which human beings deal with their closest personal relationships, covering a wider range than the genealogical assumptions on which anthropological analysis has traditionally been based.

Frances Pine has provided a detailed analysis of the Polish rural house which fits well with Lévi-Strauss's analysis. she examines the case of the Górale, people who live in the upland region to the south of Cracow. Their villages are remote and, before the impact of tourism and other off-farm employment opportunities, they were very poor. Many Górale migrated to North America, but they usually kept in close contact with their relatives at home. The focus of this identity was not the kin group as a corporation, though lineages may have operated as patrilineal descent groups in the recent past. Rather, the principal focus of identity within the village was the house, which as in many other parts of rural Europe is 'both the minimal unit of social and kinship organization and a metaphor for correct social order.'[35] Persons were referred to by their 'house name' rather than the name that appeared on their birth certificate, and the traditional name for the land that they farmed might be different again. The most important criteria for establishing and maintaining house identity were living together and working together, not biological kinship. In a situation of land shortage, the distribution of persons and land was a matter of vital concern to all. Pine showed that when male successors were lacking a son-in-law would inherit the farm, or children might be adopted within the village. Servants, too, could be readily incorporated into the house, which was and remains the focus of considerable ritual activity.

This flexibility, like the systematic practice of adoption and fostering in many West African societies, might be explained by an economist as a rational adaptation which helps to ensure the optimum distribution of persons over the land. It is difficult, however, to see any evolutionary logic at work in this case. As in much of the rest of Galicia, Górale egalitarian inheritance practices by the early twentieth century had caused the average size of farm to fall to levels where it could barely provide families with a subsistence. The culture of the house was maladaptive in Darwinian terms. Pine eschews any evolutionist approach and, unlike Lévi-Strauss, does not see the house as a transitional social arrangement, which should disappear with the emergence of the state and the consolidation of more 'complex' forms of social organisation. She stresses instead the capacity of the house to endure and its proven compatibility with the very different forms of state régime that Poland has experienced over the last few decades. In the early communist period the house was the symbolic focus of opposition to a state which imposed massive restrictions on all independent activities, including the activities of the household. These controls were relaxed in the later communist years, when households had many opportunities to diversify their economic activities. In this period, and in the post-communist years, when many household members lost their off-farm jobs, the ideal or symbolic significance of the house corresponded to its role as the focus of material reproduction. The village house therefore continued to provide the principal ideological focus for Górale identity, both as ideal and as lived reality.

24 | CONTINGENT AND PRIMORDIAL IDENTITIES

Ethnicity and nationalism as extended kinship

In this part of the book we have explored a little of the variety of human kinship, marital and household arrangements. This variety persists in new ways in the contemporary world. The loyalties of kinship in the traditional familiar sense are of the utmost importance for the great majority of human beings, but it is preferable to approach kinship flexibly and it can be instructive to broaden the study of kinship away from biological foundations.

The question arises as to how far we should go in allowing extensions of kinship. The exploration is here extended to those quasi-sacred political forms of relatedness and belonging in the modern world, ethnicity and nationalism. We examine these because they seem to be the most powerful vehicles of social identity in the contemporary world, giving persons their most binding ties and orientations in the way that, for most of human history, those bearings have been supplied by kinship in some narrower sense. There is, of course, a link in that ethnicity and ethnic varieties of nationalism are normally modelled as extensions of an ideology of common descent. Ethnicity can be viewed as 'kinship writ large', as an extension of one's personal kindred that includes many more persons than one can possibly know personally, but which like a descent group has a clear boundary against the rest of the world.

All humans also have other forms of belonging, other forms of social identity with a claim on our attention, but these can be viewed as *contingent* in the sense that that they either derive from choices persons make, or from some principle that is felt to be less compelling than that of the *primordial* claims of kinship and ethnicity. We can illustrate with regard to the Nuer, whose segmentary lineage system we described in the context of 'acephalous' politics. Descent was not the only political principle at work in this society: residence, age grade, and religion were also significant. Yet it seems that the claims of descent were of exceptional strength, so that in situations of serious strife persons would leave their residential group and take up their position in a system of alliances defined by their genealogies. The position of the Nuer today, in a post-colonial context, dogged by decades of civil war, is very different. Many new economic, regional and religious sources of identity have appeared but the old kinship system has been not so much abandoned as dramatically extended. It seems that Nuer have now acquired something they did not have when studied by Evans-Pritchard in the 1930s, a strong sense of forming an ethnic group or nation, an identity for which they are prepared to fight and die. When familiar institutions disappear and economic life becomes difficult, as was very common in the wake of European colonialism and again recently in Eastern Europe after the collapse of communism, activating primordial ties seems to be a vital survival strategy.

The term primordial is easily misunderstood. We do not argue that the identities that people typically feel to have been characteristic of them 'since time immemorial' actually possess that quality of durability. On the contrary, these identities evolve through time and are therefore themselves highly contingent. A good many of them can be readily shown to be recent constructions, with anthropologists sometimes playing a part. But even in these cases people seem to need to believe in the antiquity of claims and in the priority of kin and co-ethnics. Primordial identities are the ones that generate the strongest forms of belonging, forms which seem 'natural', or at any rate so decisively fixed that their hold over the individual is extremely strong. Many Poles in the diaspora, from Chicago to Melbourne, from London to Buenos Aires, seem to feel their Polishness in this way.

'I say I'm Polish. And when they say, 'Oh, don't you speak good English!', that's when I tell them, 'well actually I was born over here. But I do consider myself Polish, basically because both my parents were Poles'. If people say, 'No, you're not Polish', I say – 'Look if a cat has kittens in an oven, they're not biscuits.'[36]

Ethnos derives from the ancient Greek word for 'people' or 'nation'. It was originally applied to one's own nation, but after a strange trajectory it is commonly applied nowadays to minorities, to 'others'. Anthropologists reject such usages and point out that majorities also have ethnicities. Fredrik Barth and others have shown that ethnic boundaries can be crossed and do not correspond precisely to cultural boundaries, although Barth has also suggested that the core values of a culture tend to endure, even in new conditions and with changing personnel. For Barth, ethnicity provides all of us with our 'basic, most general identity'.

The connotations of the term ethnic have led some anthropologists to discard it in much the same way that others have discarded tribe. They prefer to speak only of national identities, but nation is nowadays usually taken to imply a separate state and this does not apply to all peoples aspiring to some form of collective recognition, perhaps as a 'culture'. Most therefore continue to use ethnicity as well as nationalism, recognising that the linking of states to a genealogically constructed ethnic community has been much stronger in some parts of the world than others. It has had particularly dire consequences in recent years in the Balkans where, in conditions of political uncertainty, élites have been able to mobilise large populations that had previously lived in peace alongside one another into campaigns of horrifying inter-ethnic violence. Conflicts have been especially brutal when an ethnic boundary coincided with a religious boundary. In multiethnic, multifaith communities, some people turned on their close neighbours and slaughtered them.

Can human societies dispense with primordial loyalties of this kind? It is important to maintain a balanced perspective and to note that, while some migrants and refugees develop a heightened appreciation of their 'roots', which they may then re-import to their places of origin, many others follow paths of integration and even assimilation in their new locations. Many Polish emigrants and their descendants have followed the latter courses, so that they nowadays feel an American or British patriotism rather than Polishness. Multicultural policies are usually intended to facilitate the consolidation of compromise, 'hyphenated' identities, such as Polish-American. In practice, knowledge of the minority language and culture often proves difficult to sustain. Attempts to promote it more actively can lead to tensions with the dominant culture. On the other hand, strict insistence by powerholding groups on recognising the cultural rights of minorities may also lead to difficulties, if in practice this multiculturalism entrenches ghetto-like segregation and inhibits the mobility of the members of disadvantaged groups. Such dilemmas arise not only as a result of large-scale migration. They are inherent wherever the modern state recognises cultural minorities; for example the many small indigenous peoples recognised by communist nationality policies in China and the former Soviet Union.

Many contemporary German intellectuals, reacting against the extremes to which primordialism led their predecessors, have consciously rejected notions of 'blood and soil' (*Blut und Boden*) as the basis of their nation. Some reject any cultural or emotional basis for national sentiment, upholding instead only 'constitutionalism patriotism'. But is it possible to build a genuine community and solidarity on the basis of a rational constitution and the *Rechtsstaat*? Some anthropologists are similarly committed to transcending territorial attachments and all particularist forms of community. Instead they declare their allegiance to universal human rights but whether it will ever be possible to transfer the principle of 'kinship writ large' to this level seems most doubtful. For the time being such declarations have little emotional force. The reality is that, at least for most of us, primordial loyalties are too powerful and they pull us in a different direction.

Age

Age provides a criterion for the formation of groups that deserves special attention because, although given by birth, it can in practice work to mitigate the ties that we have been describing as primordial. For example, if all the children in a multiethnic village or town go to school together and form enduring ties based on their age grade, this should counter other tendencies confining those children within their separate religious and ethnic communities. In practice, however, the age-based associations are very often formed within these communities and they may play an important role in strengthening those identities, for example when secret knowledge is transmitted in the course of elaborate initiation ceremonies. In several East African societies, such as the Borana of southern Ethiopia, 'age classes' are the dominant structures of a non-centralised political system. While the elders enjoy high prestige and are deferred to at tribal assemblies, much *de facto* power is delegated to younger men in the 'warrior' grade.

Age is also a significant principle for alliance and group formation in modern European societies, including Carpathian villages, where patterns of local violence dictated by young men who had finished school but not yet established their own household were still common in the mid-1950s. Malinowski mentioned these *bijaki* as examples of socially regulated aggression and of course this is not just a phenomenon of backward villages. Similar gangs exist in cities like London or Chicago. Loyalty to an age gang often lasts throughout one's lifetime, although the implications for actual behaviour may change as the years go by and members acquire other social commitments: i.e. they become husbands and fathers.

Associations, local and global

Quite different from groups based on kinship and age are those which a person is free to join and leave at any time. Voluntary associations are well documented in most forms of society, even some of the technologically more simple. Most hunter gatherers are not tied to a strong ideology of descent and, while kinship links normally dominate, there is a lot of flexibility in the formation of informal alliances and partnerships. In agricultural and industrial societies the opportunities for special-interest economic, religious and recreational groups are legion. As property in land and territoriality are consolidated, locality becomes a powerful source of identity. Occupational identities may be inherited or acquired by a lengthy process of apprenticeship, or they may be freely chosen by the individual. However, specialised work seldom acquires the quality of primordiality, except in cases where occupation is overlain with extra layers of custom and ritual, as in the Hindu caste system.

Voluntary associations in contemporary Europe would include the clubs, charitable foundations and non-governmental organisations that, as we saw in Chapter 11, constitute the essence of a pluralist democracy for the theoreticians of 'civil society'. They must also include a spectrum of 'subcultures', some of them approximating movements we might classify as religious sects, others uniting behind the mass-produced memorabilia of a big football club or a particular musical style, still others extracting a positive message from political rhetoric that may be far from democratic. Some people join Amnesty International and some their local Rotary Club, but others are attracted to skinhead bands. These last have sometimes been termed 'neo-tribes' but this is to give a misleading impression of tribal identity, to imply that the prime purpose of the tribe was always mobilisation for aggressive purposes. In any case there is little evidence that these 'neo-tribes' form lasting alternatives to the loyalties of kinship and ethnicity.

The role and scope of voluntary associations have increased with social complexity and the mobility of people, goods and knowledge that we have noted as the hallmark of accelerating globalisation. Transnational social movements and human rights organisations monitor the activities of global political actors and business enterprises. In every field of culture from religion to cuisine, from music to body decoration, one can select the traits one likes and, in most cases, find people with whom to discuss the enthusiasm via the internet. However, again there is little sign that such new associations can substitute for primordial loyalties. Many theorists have pointed out how local identities are reaffirmed and even strengthened in the course of globalisation. With some exceptions, among whom anthropologists may be overrepresented, the flux of international movement is no substitute for the pleasures of the homeland, the security of an intimacy that is grounded ultimately in the persons to whom one is tied from birth and in cultural ideas such as *Blut und Boden*.

Cross-cutting ties

Beginning with the ties of kinship, we have moved on to sketch other significant forms of social identity. The important question is how to put these together. Each person is likely to belong to numerous different groups and play a variety of social roles, and therefore to have a number of different social identities. We need to know how these identities reinforce each other, and to be especially sensitive to antagonistic combinations. Kinship and ethnicity may have some ultimate priority but they do not prevail over other ties in all contexts.

One influential approach, associated particularly with Max Gluckman and the 'Manchester school' in British social anthropology, concentrates on 'cross-cutting ties'. In contrast to those contemporaries who emphasised the determining structures of segmentary political systems, Gluckman was more concerned to engage with micro-level compexity. He noted, for example, that intermarriage, economic mobility and religious pluralism would all generate complex patterns of alliance which, taken together, reduce the likelihood of violent conflict. His functionalist assumption that some sort of cohesion always prevails has been rejected by later anthropologists. They tend to be especially uncomfortable with some of his southern African illustrations. For Gluckman in the 1950s, cross-cutting ties helped to explain why blacks in South Africa were not mounting effective opposition to the white minority. It is interesting to speculate how he might have adjusted his theory in the later years of the *apartheid* system, when violent conflict increased significantly. At any rate, the basic idea of cross-cutting ties has remained popular in an age when most anthropologists prefer to stress the range of options open to individual decision takers, rather than to see their actions as determined by external structures. Gluckman's idea can be more readily reconciled with those postmodern approaches that emphasise the plasticity of all identities, and continuous flux in their adoption and in their demise.

But does the existence of cross-cutting ties in fact conduce to lower levels of antagonism and violence? The existence of an orthodox Albanian minority did not prevent orthodox Serbs from pursuing ruthless policies against all Albanians in Kosovo. Violence in the wars of Yugoslav Succession generally does not seem to have been contained at lower levels in those districts where there was most ethnic intermingling – rather the contrary. The fact that many blacks shared a common religion with whites did not in the end suffice to prevent a major escalation of violence in the South African context, and arguably the apartheid regime could not have been toppled otherwise. Antagonisms existed not only between black and white but also between different groups within each 'racial' category, and these sometimes had terrible consequences in the 'ethnicisation' of politics which took place in the 1990s. In a paradoxical manner, the idea of 'separate cultures' which underpinned *apartheid* have been substantiated in the post-*apartheid* years.

A complex situation in which kinship and ethnicity do not neatly correspond has been analysed by Günther Schlee in Northern Kenya where pastoral groups have, principally by oral transmission, maintained detailed genealogies over many generations. Here the 'call of kinship' seems quite exceptionally strong, even in cases where no precise genealogical knowledge is available. One clan among the Rendille, although resembling other Rendille in language and virtually all other cultural practices, is known to have been founded some three centuries ago by a captive Gabbra. A strong principle of patrilinearity means that, after all this time of living with and intermarrying with Rendille, the people of this group are still Gabbra in terms of their 'most basic' identity, although they are Rendille in some more general cultural sense. Conflicts between these adjacent peoples have a long history. They have reached new levels of violence in the 1990s, particularly due to the availability of weapons following the disintegration of state systems in Ethiopia and Somalia. The Gabbra had easier access to these weapons. In these conflicts, some Rendille exploited their clan ties to join Gabbra, but this did not prevent the violence. Schlee found, on the contrary, that residential intermingling served only to facilitate patterns of revenge killing, while acknowledgement of a clan tie to an enemy group had negative repercussions for continuing good relationships with the rest of one's own ethnic community.

The depressing conclusion in this Rendille-Gabbra case is that the cross-cutting ties failed to preserve peace and cohesion, and may actually have accentuated opposite tendencies. If this argument can be generalised, the implication is that increasing fragmentation of identities in the course of globalisation is not in itself any reason to be optimistic about the prospects for peace and social cohesion. If claims rooted in kinship are prioritised in this way and backed up by the means of destruction, the potential of other forms of social identity to defuse conflict through cross-cutting ties cannot be realised.

SUMMARY OF PART V

Anthropological approaches to kinship were initially built on speculative evolutionist hypotheses. These have been mostly abandoned, although Lévi-Strauss has recently argued that the house is the main principle of social organisation in a specific transitional phase of evolution between what he terms elementary and complex systems.

Twentieth-century ethnographers have shown in their field studies how kinship is the dominating principle in the social organisation of tribal societies. Kinship loses this role in modern conditions, although the 'domestic domain' remains important, as feminist work on gender differences has shown. Ideas about micro levels of relatedness continue to have far-reaching consequences for the whole of social organisation, not only in the roles that family members play in the running of businesses and the transmission of property but also when close economic relationships with non-kin are described in the idiom of kinship. This raises the question of what exactly we mean by kinship. Some have insisted on grounding it in awareness of biological universals, while others have pointed out that local models of biology vary greatly and insisted on prioritising the local models. Interesting examples include 'milk siblings', where persons are considered to have a special relationship as a result of suckling from the same woman, and spiritual kinship (godparenthood), where no bodily substances are involved at all.

We also considered the alleged universality of the household, the family, marriage and the incest taboo. Much hinges on the definitions we use and cross-cultural comparisons pose so many problems that most anthropologists have abandoned them. Households form the material micro-units of all societies. Their structure must be studied dynamically, since size and composition change as the persons in them proceed through their lifecourses. When we study family we are concerned more with moral norms, with the ideology or culture that shapes and determines how people are recruited into households.

No known society tolerates free sexual access within family groups and this taboo has been held by Lévi-Strauss to be the fundamental defining moment of human culture. Once again, however, there is so much cultural variation in extensions of the taboo, not to speak of patterns of aversion among some other primates, that all generalisations are open to criticism. Marriage can be defined in terms of the union of a woman and some socially recognised partner to produce legitimate offspring; but social trends and innovations in reproductive technologies are undermining all our traditional, biologically grounded notions of marriage and the family.

Although kinship in the traditional sense plays a reduced role in contemporary societies, we suggested that relations considered to be primordial (whether actually very old or not) have a continuing potential to dominate over other ties, such as those based on common age or on voluntary affiliation. Ethnicity and nationalism can in this sense be viewed as extensions of kinship as well as forms of secular religion. In all societies, whether dominated by kinship or by its modern extensions, ethnicity and nationalism, multiple principles of identity constantly intersect or 'cross-cut' each other. We do not as yet have a general theory to predict when such cross-cutting will lead to the defusion of conflict and when appeal to a primordial tie is likely to trigger violence.

Part VI
CONCLUSION

25 | ANTHROPOLOGICAL EDUCATION

Holism and 'total social facts'

By now, it should be clear what we mean when we say that social anthropology aims to be holistic. Of course it would be possible to devise a project which concentrated on, say, the economic aspects of life in a community in Poland. But economic decisions can have complex motivations and need to be understood in their context. We need some knowledge of political conditions in order to understand continuing peasant grievances. We need knowledge of the history of ethnic relations to understand why some people feel aggrieved about the loss of certain rights. The rich symbolism of Polish Catholicism has been modified over time and the church as an institution is in a quite different situation nowadays from that in which it found itself under communism. A study of its symbols and rituals is bound to reflect these changes, at any rate if it concerns itself with how these are now practised and understood by Polish people. It is possible to imagine an investigation, perhaps one that aimed to find the deeper logic of these symbols, that did not depend on fieldwork at all, since all the data could be readily accessed in books or even from the internet. But that would not be a social anthropological study, as we define the discipline.

The goal of holism is elusive: as academics we have to divide things up, impose discontinuities, where ideally we would always be emphasising the connections. However the fourfold division that we have followed is not our arbitrary creation. The branches of economic anthropology, political anthropology, religion and kinship have been well established in teaching and research for a long time. You might feel that subdivisions of this kind undermine the aspiration to holistic social analysis. Rather than thinking of 'subsystems' of social life it may be much better to think of all social behaviour as having four different *aspects* or *dimensions* to it. The economic aspect is the attribution of *rationality* in human decision taking. Defined in this way, the economic dimension extends well beyond our work and market relationships. But these decisions are made in social contexts, above all contexts of *power* relationships, which is where the political dimension comes in. We must also recognise the tremendous significance of a *symbolic* dimension of social life, in the most advanced capitalist societies as among the simplest societies of food collectors. Finally, we are always concerned with the collective *identities* of the human beings whose social behaviour we study.

In short, the fieldworker must be sensitive to the specific temporal and spatial coordinates of the object of the research, and to all the complex interactions that take place between the fields that we have carved out as 'subsystems' of social relations. We have not the space in this volume to address other possible subsystems and many topics have had to be ignored. It is possible nowadays to speak of 'the anthropology of' just about anything at all. Usually this means little more than the use of ethnographic methods to understand some aspect of social life in a holistic way. However, branches such as medical anthropology and environmental anthropology have developed into exciting branches of study in their own right. They are useful to policymakers trying to solve contemporary social problems, and yet they connect back to central intellectual issues in the development of the discipline.

Malinowski's holistic project was tremendously ambitious, perhaps over-ambitious since he never managed to write a single synthesising study to spell out all the connections that mattered in the case of the Trobriand Islanders. Anyway, it may not be such a good idea to emphasise holism if it leads us to assume that all the connections must be positive and harmonious. This is a standard criticism of all versions of functionalism. But there is no need to assume harmony. It ought to be possible to carry out holistic studies and be sensitive to conflicts and contradictions, in accordance with the precepts of Marxist and other non-functionalist approaches.

The deeper problem with holistic approaches is that they force us to focus on bounded units, for only in this way, by defining a bounded whole, can we proceed to show how all the parts either fit together or become entangled in relations of contradiction or whatever. The holistic approach leads us willy nilly to Malinowski's strong notion of culture. He didn't only see the Trobrianders as 'a culture'. He applied the same model to his native Poland, and indeed to the entire world. But was there in his lifetime a unique Polish culture to which all speakers of Polish belonged and with which they identified? Some evidence suggests that the distinctiveness is actually rather new, that in the nineteenth century the Polish speaking peasant and the Ukrainian-speaking peasant had far more in common culturally than either could ever share with a university intellectual from Cracow. Malinowski was careful to distinguish his cultural nationalism from any form of political nationalism, but it seems to me that even cultural nationalism should be highly suspect. After all it accepts the nationalist's basic assumption, when this is what anthropology should be challenging.

Other schools in anthropology also encountered this problem. In particular, the Durkheimian emphasis upon society is open to some of the same objections as the Malinowskian concept of culture. There is, however, in the rich heritage of the Durkheimian school, an idea that can help us to answer the objections. Mauss described the gift as an example of a 'total social fact' because of the way it linked economic transactions to political relations and reaffirmed the identity of groups. The boundaries of these collectivities are real enough, but they are all part of a larger encompassing system. The 'total social fact' provides insight into a general principle of social order, in which the economic cannot be distinguished from the political, or the religious from the legal. In this sense Mauss is holistic, but he draws our attention to phenomena of central significance without requiring us to view culture or society itself as a self-sufficient totality. Try to think of equivalent examples of 'total social facts' from your own social experience.

The uses of anthropology

Anthropological knowledge can have very pragmatic uses. It is not a substitute for the precise technical skills of engineers, soil scientists etc. but it can facilitate the optimum deployment, or the 'translation' of scientific knowledge into different cultural settings. It can also help outside 'experts' to appreciate local knowledge, not only for solving 'technical' problems in the local environment but also for its own sake, as a cultural value. Happily, it seems that recognition of the usefulness of anthropology in this sense has increased more or less continuously since Malinowski made the case for 'applied anthropology' in the 1920s. Nowadays many anthropologists are employed by governmental and international bodies such as the World Bank. Their expertise in sensitive observation can also be focused on bureaucratic organisations, including those which employ them. This can both extend our knowledge of how such institutions work and increase their efficiency. It follows that to invest in anthropological expertise may be a smart decision for a rational profit-maximising corporation as well as for governments and non-governmental organisations.

The basic point does not apply only to remote places with traditions very different from European societies. Anthropological enquiries can also make a real difference in post-socialist Eastern Europe. For example, work on the new minorities taking shape in the big cities might help to ensure better inter-cultural understanding than has been achieved so far in Britain, France and Germany. In the rural context, anthropological work could be highly relevant to the decisions taken in Brussels on European farm policy, or at least to mitigating their effects for millions of European peasants.

Anthropologists may also be able to give advice on the causes and the motivations behind violent conflicts. Malinowski believed that warfare was yet another field to which the anthropologist might make a distinctive contribution. Where he spoke of nationality conflicts we are likely nowadays to speak of 'ethnic cleansing', but the patterns of behaviour have not changed so much. Anthropologists can help to explain this behaviour and its evocation through the use of myths and symbols. They can point out the contingent nature of the groups that engage in violent conflict and their long-term inderdependencies with their opponents, and this is very important at times when the groups' own representations emphasise the opposite. In cases such as this there is a need to go beyond the 'local model'.

Of course, many applications of anthropological knowledge involve simplification. The consultant who prepares a report on a development project usually has to gloss over at least some elements of the internal diversity among the people affected by the project. Such simplification may be justified if it leads to outcomes that all observers may agree are better than those which would occur without any anthropological input at all, but many people might wonder why anthropologists should favour intervention in the first place, if they are associated with the study of human diversity. It is confusing if people think anthropologists are actively engaged in efforts to 'modernise' and 'develop' people in remote parts of the world if this is understood to mean making them more like ourselves. Indeed, whatever Malinowski may have written about the importance of 'applied anthropology', he did not do much of it himself. In their heart of hearts, most social anthropologists want to keep people different, not make them more like each other.

Cultural diversity and human rights

Whatever they are, nowadays cultures do not correspond neatly to nations and territories. There are many kinds of cultural diversity, not only the sort that we call ethnic. Ethnic and national groups are very important forms of identity in the contemporary world, but cannot form no more than a subset of culture. There is much confusion here, and colleagues in other disciplines often criticise anthropologists for defending cultural practices which they find abhorrent. They take phenomena such as female circumcision, which the great majority of people in Europe and America reject though it is culturally valued by many people in Africa, and they say: anthropologists want to sustain barbaric customs. That is nonsense, but it can never be the business of anthropologists to condemn practices which have evolved as part of a people's cultural tradition. That is what the British colonisers used to do before the impact of anthropology, in their ignorance of local custom. Since Malinowski we have done better than this and even clitoridectomy deserves to be assessed in its cultural context. Above all, we can promote dialogues. The more that African women discuss issues with their European and American sisters, the more likely it is that changes will take place. Change can then take the form of adaptations, rather than the destruction of cultures, and westerners may learn as much from African women as vice versa.

Anthropology does not have a ready answer to every controversial moral issue that comes along. On issues such as the new reproductive technologies, experiments on animals or euthenasia, and many other issues, anthropologists can be found in almost every corner of the more general arena of debate. But this does not matter. The important thing is to be able to have the debates, to understand how people quite different from ourselves might view the issue, and to probe the local models behind all the arguments brought forward. These are the principles that should underpin all levels of anthropological education, and some anthropologists argue that the subject should be more widely taught in schools as well as in universities.

The danger remains, however, that the study of anthropology is still widely linked to the exotic, to romantic notions of primitive folk at home with nature, and so on. The anthropologists are perceived as keepers of a human zoo. Malinowski warned of the dangers of this a long time ago:

> Obviously the anthropologist must not appear merely as… the clown of social science, amusing the symposium with anecdotes on cannibalism or head-hunting, on preposterous magical rites or quaint war dances.[37]

Exoticism blends easily with notions of the world as made up of bounded blocks, or stones in a mosaic. Accelerating globalisation is increasing many people's preoccupation with identity and fostering this sense of boundedness in their consciousness, even when it is being undermined in the daily reality of their lives. People somehow want to believe that, even if we are all vaguely much the same nowadays, there was a time not so long ago when cultures were built on deep and genuinely radical difference. And it is indeed the case that some, anthropologists, especially those of the cultural anthropology school, have exaggerated differences, and understated commonalities.

In other words the anthropologist's concept of culture, as it has developed over the last two centuries or so, is too close for comfort to the way that nationalist ideologies have developed over the same period. It is a mistake, and politically a very dangerous one, to divide up the people of the world like this. At worst, as with Serbian national myths about Kosovo, this can provide the justification for ethnic cleansing. But it is now well documented that even well-intentioned 'multicultural' régimes such as those of Scandinavia did not do immigrants any favours by classifying them as possessed of a unique and distinct *culture*. In practice this policy masked processes of discrimination and subordination, particularly of women.

Of course anthropologists do not mean to use the word culture in this sense. They are well aware that cultures do not conform tidily to social and political units, but it is this distorted view that is now widely accepted. The more subtle, *processual* arguments of anthropologists are not very effective in public debates. Perhaps the term has outlined its scientific usefulness. Does it really make sense to talk of 'the culture of Buddhism', or the 'culture of communism'? This is hardly any better than the sort of sloppy ephemeral usage that you can find in newspaper articles, for example on the 'culture of political correctness in western society' or the 'enterprise culture'. Moreover, it is impossible to maintain that only humans have culture, for it is now well demonstrated that many animals also pass on information in complex, non-genetic ways. Pascal Boyer therefore concludes as follows.

> By dispensing with the ontologically vague, quasi-mystical notion of 'culture,' it is possible to have a clearer understanding of these two types of causal structures that are likely to account for particular cultural phenomena, namely the biological history of the species... and the historical history of human groups.[38]

Om the other hand, are these sufficient reasons for abandoning the concept of 'culture' altogether? We still have no better term to grasp all that human beings create beyond that which is required by the factors of biology and environment. We have no better term for recognising and describing the diversity of human populations than to speak of differences in culture. It is both indispensable for our *external* analyses and an encapsulation of *local* models of group difference which pre-date modern forms of ethnicity and nationalism and have always been basic to human social life.

So, to conclude, what is social anthropology and what are its prospects at the turn of the millennium? We have tried to show how the discipline has developed, and to set this intellectual history in the context of more general processes, notably the rise and fall of colonial empires and intensifying globalisation. This is, in a sense, to apply the anthropological approach to social anthropology itself: the bottom line is that everything must be understood in its full context.

Perhaps the best definition is that social anthropology is whatever the people who call themselves social anthropologists do. As we have seen, they pursue a tremendous variety of research directions, but there is a common core. It consists on the one hand of an appreciation of both the unity and the cultural diversity of the human species and on the other of a commitment to fieldwork methods. The work of Malinowski in the Trobriand Islands was one of the pioneering contributions to this subject. Anthropology has matured since his era. Its applicability to all human communities, not only to the exotic 'other', is no longer just a pious declaration, it is reality.

Having said this, we nonetheless make the following practical suggestion. Before you undertake anthropological research in a setting with which you have some personal familiarity, for example, because you yourself were brought up in the same country, it helps if you have some experience of tackling a project in an unfamiliar setting. Of course there are many degrees of familiarity. Often the linguistic factor is more important than spatial location. The challenge of mastering a language quite different not only from your native tongue but also from others related to it, can itself take you a long way to acquiring the perspective of an anthropologist, and help you to prepare for applying this perspective later in other settings.

> The whole difficulty and art of fieldwork consists of starting from those elements which are familiar in the foreign culture and gradually working the strange and diverse into a comprehensible scheme. In this the learning of a foreign culture is like the learning of a foreign tongue: at first mere assimilation and crude translation, at the end a complete detachment from the original medium and a mastery of the new one.[39]

There is one final pragmatic reason why European anthropologists should give priority to the study of societies and languages remote from their own. That is the simple fact that, compared to what is known and meticulously documented for virtually all regions of Europe, our knowledge of the immense creative diversity of many regions of this planet is still rather limited. There are no 'savages' left to be discovered and wherever he or she works the anthropologist is likely to encounter other outsiders – businessmen, missionaries, peacekeeping soldiers, tourists, journalists and so on. But none of these can generate the knowledge that results from anthropological fieldwork.

NOTES

[1] Tylor, E. *Primitive Culture: researches into the development of mythology, philosophy, religion, language, art and custom*, London, Murray, 1871, p.1.

[2] Firth, R. 'The sceptical anthropologist? Social anthropology and Marxist views on society' in M. Bloch (ed.) *Marxist Analyses and Social Anthropology*, London, Malaby Press, 1975, pp. 29–60.

[3] Malinowski, B. *Argonauts of the Western Pacific: an account of native enterprise and adventure in the archipelagoes of Melanesia New Guinea*, London, Routledge, 1922, p. 25.

[4] Malinowski, B. *Coral Gardens and Their Magic: a study of the methods of filling the soil and of agricultural rites in the Trobriand Islands*, vol. 1, Appendix, London: Allen & Unwin; 1935.

[5] Malinowski, B. *Freedom and Civilization*, New York, Roy, 1994

[6] Maitland, F.W. *The Collected Papers of Frederic William Maitland, Downing Professor of the Laws of England*, vol. 3 Cambridge, Cambridge University Press, 1911, p. 295

[7] Kroeber, A.L. *Anthropology; cultural processes and patterns*, New York, Harcourt, Brace and Jovanovich, 1943, p. xiii.

[8] Malinowski. B. 'Tribal male associations in Australia' in R. Thornton and P. Skalnik (eds.), *The Early Writings of Bronislaw Malinowski*, Cambridge, Cambridge University Press, 1993, p. 206.

[9] Robbins, L. *An Essay on the Nature and Significance of Economic Science*, London, Macmillan & Co., 1932.

[10] Firth, R. *Primitive Polynesian Economy*, London: 1965 (1st edn), London, Routledge, 1939, p. 13.

[11] Polanyi, K. 'The economy as instituted process', in K. Polanyi, C. Arensberg and H. Pearson (eds) *Trade and Market in the Early Empires*, Glencoe, IL, Free Press, 1957

[12] Marx, K. *Preface to the Contribution to the Critique of Political Economy*, London, 1857.

[13] Gudeman, S. and Rivera, A. *Conversations in Colombia*, Cambridge, Cambridge University Press, 1990, p. 189.

[14] Malinowski, B. *Coral Gardens and Their Magic*, London, Allen & Unwin, 1935, p. x

[15] Sahlins, M. *Stone Age Economics*, Chicago and New York: Aldine, Atherton, 1972, Ch. 3.

[16] Donham, D. *History, Power, Ideology; central issues in Marxism and anthropology*, Cambridge, Cambridge University Press, 1990.

[17] Evans-Pritchard, E.E. *The Nuer. A description of the modes of livelihood and political institutions of a Nilotic people*. Oxford, Clarendon Press, 1940, p. 144.

[18] Malinowski, B. 'An anthropological analysis of war' in *Magic, Science and Religion and Other Essays*, Boston, MA, Beacon Press; 1948, pp. 289–90, 299.

[19] ibid., p. 308

[20] Hoebel, E.A, *Anthropology*, New York, McGraw-Hill, 1996, p. 440.

[21] Hasluck, M. *The Unwritten Law in Albania*, London, Cambridge University Press, 1954.

[22] ibid., p. 266

[23] Malinowski, B. 'Myth in primitive psychology' in *Magic, Science and Religion and Other Essays*, Glencoe, IL, Free Press, pp. 72–124, at p. 122.

[24] Geertz, C. Negara: *the theatre state in nine-teenth century Bali*, Princeton, NJ, Princeton University Press, 1980. p. 13.

[25] Malinowski, B. 'Totemism and exogamy' in R. Thornton and P. Skalnik (eds.), *The Early Writings of Bronislaw Malinowski*, Cambridge, Cambridge University Press, 1950, p. 166.

[26] Malinowski, B. *Magic Science and Religion and Other Essays*, Boston, Beacon Press, 1948, p. 1.

[27] Geertz, C. 'Religion as a cultural system' in M. Banton (ed.) *Anthropological Approaches to Religion*, London, Tavistock, 1966, p. 4.

[28] Douglas, M. 'Purity and Danger'. Cited in M. Stewart, *The Time of the Gypsies*, Boulder, CL Westview Press, 1997, p. 204.

[29] Kertzer, D.I. *Ritual, Politics and Power*, New Haven, CT, Yale University Press, 1988, p. 76.

[30] Leach, E., *Culture and Communication*, Cambridge, Cambridge University Press, 1976, p. 78.

[31] Lewis, G. *Day of Shining Red; an essay on understanding ritual*, Cambridge, Cambridge University Press, 1980, p. 198.

[32] Radcliffe-Brown A.R. 'Introduction' in A. R. Radcliffe-Brown and D. Forde (eds.), *African Systems of Kinship and Marriage*, London, Oxford University Press, 1950, p. 13.

[33] Malinowski, B. *The Father in Primitive Psychology*, London, Trench & Trubner, 1927, p. 7.

[34] Leach, E. *Social Anthropology*, London, Fontana, 1982, pp. 210–11.

[35] Pine, F. 'Naming the house and naming the land: kinship and social groups in highland Poland', *Journal of the Royal Anthropological Institute*, 1996 2 (3), 443–60.

[36] Anonymous interviewee, quoted in K. Sword, *Identity in Flux. The Polish Community in Britain*, London, School of Slavonic and East European Studies, 1966, p. 224.

[37] Malinowski, B. 'An anthropological analysis of war' in *Magic, Science and Religion and Other Essays*, Boston MA, Beacon Press, 1948, p. 277.

[38] Boyer, P. *The Naturalness of Religious Ideas: a cognitive theory of religion*, Berkeley: University of California Press, 1994, p. 296.

[39] Malinowski, B. *The Sexual Life of Savages in North-Western Melanesia*, London, Routledge, 1929, p. xxi.

ACKNOWLEDGEMENTS

I wrote most of this book during a Fellowship at the Wissenschaftskolleg zu Berlin in 1997–1999. To write an introductory book at an Institute for Advanced Study must have seemed an odd undertaking to my colleagues there, although they were too polite to say so. In fact, being away from familiar libraries and enjoying the company of Fellows with very different backgrounds helped a great deal, as did contacts with numerous Berlin colleagues in *Ethnologie* and *europäische Ethnologie*. I must especially thank Ray Abrahams, Raymond Firth, Chris Gregory, Ildi Hann, Zdzislaw Mach, Frances Pine, Günther Schlee, Michael Stewart and anonymous reviewers for making helpful comments on parts of an earlier draft.

From Berlin it is but an overnight train journey to Cracow, so it has been easy for me to renew contacts with a city and university that I have known since the 1970s. Social anthropology is securely established in Malinowski's *alma mater*, which is hosting the biennial conference of the European Association of Social Anthropologists in the last year of the second Christian millennium.

CH
Halle, December 1999

FURTHER READING

PART I

Chapter 1

General reference works

T. Barfield (ed.), *Dictionary of Anthropology* (Oxford, Blackwell, 1997)

A. Barnard and J. Spencer (eds.), *Encyclopedia of Anthropology* (London, Routledge, 1996)

T. Ingold (ed.), *Companion Encyclopedia of Anthropology* (London, Routledge, 1994)

Chapter 2

M. Bloch, *Marxism and Anthropology; the history of a relationship* (Oxford, Clarendon Press, 1983)

J. Clifford and G. Marcus (eds.), *Writing Culture; the poetics and politics of ethnography* (Berkeley, CA, University of California Press, 1986)

R.Ellen, E. Gellner, G. Kubica and J. Mucha (eds.), *Malinowski Between Two Worlds; the Polish roots of an anthropological tradition* (Cambridge, Cambridge University Press, 1988)

C. Geertz, *Works and Lives; the anthropologist as author* (Cambridge, Polity Press, 1988)

A. Kuper, *Anthropology and Anthropologists; the modern British School,* 3rd edn (London, Routledge, 1996); *The Invention of Primitive Society; transformations of an illusion* (London, Routledge, 1988)

E. Leach, *Claude Lévi-Strauss* (London, Fontana, 1970)

G. Marcus and M. Fischer, *Anthropology as Cultural Critique; an experimental moment in the human sciences* (Chicago, IL, University of Chicago Press, 1986)

H. Moore, *Feminism and Anthropology* (Cambridge, Polity Press, 1988)

Chapter 3

F. Engels, *The Origins of the Family, Private Property and the State* (Harmondsworth, Penguin, 1985)

J. Friedman, *Cultural Identity and Global Process* (London, Sage, 1994)

E. Gellner, *Plough, Sword and Book; The structure of human history* (London, Collins Harvill, 1988)

A. Jackson (ed.), *Anthropology at Home* (London, Tavistock, 1987)

W. G. Runciman, *The Evolution of Society* (London, Routledge, 1997)

Chapter 4

R. Ellen (ed.), *Ethnographic Research; a guide to general conduct* (London, Academic Press, 1984)

E. Evans-Pritchard, *The Nuer: A description of the modes of livelihood and political institutions of a Nilotic people* (Oxford, Clarendon Press, 1940)

S. Hutchinson, *Nuer Dilemmas; coping with money, war and the state*, (Berkeley, CA, University of California Press, 1996)

Z. Mach, *Symbols, Conflict and Identity* (Albany, NY, State University of New York Press, 1993)

PART II

General reference works

S. Narotzky, *New Directions in Economic Anthropology* (London, Pluto, 1997)

S. Plattner (ed.), *Economic Anthropology* (Stanford, CA, Stanford University Press, 1989)

R. Wilk, *Economies and Cultures; foundations of economic anthropology* (Boulder, CL, Westview Press, 1996).

Chapter 5

M. Bloch (ed.), *Marxist Analyses and Social Anthropology* (London, Malaby Press, 1975)

R. Firth, *Primitive Polynesian Economy* (London, Routledge, 1939)

R. Firth (ed.), *Themes in Economic Anthropology*, (London, Tavistock, 1967)

M. Godelier, *Perspectives in Marxist Anthropology* (Cambridge, Cambridge University Press, 1977)

S. Gudeman, *Economics as Culture; models and metaphors of livelihood* (London, Routledge & Kegan Paul, 1986)

S. Gudeman and A. Rivera, *Conversations in Colombia; the domestic economy in life and text* (Cambridge, Cambridge University Press, 1990)

B. Malinowski, *Coral Gardens and Their Magic* (London, Allen & Unwin, 1935)

B. Malinowski, *Argonauts of the Western Pacific* (London, Routledge & Kegan Paul, 1978)

K. Polanyi, C. Arensberg and H. Pearson (eds.), *Trade and Market in the Early Empires; economies in history and theory* (Glencoe, IL, Free Press, 1957)

Chapter 6

N. Bird-David, 'Beyond the hunting and gathering mode of subsistence: observations on the Nayaka and other modern hunter-gatherers', *Man*, 1992, vol. 27, no. 1, pp. 19–44

S. Day, E. Papataxiarchis and M. Stewart (eds.), *Lilies of the Field; marginal people who live for the moment* (Boulder, CL, Westview, 1999)

K. Hart, 'Informal income opportunities and urban employment in Ghana', *Journal of Modern African Studies*, 1973, vol. 11, no. 1, pp. 61–89

K. Hart, *The Political Economy of West African Agriculture* (Cambridge, Cambridge University Press, 1982)

M. Holmstrom, *Industry and Inequality; the social anthropology of indian labour* (Cambridge, Cambridge University Press, 1984)

L. Howe, *Being Unemployed in Northern Ireland; an ethnographic study* (Cambridge, Cambridge University Press, 1990)

M. Sahlins, *Stone Age Economics* (London, Tavistock, 1974)

D. Thorner, B. Kerblay, R. E. F. Smith, *A. V. Chayanov on the Theory of Peasant Economy* (Manchester, Manchester University Press, 1986)

J. Woodburn, 'Egalitarian Societies', *Man,* 1982, vol. 17, no. 4, pp. 431–451

Chapter 7

P. Bohannan and L. Bohannan, *Tiv Economy* (London, Longman, 1968)

P. Bohannan and G. Dalton, *Markets in Africa* (Evanstone, IL, Northwestern University Press, 1961)

J. Carrier (ed.), *A Critique of the Market Concept* (Oxford, Berg, 1997)

G. Dalton, 'Primitive Money' in *American Anthropologist,* 1965, vol. 67, pp. 44–65

G. Dalton (ed.), *Tribal and Peasant Economies* (Austin, TX, University of Texas Press, 1976)

J. Davis, *Exchange* (Milton Keynes, Open University Press, 1992)

R. Dilley (ed.), *Contesting Markets; analyses of ideology, dicourse and practice* (Edinburgh, Edinburgh University Press, 1992)

M. Douglas, 'Rafia cloth among the hole' in G . Dalton (ed.) *Tribal and Peasant Economies* (Garden City, NY, Natural History Press, 1967)

R. Firth, *Primitive Polynesian Economy* (London, Routledge & Kegan Paul, 1965)

R. Hodges, *Primitive and Peasant Markets* (Oxford, Blackwell, 1988)

B. Malinowski, *Argonauts of the Western Pacific* (London, Routledge & Kegan Paul, 1978)

M. Mauss, *The Gift; the form and reason for exchange in archaic societies* (London, Routledge, 1990)

J. Parry and M. Bloch (eds.), *Money and the Morality of Exchange* (Cambridge, Cambridge University Press, 1989)

K. Polanyi, *The Great Transformation* (Boston, MA, Beacon Press, 1957)

H. Schneider, *Economic Man; the anthropology of economics,* (New York, Free Press, 1974)

J. Woodburn, 'Egalitarian Societies', *Man*, 1982, vol. 17, no. 4, pp. 431–451

J. Woodburn, 'Sharing is not a form of exchange; an analysis of property-sharing in immediate-return hunter-gatherer societies' in C. M. Hann (ed.), *Property Relations; renewing the anthropological tradition* (Cambridge, Cambridge University Press, 1998), pp. 48–63

Chapter 8

R. Abrahams (ed.), *After Socialism; land reform and social change in Eastern Europe* (Oxford, Berghahn Books, 1996)

R. Firth, *Primitive Polynesian Economy* (London, Routledge, 1939)

M. Gluckman, *The Ideas in Barotse Jurisprudence* (New Haven, CT, Yale University Press, 1965)

C. M. Hann (ed.), *Property Relations; renewing the anthropological tradition* (Cambridge, Cambridge University Press, 1998)

C. Humphrey, *Karl Marx Collective* (Cambridge, Cambridge University Press, 1983)

B. Malinowski, *Coral Gardens and Their Magic; a study of the methods of tilling the soil and of agricultural rites in the Trobriand Island* (London, Allen & Unwin, 1935)

M. Strathern, *Property, Substance and Effect*; *anthropological essays on persons and things* (London, Athlone Press, 1999)

Chapter 9

P. Anwalt, 'Costume and Control; Aztec sumptuary laws', *Archaeology,* 1980, vol. 33, no. 1, pp. 33–43

P. Bourdieu, *Distinction; a social critique of the judgement of taste* (London, Routledge & Kegan Paul, 1984)

M. Douglas and B. Isherwood *The World of Goods; towards an anthropology of consumption* (London, Allen Lane, 1979)

J. Friedman, *Cultural Identity and Global Process* (London, Sage, 1994)

J. Griedman, *Cultural Identity and Global Process* (London, Sage, 1994)

A. Gell, 'Newcomers in the world of goods' in A. Appadurai (ed.), *The Social Life of Things* (Cambridge, Cambridge University Press, 1988), pp. 110–138

J. Goody, *The Culture of Flowers* (Cambridge, Cambridge University Press, 1993)

D. Miller (ed.), *Acknowledging Consumption* (London, Routledge, 1995)

S. Mintz, *Sweetness and Power* (New York, Viking, 1986)

PART III

General reference works

J. Gledhill, *Power and Its Disguises; anthropological perspectives on politics* (London, Pluto, 1994)

T. Lewellen, *Political Anthropology; an introduction* (South Hadley, MA, Bergin & Carvey, 1983)

L. Mair, *Primitive Government* (Harmondsworth, Penguin, 1962)

Chapter 10

F. Bailey, *Stratagems and Spoils; a social anthropology of politics* (Oxford, Blackwell, 1969)

F. Barth, *Political leadershp among Swat Pathans* (London, Athlone, 1959)

F. Barth, *Collected Essa*ys, vol. 1, (London, Routledge & Kegan Paul, 1981)

A. Cohen, *Two Dimensional Man* (Berkeley, CA, University of California Press, 1974)

M. Fortes and E. Evans-Pritchard (eds.), *African Political Systems* (London, Oxford University Press, 1940)

J. Kubik, *The Power of Symbols against the Symbols of Power; the rise of solidarity and the fall of state socialism in Poland* (Pennsylvania, Pennsylvania State University Press, 1994)

Chapter 11

I. Bellér-Hann and C. Hann, *Turkish Region* (Oxford, James Currey, 2000)

H. Claessen and P. Skalnik (eds.), *The Early State*, (The Hague, Mouton, 1978)

P. Clastres, *Society Against the State; the leader as servant and the humane uses of power among the Indians of the Americas* (New York, Urizen Books, 1977)

J. Davis, *Libyan Politics. Tribe and revolution; an account of the Zuwaya and their government* (London, Tauris, 1987).

T. Earle (ed.), *Chiefdoms; power, economy and ideology* (Cambridge, Cambridge University Press, 1991)

M. Fried, *The Evolution of Political Society; an essay in political anthropology* (New York, Random House, 1967)

C. Hann and E. Dunn (eds.), *Civil Society; challenging western models* (London, Routledge, 1996)

T. Ingold, D. Riches and J. Woodburn (eds.), *Hunters and Gatherers* (2 Volumes, Oxford, Berg, 1988)

M. Mundy, *Domestic Government; kinship, community and policy in North Yemen* (London, Tauris, 1995)

G. Schlee, *Identities on the Move; clanship and pastoralism in northern Kenya* (Nairobi, Gidean S. Were Press, 1994)

A. Strathern, *The Rope of Moka; big-men and ceremonial exchange in Mount Hagen, New Guinea* (Cambridge, Cambridge University Press, 1967)

R. Tapper, *Frontier Nomads of Iran; a political and social history of the Shahsevan* (Cambridge, Cambridge University Press, 1997)

J. Woodburn, 'Minimal Politics: The Political Organisation of the Hadza of Tanzania', in W. Shack and P. Cohen (eds.), *Politics in Leadership; a comparative perspective* (Oxford, Clarendon Press, 1979), pp. 244–66

Chapter 12

R. Abrahams, *Vigilant Citizens; vigilantism and the state* (Cambridge, Polity Press, 1998)

A. Blok, *The Mafia of a Sicilian Village 1860-1960; a study of violent peasant entrepreneurs* (Oxford, Blackwell, 1974)

T. Bringa, *Being Muslim the Bosnian Way; identity and community in a central Bosnian village* (Princeton, NJ, Princeton University Press, 1995)

N. Chagnon, *Yanomami; the fierce people* (New York, Holt & Winston, 1968)

R. Ferguson and N. Whitehead (eds.), *War in the Tribal Zone; expanding states and indigenous warfare* (Santa Fe, School of American Research Press, 1992)

T. Gibson, *Sacrifice and Sharing in the Phillipine Highlands* (London, Athlone, 1985)

J. Goody, *Technology, Tradition and the State in Africa* (London, Oxford University Press, 1971)

J. Haas (ed.), *The Anthropology of War* (Cambridge, Cambridge University Press, 1990)

E. Hobsbawm, *Primitive Rebels; Studies in archaic forms of social movement in the 19th and 20th centuries* (Manchester, Manchester University Press, 1974)

E. Hobsbawm, *Bandits* (Harmondsworth, Penguin, 1972)

S. Howell and R. Willis (eds.), *Societies at Peace; anthropological perspectives* (London, Routledge, 1989)

J. Lizot, *Tales of the Yanomami; daily life in the Venezuelan forest* (Cambridge, Cambridge University Press, 1985)

J. Overing, *The Piaroa; a people of the Orinoco Basin* (Oxford, Clarendon Press, 1975)

S. P. Reyna and R. E. Downs (ed.), *Studying War: anthropological perspectives* (Reading, Gordon and Breach, 1994)

D. Riches (ed.), *The Anthropology of Violence* (Oxford, Blackwell, 1986)

C. M. Turnbull, *Wayward Servants; the two worlds of the African Pygmies* (London, Eyre & Spottiswoode, 1966)

Chapter 13

J. Borneman, *Settling Accounts; violence, justice and accountability in post-socialist Europe* (Princeton, NJ, Princeton University Press, 1997)

M. Hasluck, *The Unwritten Law in Albania* (Cambridge, Cambridge University Press, 1954)

H. Maine, *Ancient Law* (London, Murray, 1906)

B. Malinowski, *Crime and Custom in Savage Society* (London, Routledge & Kegan Paul, 1926)

S. Roberts, *Order and Dispute; an introduction to legal anthropology* (Oxford, Martin Robertson, 1979)

J. Starr, *Law as Metaphor; from Islamic Courts to the Palace of Justice* (Albany, NY, State University of New York Press, 1992)

Chapter 14

B. Anderson, *Imagined Communities; reflections on the spread of nationalism* (London, Verso, 1983)

M. Bloch, *From Blessing to Violence* (Cambridge, Cambridge University Press, 1986)

M. Bloch, *Ritual, History and Power; selected papers in anthropology* (London, Athlone. 1989)

A. Cohen, *Two Dimensional Man* (London, Routledge & Kegan Paul, 1974)

E. Evans-Pritchard, *The Divine Kingship of the Shilluk* (Cambridge, Cambridge University Press, 1948)

C. Geertz, *Negara; the Theatre State in Nineteenth Century Bali* (Princeton, NY, Princeton University Press, 1980)

M. Gluckman (ed.), *Essays on the Ritual of Social Relations* (Manchester, Manchester University Press, 1962)

D. Kertzer, *Ritual, Politics and Power* (New Haven, CT, Yale University Press, 1988)

D. Kertzer, *Comrades and Christians; religion and political struggle in communist Italy* (New Haven, CT, Yale University Press, 1980)

J. Kubik, *The Power of Symbols against the Symbols of Power; the rise of Solidarity and the fall of state socialism in Poland* (Pennsylvania, Pennsylvania State University Press, 1994)

D. Lan, *Guns and Rain; guerrillas & spirit mediums in Zimbabwe* (London, Currey, 1987)

C. Lane, *The Rites of Rulers; Ritual in industrial society – the Soviet case* (Cambridge, Cambridge University Press, 1981)

E. Leach, *Political Systems of Highland Burma* (London, Bell, 1954)

Z. Mach, *Symbols, Conflict and Identity* (Albany, NY, State University of New York Press, 1993)

T. Nairn, *The Enchanted Glass; Britain and its monarchy* (London, Vintage, 1994).

J. Scott, *Weapons of the Weak; everyday forms of peasant resistance* (New Haven, CT, Yale University Press, 1985)

J.Scott, *Domination and the Arts of Resistance; hidden transcripts* (New Haven, CT, Yale University Press, 1990)

PART IV

General reference works

E. Evans-Pritchard, *Theories of Primitive Religion*, (Oxford, Clarendon Press, 1965)

R. Firth *Religion: a humanist interpretation* (London, Routledge, 1996)

M. Klass, *Ordered Universes* (Boulder, CO, Westview Press, 1995)

B. Morris, *Anthropological Studies of Religion; an introductory text* (Cambridge, Cambridge University Press, 1987)

Chapter 15

J. Comaroff, *Body of Power, Spirit of Resistance; the culture and history of a South African people* (Chicago, IL, University of Chicago Press, 1985)

E. Durkheim, *The Elementary Forms of the Religious Life,* 2nd edn, (London, Allen & Unwin, 1976)

E. Evans-Pritchard, *Nuer Religion* (Oxford, Clarendon Press, 1981)

J. G. Frazer, *The Golden Bough; a study in magic and religion* (London, Macmillan, 1890)

C. Geertz, 'Religion as a cultural system' in M. Banton (ed.), *Anthropological Approaches to the study of Religion* (London, Tavistock, 1966)

C. Humphrey, 'Shamans in the city', *Anthropology Today,* 1999, no. 3, pp. 3–10

C. Humphrey and N. Thomas, *Shamanism, History and the State* (Ann Arbor, University of Michigan Press, 1994)

C. Lane, *The Rites of Rulers* (Cambridge, Cambridge University Press, 1981)

G. Lewis, *Day of Shining Red; an essay of understanding ritual* (Cambridge, Cambridge University Press, 1980)

I. Lewis, *Ecstatic Religion; an anthropological study of spirit possession and shamanism* (Harmondsworth, Penguin, 1975)

E. B. Tylor, *Primitive Culture; researches into the development of mythology, philosophy, religion, language, art and custom* (London, Murray, 1871)

M. Weber, *The Sociology of Religion* (Boston, MA, Beacon Press, 1963)

P. Worsley, *The Trumpet Shall Sound; a study of 'cargo cults' in Melanesia,* 2nd edn (London, MacGibbon & Kee, 1968)

Chapter 16

M. Douglas, *Purity and Danger* (London, Routledge, 1966)

M. Douglas, *Natural Symbols* (Harmondsworth, Penguin, 1970)

E. Durkheim and M. Mauss, *Primitive Classification* (Chicago, IL, University of Chicago Press, 1963)

E. Evans-Pritchard, *Witchcraft, Oracles and Magic Among the Azande* (Oxford, Clarendon Press, 1937)

J. Goody, 'A kernel of doubt' in *Food and Love; a cultural history of east and west* (London, Verso, 1998), pp. 203–221

R. Horton, 'African traditional thought and western science' in B. Wilson (ed.), *Rationality* (Oxford, Blackwell, 1970), pp. 131–171

S. Hugh-Jones, *The Palm and the Pleiades* (Cambridge, Cambridge University Press, 1979)

I. Jarvie, 'Explaining Cargo cults', in B. Wilson (ed.), *Rationality* (Oxford, Blackwell, 1970), pp.50–61

P. Lawrence, *Road Belong Cargo; a study of the cargo movement, Southern Madang District* (Manchester, Manchester University Press, 1964)

E. Leach (ed.), *The Structural Study of Myth and Totemism* (London, Tavistock, 1967)

E. Leach (ed.), *Genesis as Myth and other Essays* (London, Cape, 1969)

C. Lévi-Strauss, *Totemism* (Harmondsworth, Penguin, 1969)

C. Lévi-Strauss, *The Savage Mind* (Chicago, IL, Chicago University Press, 1966)

L.Levy-Bruhl, *Hoe Natives Think* (London, Allen & Unwin, 1926)

A. Macfarlane, *Witchcraft in Tudor and Stuart England* (London, Routledge, 1970)

M. Marwick, *Sorcery in its Social Setting. A Study of the Northern Rhodesian Cewa* (Manchester, Manchester University Press, 1964)

F. Steiner, *Taboo* (Harmondsworth, Penguin, 1966)

M. Stewart, *The Time of the Gypsies* (Boulder, CO, Westview Press, 1997)

Chapter 17

E. Evans-Pritchard, *Theories of Primitive Religion* (Oxford, Clarendon Press, 1965)

C. Geertz, *The Interpretation of Cultures* (New York, Basic Books, 1973)

A. van Gennep, *The Rites of Passage* (Chicago, IL, University of Chicago Press, 1960)

D. I. Kertzer, *Ritual, Politics and Power* (New Haven, CT, Yale University Press, 1988)

E. Leach, *Culture and Communication* (Cambridge, Cambridge University Press, 1976)

G. Lewis, *Day of Shining Red; an essay on understanding ritual* (Cambridge, Cambridge University Press, 1980)

V. Turner, *The Forest of Symbols; aspects of Ndembu ritual* (Ithaca, NY, Cornell University Press, 1967)

V. Turner and E. Turner, *Image and Pilgrimage in Christian Culture* (New York, Columbia University Press, 1978)

K. Verdery, *The Political Lives of Dead Bodies; reburial and post-communist change* (New York, Columbia University Press, 1999)

Chapter 18

F. Cancian, *Economics and Prestige in a Maya Community; the religious cargo system in Zinacantan* (Stanford, CA, Stanford University Press, 1965)

G. Evans, *Lao Peasants under Socialism* (New Haven, CT, Yale University Press, 1990)

C. Geertz, *Islam Observed; religious development in Morocco and Indonesia* (New Haven, CT, Yale University Press, 1968)

E. Gellner, *Muslim Society* (Cambridge, Cambridge University Press, 1981)

J. Goody, *The Domestication of the Savage Mind* (Cambridge, Cambridge Univeristy Press, 1977)

J. Goody, *The Logic of Writing and the Organization of Society* (Cambridge, Cambridge University Press, 1986)

E. Leach (ed.), *Dialectic in Practical Religion* (Cambridge, Cambridge University Press, 1968)

C. Markschies, *Between Two Worlds; Structures of Earliest Christianity* (London, SCM, 1999)

M. Spiro, *Buddhism and Society; a Great Tradition and its Burmese Vicissitudes* (Berkeley, CA, University of California Press, 1982)

Chapter 19

B. Anderson, *Imagined Communities; reflections on the origin and spread of nationalism*, 2nd edn (London, Verso, 1991)

R. Bellah, 'Civil religion in America' in *Daedalus*, 1967, vol. 96, pp.1–21

M. Billig, *Banal Nationalism* (London, Sage, 1995)

G. Bowman 'Nationalizing the Sacred; shrines and shifting identities in the Israeli-occupied territories', *Man*, vol. 28, no.3, pp. 431–460

E. Gellner, *The Psychoanalytic Movement* (London, Granada, 1985)

P. van der Veer, *Religious Nationalism: Hindus and Muslims in India* (Berkeley, CA, University of California Press, 1994)

K. Verdery, *National Ideology under Socialism* (Berkeley, CA, University of California Press, 1991)

PART V

General reference works

A. Barnard and A. Good, *Research Practices in the Study of Kinship* (London, Academic Press, 1984)

C. Harris, *Kinship* (Milton Keynes, Open University Press, 1990)

L. Holy, *Anthropological Perspectives on Kinship* (London, Pluto, 1996)

R. Keesing, *Kin Groups and Social Structure* (New York, Holt Rinehart and Winston, 1975)

R. Parkin, *Kinship: an introduction to the basic concepts*, (Oxford, Blackwell, 1997)

Chapter 20

J. A. Barnes, *Three Styles in the Study of Kinship* (London, Tavistock, 1971)

J. A. Barnes, 'African Models in the New Guinea Highlands' in *Models and Interpretations; selected essays*, (Cambridge, Cambridge University Press, 1990), pp. 44–55

E. Friedl, *Women and Men; an anthropologist's view* (New York, Holt Rinehart and Winston, 1975)

J. Goody, *Production and Reproduction* (Cambridge, Cambridge University Press, 1961)

J. Goody, *The development of the Family and Marriage in Europe* (Cambridge, Cambridge University Press, 1983)

A. Kuper, *The Invention of Primitive Society* (London, Routledge 1988)

E. Leach, *Pul Eliya; a village in Ceylon* (Cambridge, Cambridge University Press, 1961)

S. Ortner and H. Whitehead (eds.), *Sexual Meanings: the cultural construction of gender* (Cambridge, Cambridge University Press, 1981)

F. Pine, 'Kinship, work and the state in post-socialist rural Poland', in *Cambridge Anthropology*, vol.18, no. 2, pp.47–58

M. Rosaldo and L. Lamphere (eds.), *Nature, Culture and Gender* (Stanford, CA, Stanford University Press, 1974)

D. Schneider, *American Kinship; a cultural account* (Eaglewood Cliffs, NJ, Prentice-Hall, 1968)

D. Schneider, *A Critique of the Study of Kinship* (Ann Arbor, University of Michigan Press, 1984)

P. Worsley, 'The kinship system of the Tallensi; a re-evaluation', in *Journal of the Royal Anthropological Institute*, 1986, vol.1, pp. 37–75

Chapter 21

J. A. Barnes, 'Genetrix: Genitor: Nature: Culture?' in *Models and Interpretations; selected essays* (Cambridge, Cambridge University Press, 1990), pp.29–43

C. Delaney, *The Seed and the Soil* (Berkeley, CA, University of California Press, 1991)

C. Delaney, 'The meaning of paternity and the virgin birth debate', *Man,* 1986, vol. 21, no. 3, pp. 494–513

C. D. Forde, 'Double descent among the Yako', in A. R. Radcliffe Browne and C.D. Forde (eds.), *African Systems of Kinship and Marriage* (London, Oxford University Press, 1950), pp. 285–332

M. Fortes, *The Web of Kinship among the Tallensi* (London, Oxford University Press, 1949)

M. Fortes, *Kinship and the Social Order; the legacy of Lewis Henry Morgan* (London, Routledge & Kegan Paul, 1969)

E. Leach, 'Virgin Birth' in *Genesis as Myth and Other Essays* (London, Cape, 1969)

P. Loizos and P. Heady (eds.), *Conceiving Persons; ethnographies of procreation, fertility and growth.* (London, Athlone, 1999)

D. Schneider and K. Gough (eds.), *Matrilineal Kinship* (Berkeley, CA, University of California Press, 1961)

Chapter 22

W. Arens, *The Original Sin: Incest and its meaning* (Oxford, Oxford University Press, 1986)

J. Comaroff (ed.), *The Meaning of Marriage Payments* (London, Academic Press, 1980)

E. Evans-Pritchard, *Kinship and Marriage Among the Nuer* (Oxford, Clarendon Press. 1951)

J. S. LaFontaine, *Child Sexual Abuse*, (Cambridge, Polity Press, 1990)

R. Fox, *Kinship and Marriage* (Harmondsworth, Pelican, 1967)

R. Fox, *The Red Lamp of Incest* (New York, E. P. Dutton, 1980)

J. Goody, 'Incest and adultery in comparative perspective', in J. Goody (ed.), *Kinship; selected readings* (Harmondsworth, Penguin, 1971)

J. Goody, 'Bridewealth and Dowry in Africa and Eurasia' in J. Goody and S. N. Tambiah, *Bridewealth and Dowry* (Cambridge, Cambridge University Press, 1973)

C. Lévi-Strauss, *The Elementary Structures of Kinship* (Boston, Beacon Press, 1969)

L. Mair, *Marriage* (Harmondsworth, Penguin, 1971)

E. Tylor, 'On a method of investigating the development of institutions; applied to laws of marriage and descent', in *Journal of the Royal Anthropological Institute*, 1889, vol.18, pp. 245–269

A.Wolf and C. Huang, *Marriage and Adoption in China 1845–1945* (Stanford, CA, Stanford University Press, 1980)

N. Yalman, *Under the Bo Tree* (Berkeley, CA, University of California Press, 1967)

Chapter 23

J. Carsten and S. Hugh-Jones (eds.), *About the House* (Cambridge, Cambridge University Press, 1995)

C. Lévi-Strauss, *The Way of the Masks* (London, 1983)

G. Murdock, *Social Structures* (New York, MacMillan, 1949)

R. M. C. Netting, R. R. Wilk (eds.), *Households; comparative and historical studies of the domestic group* (Berkeley, CA, University of California Press, 1984)

F. Pine, 'Naming the house and naming the land: kinship and social groups in highland Poland', *Journal of the Royal Anthropological Institute*, 1996, vol. 2, no. 3, pp.443–460

D. Pitkin, *The Home that Giacomo built; history of an Italian family, 1878–1978*, 2nd edn (Dowling College Reprints Series, 1999)

J. White, *Money Makes us Relatives; women's labor in urban Turkey* (Austin, TX, University of Texas Press, 1994)

P. Willmott and M. Young, *Family and Kinship in East London* (London, Routledge, 1957)

Chapter 24

F. Barth (ed.) *Ethnic Groups and Boundaries, the social organization of cultural difference* (Bergen, Universitetsforl, 1969)

B. Bernardi, *Age Class Systems: social institutions and polities based on age* (Cambridge, Cambridge University Press, 1985)

T. Bringa, *Being Muslim the Bosnian Way; identity and community in a central Bosnian village* (Princeton, NJ, Princeton University Press, 1995)

T. H. Eriksen, *Ethnicity and Nationalism; anthropological perspectives* (London, Pluto, 1993)

R. G. Fox (ed.), *Nationalist Ideologies and the Production of National Cultures* (Washington, American Anthropological Association, 1990)

M. Gluckman, *Custom and Conflict in Africa* (Oxford, Blackwell, 1966)

I. Lewis, *Blood and Bone; the call of kinship in Somali society* (Lawrenceville, NJ, Red Sea Press, 1994)

G. Schlee, *Identities on the Move; clanship and pastoralism in Northern Kenya* (Nairobi, Gideon S. Were Press, 1994)

P. Spencer (ed.), *Age and the Riddle of the Sphynx; paradox and change in the life course* (London, Routledge, 1990)

K. Sword, *Identity in Flux. The Polish Community in Britain* (London, School of Slavonic and East European Studies, 1996)

E. Tonkin, M. McDonald and M. Chapman (eds.), *History and Ethnicity* (London, Routledge, 1989)

PART VI

Chapter 25

Many more detailed introductions to anthropology are available nowadays as a next step for those wishing to continue their anthropological education. Among British volumes: John Beattie, *Other Cultures* (Oxford, Cohen & West, 1964) and David Pocock, *Teach Yourself Understanding Social Anthropology* 2nd edn (London, Athlone,1998). A more up-to-date European's perspective is offered by Thomas Hylland Eriksen, *Small Places, Large Issues; an introduction to social anthropology* (London, Pluto, 1996). A comprehensive introduction in the American style is Roger Keesing and Andrew J. Strathern, *Cultural Anthropology; a contemporary perspective*, 3rd edn, (Fort Worth, Harcourt Brace, 1998).

For contrasting approaches to the concept of culture see Michael Carrithers, *Why Humans Have Cultures; explaining anthropology and social diversity* (Oxford, Oxford University Press, 1993) and Adam Kuper, *Culture; the anthropologist's account* (Cambridge, MA, Harvard University Press, 1999).

For further reading suggestions and practical information about studying social anthropology in Britain see S. Coleman and B. Simpson (eds.): *Discovering Anthropology; a resource guide for teachers and students* (5th edn., London 1998). (Available price £12 from Royal Anthropological Institute, 50 Fitzroy Street, London W1P 5HS.)

INDEX

TEACH YOURSELF

CULTURAL STUDIES

Will Brooker

Teach Yourself Cultural Studies provides a comprehensive introduction to this exciting subject. The key theorists and issues are discussed in a lively and easy-to-follow style – suitable for both beginners and first-level students.

The book:

- introduces and explains Cultural Studies from its historical origins to recent work on video games, TV fandom and the Internet.
- summarizes, examines and critiques the work of key theorists.
- communicates complex ideas in a clear and concise way.

Will Brooker has lectured in Media, Film and Communication Studies and is currently researching and teaching at the University of Wales, Cardiff.

Other related titles

TEACH YOURSELF

POSTMODERNISM

Glenn Ward

One of the most fiercely disputed terms of the late twentieth century, postmodernism has had an impact in most fields, from literature and the visual arts to cultural studies and sociology. In each of these areas, the meanings of postmodernism are flexible, but in all cases it forces us to question some of our most cherished assumptions. Postmodernist debates suggest that our most ingrained ideas about the nature of history, culture, meaning and identity can no longer be taken for granted. As such, it has far-reaching implications for how we think about the world today.

Glen Ward's informative text:

- introduces the most important theorists in a number of different disciplines;
- links theoretical questions to an eclectic range of examples, from both 'high' and 'popular' cultures;
- is an indispensable guide to the sometimes demanding terrain of postmodernism;
- places postmodernism in a wide context.

Glenn Ward is a lecturer in the Faculty of Art and Music at Bath College of Art and Design.

TEACH YOURSELF

PSYCHOLOGY

Nicky Hayes

Teach Yourself Psychology explains basic psychological processes and how they influence us in all aspects of everyday life. It explores why human beings are as they are, how they came to be that way and what they might do to change seemingly fundamental traits. This book puts psychology in context using non-technical language to analyze everyday situations. It is a comprehensive introduction that shows how human experience can be understood on many levels.

- Learn what psychology is.
- Explore the psychology of teaching and learning.
- Investigate different research methods used to investigate a broad spectrum of human experience.
- Read about psychology and the environment.
- Study psychology in the workplace.
- Find out more about biological rhythms.

Nicky Hayes has a particular interest in shared beliefs and in the teaching and understanding of psychology. She has written undergraduate textbooks as well as research papers and articles.